The Negro in the
Reconstruction of Florida, 1865-1877

Florida State University Studies

Number Forty-six

THE NEGRO IN THE RECONSTRUCTION

OF FLORIDA, 1865-1877

By

Joe M. Richardson

THE FLORIDA STATE UNIVERSITY

Tallahassee

1965

THE FLORIDA STATE UNIVERSITY

Published under the Auspices
of
THE RESEARCH COUNCIL
The Florida State University

vii

TABLE OF CONTENTS

PREFACE

Studies of Reconstruction in Florida have usually ignored the Negro or have portrayed him as shiftless, incompetent, and if a politician, corrupt. Certainly the ex-slaves were ill trained for their status as free men, but they made remarkable adjustments and progress within a decade. Several Negro politicians, though unprepared for their new positions, were surprisingly able. This book is not a thorough history of Reconstruction. It is an attempt to picture the role played by the freedmen in the State from 1865 to 1877, and to show how they reacted to the many problems encountered after emancipation.

The assistance of the staff of the following institutions is gratefully acknowledged: The Robert Manning Strozier Library at Florida State University, Tallahassee; The P. K. Yonge Library of Florida History, Gainesville; The Library of Congress and National Archives; the Florida State Library, Tallahassee; the Southern Historical Collection at the University of North Carolina, Chapel Hill; the Flowers Collection at Duke University, Durham; the David S. Walker Library, Tallahassee; Fisk University Library, Nashville, and the University of South Florida Library, Tampa.

I wish to thank the clerks of circuit court of Leon, Jefferson, and Gadsden counties, and the Departments of State, Education and Agriculture for their co-operation. I am indebted to Professor Weymouth T. Jordan, Professor James P. Jones, Jr., and Dr. Dorothy Dodd, all of whom read the manuscript and made useful suggestions. Such errors as appear are my responsibility.

CHAPTER I

FLORIDA AFTER THE WAR

Florida, once called the "smallest tadpole in the dirty pool of secession," had the smallest population of any Confederate State. At the outbreak of the Civil War, Florida had little more than one-third as many free people as the city of Cincinnati.[1] In 1860 the State had 140,424 inhabitants and by 1870 they had increased to only 187,746. The 1870 census listed 96,057 whites and 91,689 Negroes.[2] Eight of the thirty-nine settled counties had a majority of freedmen.[3] The two largest, Alachua and Leon, with 17,328 and 15,236 residents respectively, contained almost one-fifth of the total population.

Most of the citizens were concentrated in North Florida, with almost half of them dwelling in the seven northern counties.[4] One traveler said it was difficult to realize just how sparsely settled Florida was until the towns were examined. Key West had the largest number of whites of any city with a total of 2,241 while Tallahassee, the capital city, could count only about 2,000. Tallahassee was described by a newspaper correspondent in August, 1865, as having unpretentious public buildings, and generally poor and neglected private dwellings and stores. The walks were dilapidated and broken, he said, but the town was, "in its location, surroundings and appearance, cheerful and pleasant."[5] Florida's population of less than 200,000 was scattered over an area of nearly 60,000 square miles. Agriculture had been the primary pursuit of Floridians, and there had been little disposition to settle in villages and communities, but rather a tendency toward a dissipation of population.[6] Florida was an unsettled frontier

---

[1] Whitelaw Reid, *After the War: A Southern Tour* (New York, 1866), 159-60.

[2] *Eighth Census of the United States*, 1860, I, 54; *Ninth Census of the United States*, 1870, I, 19.

[3] Alachua, Duval, Gadsden, Jackson, Jefferson, Leon, Madison, and Marion. These eight counties had Negro majorities by 1870, but General John G. Foster reported that in 1866 only six counties had a majority of freedmen. J. G. Foster to O. O. Howard, October 1, 1866, in Records of the Freedmen's Bureau, Florida, National Archives, Washington, D. C. (Cited hereafter, Bureau Records, Florida.)

[4] *Ninth Census of the United States*, 1870, I, 19.

[5] Reid, *op. cit.*, 159-60; New York *Times*, August 1, 1865.

[6] *Florida, Its Climate Soil and Production With a Sketch of Its History, Natural Features and Social Condition* (Jacksonville, Florida, 1868), 9.

state. An observer declared in December, 1866, that the frontier extended from the Tampa Bay area east to St. Augustine. That portion of the State, he asserted, was "infested with bands of renegades and desperados" who stole from and murdered other whites.[7]

Florida was a poor state and before the war had been dominated by a few wealthy planters. Indeed, it has been said that until 1868 the State was in the "hands and pockets of a baker's dozen" of such men as David L. Yulee and David S. Walker.[8] After the war several of the former leaders claimed they had opposed the war, but had felt obligated to follow their State.[9] An *original secesh*" was hard to find, a Marianna man wrote in August, 1865. Even former Governor John Milton, he added, who "was the secesh leader" denied he was in favor of secession shortly before he committed suicide.[10] In May, 1865, acting Governor Abraham K. Allison informed General Edward M. McCook, Union Commander at Tallahassee, that citizens of Florida recognized the requirements of the Constitution of the United States, and were ready to "resume the duties and privileges created by that instrument in a spirit of perfect good faith, with the purpose to abide therein."[11] Allison, Yulee and "other prominent citizens" accepted the termination of the war with apparent cheerfulness, and were gratified with the policy followed by the military.[12] A Union captain failed to understand how the State had seceded, so many people claimed to be Unionists.[13] Acquiescence did not necessarily mean that all Floridians agreed with the outcome of the war. According to a contemporary the young men and women were especially determined never to surrender, but by the time Union forces arrived

---

[7] J. T. Sprague to O. O. Howard, December 31, 1866, in Bureau Records, Florida.

[8] New York *Tribune*, February 20, 1868.

[9] M. A. Williams to W. Marvin, August 9, 1865, in David L. Yulee Papers P. K. Yonge Library of Florida History, Gainesville, Florida.

[10] Milton was governor of Florida during the war but assumed office after secession. E. Philips to J. J. Philips, August 2, 1865, in James J. Philips Papers, Southern Historical Collection, University of North Carolina, Chapel Hill, North Carolina.

[11] A. K. Allison to E. M. McCook, May 13, 1865, in Governor's Letterbook, Florida State Library, Tallahassee, Florida.

[12] U. S. Department of War, *The War of the Rebellion: a compilation of the official records of the Union and Confederate armies* (70 vols., Washington, 1880-1901), I Series, XLIX, pt. 2, 747.

[13] E. Philips to J. J. Philips, August 2, 1865, in James J. Philips Papers.

"one and all had come to the conclusion—that *Yankee* military government was better than none."[14]

Former leaders of the State appeared to be more reconciled to the outcome of the war than the population at large. Some of the young men believed they could not live "under yankee rule." There were frequent bitter comments about Northerners in Florida. A former resident of Jacksonville wrote that the city would be a "worse yankee hole than ever," and swore he would never live there again. He intended, he added, to leave the United States. Lake City was "beset with yankees," another Floridian said, and with Southerners who were worse.[15] Several observers declared that Floridians were not reconciled. A visitor to Jacksonville in late 1866 found Southerners "universally very bitter" against the current Congress and Northern correspondents, while a Bureau agent asserted, that Unionists could not "freely express their love or admiration" for the country without incurring displeasure and sometimes actual enmity of the whites. As late as 1867 Northern people were said to be safe, but not welcome in certain sections of Florida.[16]

The citizens of the State were bitter against the government, two Floridians testified before the Reconstruction Committee, and they had no regard for the Union. They talked treason, the testimony indicated, and felt beaten but not conquered.[17] According to reports, women were more bitter toward the United States than men. There was a "certain number of reasonable individuals" among the better class of Floridians, a Bureau agent wrote in 1866, but the female members of the same families were not included. Another agent said most of the men were "well disposed" toward the government, but the "old women, silly girls, and men" who remained at home during the war were less willing

---

14 Ellen Call Long, History of Florida, 345. Unpublished manuscript in the Florida Historical Society Collection, University of South Florida, Tampa, Florida.

15 F. P. Fleming to M. Seton, May 3, 1865, in Fleming Papers, Florida Historical Society Collection, University of South Florida, Tampa, Florida; F. F. L'Engle to E. M. L'Engle, June 26, 1865, in Edward M. L'Engle Papers, Southern Historical Collection, University of North Carolina, Chapel Hill, North Carolina.

16 A. B. Hart to B. H. Hart, December 18, 1866, in A. B. Hart Letters, P. K. Yonge Library of Florida History, Gainesville, Florida; U. S. Congress, *House Executive Documents*, 40th Cong., 2nd Sess., No. 57, 77.

17 U. S. Congress, *House Reports*, 39th Cong., 1st Sess., No. 30, pt. 4, 1-2; Tallahassee *Semi-Weekly Floridian*, March 20, 1866.

to submit.[18] It was not surprising that antagonism toward the Union still existed such a short time after the war. Many problems of Reconstruction can be attributed to bitterness and misunderstandings that were present before Reconstruction began.

The variations in attitude toward the Union can be found in the interests of different classes. General Israel Vogdes, Union Commander at Jacksonville, divided Florida whites into three classes, the wealthy and best educated, the partially educated, and the poor whites. The first class, he said, was small and had lost much of its wealth during the war and through abolition, but was anxious to recover its lost position, and as a body would comply with rules adopted by the United States. The partially educated were more numerous and less submissive. They admitted defeat but were not loyal, Vogdes maintained, and would cause trouble whenever an opportunity occurred. The partially educated included nearly all of the subordinate Confederate officers, and had the sympathy of the women of the better class, he added. The third group, poor whites, Vogdes continued, was tired of war, but hated the freedmen, was idle and vicious, and was but little in advance of the ex-slaves in intelligence and education. This class appeared to be more opposed to the Negro than to the Union. It felt little sympathy for former state leaders whom it was reputed to hate.[19]

The so-called poor whites composed a considerable portion of Florida's population, and lived on a level little, if any, higher than the Negro. The whites were as dirty, poor, and destitute as the freedman, a white lady wrote from Jacksonville in February, 1865. They had, she added, a "hopeless, listless appearance" and were not averse to begging. Another observer expressed hope that when slavery was dead and the "spirit of caste" banished, poor whites might "arise" and "be equal to the colored people."[20] The area around Palatka, a visitor wrote, was a pine forest containing "miserable little log cabins" with numerous "dirty children and lean-porkers." The residents demonstrated no signs of energy,

---

[18] J. E. Quentin to T. W. Osborn, April 24, 1866, H. W. Wessells, Jr. to E. C. Woodruff, April 1, 1867, in Bureau Records, Florida.

[19] I. Vogdes to O. O. Howard, July 31, 1865, in Bureau Records, Florida.

[20] *The Freedmen's Record*, I (March, 1865), 39; E. B. Eveleth to L. L. Jocelyn, February 4, 1865, in American Missionary Association Archives, Fisk University, Nashville, Tennessee.

he added, and everything betokened "poverty and wretched shift-lessness."

People ate, talked, slept, and existed. In the richer counties of middle and West Florida, conditions might be a little different, but not much, the visitor continued.[21] In Volusia County citizens reportedly lived in log shanties, and were so poor three-fourths of the women went barefoot half of the time. Several of the county officers were illiterate and unfamiliar with their duties. There were no justices of the peace or magistrates, thus marriages were slighted, with partners marrying or remarrying "to suit their fancy." One man had two wives in the same house, with six children by one and seven by the other.[22] It was the poor whites who were, as a group, most bitter in their hatred of the Negro. Their hatred was undoubtedly based on economic, as well as racial and caste motives.

The large class of poverty stricken whites was not created by the war, though the war did cause hardship. The assessed value of real and personal property excluding slaves declined from $47,000,000 in 1860 to $27,000,000 in 1865.[23] However, all of the decline was not caused by destruction. Planters had been injured by the Confederacy's economic policy and many of the estates had decayed from lack of care.[24] Disruption of the economy was more responsible for the decline in property values than was destruction of war. Some of the loss was caused by Union men who abandoned their homes for safety. Florida was so far removed from the scene of war, that little devastation occurred. As the Gainesville *New Era* reported in August, 1865, the condition of Florida was "vastly superior" to the rest of the South. With the exception of slaves, the paper added, "the loss of property in Florida during the four years of war" was "a mere cipher compared to other States."[25] A newspaper correspondent said "the suffering in the State during and after the war was relative only. Florida was too far from the theater of strife to feel the terrible blows that brought down the

---

21 W. N. Hart to M. Hart, February 18, 1867, in Walter N. Hart Letters, P. K. Yonge Library of Florida History, Gainesville, Florida.

22 Jacksonville *Florida Union*, September 14, 1867.

23 Kathryn T. Abbey, *Florida Land of Change* (Chapel Hill, 1941), 293.

24 In 1862 the Confederate Congress "passed a joint resolution that absolutely no cotton ought to be planted in 1862." A traveler in Florida reported that "little cotton" had been raised in Florida in keeping with desires of the Confederacy. A. E. Kinne to T. W. Osborn, October 15, 1866, in Bureau Records, Florida; Frank L. Owsley, *King Cotton Diplomacy* (Chicago, 1931), 47.

25 Quoted in Jacksonville *Florida Union*, August 19, 1865.

revolt."[26] Moreover, little property was confiscated in Florida, and the small amount seized was rapidly returned.[27]

Conditions in Florida were not as bad as generally painted by contemporaries. Farming had been disrupted, and trade was somewhat paralyzed, but by August, 1865, "large quantities of goods" were being sold, and people were reportedly "gradually assuming a business-like and cheerful attitude." Trade was stimulated by the United States government, which repaired some Florida railroads.[28] Some Floridians appeared to be more interested in sound investments than in the war. In April, 1865, Samuel A. Swann, a native white businessman was hoping for an honorable peace, and looking for something in which to invest a few thousand dollars. Many holders of Confederate currency were investing their money in cotton, and some, who apparently had not given up the idea of slavery, in Negroes, Swann said.[29] By June Swann was acting as a cotton agent, and considered business prospects promising. Lumber mills were being erected, turpentine plantations opened, and timber operations were being put under way by "dozens of men." Turpentine farms and steam saw mills were "all the go" around North Central Florida.[30] Many sawmills were opening near Cedar Keys, according to a report made to Yulee in August. Silas L. Niblack, a political cohort of Yulee, wrote that Florida had "good signs of prosperity," with trade opening in East and Middle Florida. Cotton was bringing a good price, and money was circulating freely in the interior, Niblack continued.[31]

Even the railroads were making money. From June 1 to August 1, 1865, the Florida Railroad Company earned $9,059.69. The railroad company in Jacksonville was doing a larger business than even during the war with an income of about $1,000 per day.[32]

---

[26] New York *Tribune*, February 20, 1868.

[27] Paul S. Peirce, *The Freedmen's Bureau* (Iowa City, Iowa, 1904), 129; J. G. Foster to O. O. Howard, October 1, 1866, in Bureau Records, Florida.

[28] Jacksonville *Florida Union*, August 19, June 3, 1865.

[29] S. A. Swann to (?) Sprott, April 25, 1865, in Samuel A. Swann Papers, P. K. Yonge Library of Florida History, Gainesville, Florida.

[30] S. A. Swann to R. Erwin, June 10, 1865, S. A. Swann to G. Savage, June 22, 1865, S. A. Swann to F. Dibble, June, n.d., 1865, S. A. Swann to D. McRae, June 23, 1865, S. A. Swann to (?) Sprott, June 27, 1865, in Samuel A. Swann Papers.

[31] R. D. Meader to D. L. Yulee, August 13, 1865, S. L. Niblack to D. L. Yulee, August 18, 1865, in David L. Yulee Papers.

[32] Statement of Earnings and Expenditures of the Florida Railroad; S. A. Swann to D. L. Yulee, August 27, 1865, in David L. Yulee Papers.

Business was still unsettled, Swann wrote a friend in Cuba in August, but he thought the resources of the State would "soon be more fully developed than ever before."[33] Business prospects were still improving in September. According to a Jacksonville newspaper, 6,000 bales of cotton, 380,000 feet of sawed timber, 1,027 barrels of tar, 20 barrels of spirits turpentine, 222 barrels of crude turpentine, and some timber had been shipped from Jacksonville since the port had been reopened.[34] Many other comments were made concerning the general prosperity in Florida soon after the war.

These harbingers of prosperity were too optimistic. Though Florida suffered less from the war than other states, it did have many problems. Considerable economic dislocation had resulted from the war, numerous productive men and potential leaders had been killed, a new labor system had to be devised, and the State experienced some poor crop years. Furthermore, Florida was a frontier state with a small, poor population. Railroads had to be built, roads constructed and repaired, and capital brought into the State. The early optimism began to decline long before Radical Reconstruction, which has been used as a scapegoat for Southern economic problems. As early as 1866 a shortage of currency had caused the beginning of later evils. It was said that in 1866 at least two-thirds of the planters were under mortgage or other obligations to merchants for advances. Planters were complaining of the merchants' unreasonable prices. By April, 1867, Swann, who had been one of the most optimistic about recovery in Florida, became "every day more and more impressed with the idea that capital alone" could and would control business in Florida,[35] and capital proved to be scarce in the State for several years. In such an underdeveloped area any government, Democratic or Republican, was destined to encounter serious problems in an attempt to bring prosperity to the State.

---

33 S. A. Swann to R. Perez, August 3, 1865, in Samuel A. Swann Papers.
34 Jacksonville *Florida Union*, September 9, 1865.
35 S. A. Swann to D. L. Yulee, April 5, 1867, in Samuel A. Swann Papers.

CHAPTER II

EMANCIPATION

The first attempt to emancipate Florida's slaves came on May 9, 1862, when Major General David Hunter, Commander of the Department of the South, proclaimed the freedom of slaves in Florida, Georgia and South Carolina. His order was overruled by President Lincoln, and most Florida Negroes probably were never aware of the proclamation. A majority of Florida slaves remained on their plantations during the war. Before Appomattox, the disappearance of a number of slaves usually indicated the presence of a Union Army in the vicinity. Florida was little traversed by troops, but a few Negroes were freed by soldiers. On March 7, 1865, a small colored detachment left Jacksonville, penetrated the interior through Marion County, and rescued ninety-one Negroes from slavery.[1] In this way enough Negroes left their homes to cause comment. Brigadier General Thomas J. McKean, Commander of the District of West Florida, wrote in January, 1865, of large numbers of refugees of all colors at Barrancas, and on April 20, 1865, the commander of Confederate forces in Florida asked Governor A. K. Allison to call a portion of the State Militia into service to protect against deserters, "and to retain and maintain proper subordination among the slaves." There was a slight accumulation of freedmen at Fernandina, Jacksonville, and St. Augustine, towns held by Union Troops, but "as a general thing they were at their homes on the plantations." Even Florida whites insisted that the Negroes generally remained loyal to their masters, and stayed on the plantation caring for the families and crops of Confederate soldiers.[2]

---

[1] The Union Army recruited 1.044 Negroes in Florida. *Official Records*, III Series, V, 662; John Hope Franklin, *From Slavery to Freedom* (New York, 1945), 289; H. B. Greely to G. Whipple, March 18, 1864, in American Missionary Association Archives.

[2] In a study of Negroes during the war Bell I. Wiley concluded that most of the slaves were neither loyal nor disloyal, but simply awaited the outcome of the war. Bell I. Wiley, *Southern Negroes 1861-1865* (New Haven, 1938), 83; T. J. McKean to L. Thomas, January 1, 1865, in U. S. Army Commands, Florida, National Archives; *Official Records*, I Series, XLVII, pt. 3, 819; T. W. Osborn to O. O. Howard, November 1, 1865, in Bureau Records, Florida;

As soon as it became evident the war was over, a few owners began to free their slaves. On April 16, a Tallahassee planter called his slaves to the house and told them: " 'you are *my* people no longer; the fortunes of war have taken you out of my hands—you are free men now.' "[3] However, many of the masters were hesitant to give up their Negroes. The Jacksonville *Florida Union* claimed some planters around Tallahassee clung to the hope they could keep their slaves, and have some kind of gradual emancipation. They were disappointed, "some even bitterly," when on May 14, Union Major General Quincy A. Gilmore issued an emancipation proclamation in Florida.[4] As late as May 19, Brigadier General Edward M. McCook, Union Commander at Tallahassee, believed it necessary to issue a statement, "in order to avoid further importunities from citizens of this vicinity," that the Negro was no longer a slave.[5] On the next day the various commanders in Florida received orders to inform those lately held in bondage of their freedom.[6] The soldiers and "yankee followers," said one contemporary, then "penetrated to our kitchens and plantations informing the negroes who in wonderment left hearth and field to hang around the Yankee camp to know more about 'dis here freedom.' "[7]

The Negro reaction to emancipation was varied. When the slaves of Susan Bradford's family were informed of their freedom "some of the men cried, some spoke regretfully . . . only two looked surly and had nothing to say. . . ." That night the maid came as usual to see Miss Bradford safe in bed and after telling her mistress goodnight the former slave declared: "I'm always going to love my child. . . .' "[8] Some of the ex-slaves, especially those who lived on plantations, appeared to think an apology due the master "for such summary appropriation of property." The town dwellers were more ready for the change. Ellen Call Long wrote in her diary on the day of emancipation that,

---

Florida, *House Journal*, 1865, 32-34.

[3] Susan Bradford Eppes, *Through Some Eventful Years* (Macon, Georgia, 1926), 271.

[4] Jacksonville *Florida Union*, May 27, 1865; New York *Tribune*, June 20, 1865.

[5] Ellen Call Long, *Florida Breezes* (Jacksonville, Florida, 1883), 382.

[6] I. Vogdes to B. C. Tilghman, May 20, 1865, in U. S. Army Commands, Florida, National Archives.

[7] Long, *op. cit.*, 381.

[8] Eppes, *op. cit.*, 271-72.

a saturnalia was held by the Negroes. . . . There was a broad grin on every countenance; shaking of hands, and a general air of extreme satisfaction, but no outbreak, no offensiveness; nothing to indicate a feeling of triumph, or joy of escape from thraldom.

"As a matter of history it should be recorded," Mrs. Long wrote years later, "that the Negroes of Florida except under evil influence conducted themselves with remarkable patience and good sense." "While freedom was welcomed by them," she added, "there was . . . no indecent outburst of congratulations. . . ."[9] A former slave reported the Negroes "were happy at the news, as they had hardly been aware that there was a war going on." Other ex-slaves were described as "jubilant, but not boastful."[10] It is generally conceded that although Florida Negroes greeted emancipation with obvious satisfaction there was little offensiveness on their part. Native whites were surprised at the ex-slaves' reaction. Former Senator David L. Yulee received a letter from his wife in June saying "the Negroes are all doing better than could be expected," and an ex-Confederate soldier wrote in the same month that the freedmen "are all conducting themselves much better than was feared."[11]

Some of the Negroes were merely bewildered at the reception of freedom. At first the ex-slaves could not comprehend emancipation, W.E.B. Dubois wrote with characteristic color, "but slowly, continuously, the wild truth, the bitter truth, the magic truth came surging through."[12] A Confederate soldier returning to Florida in early May "found the Negroes on the plantations and while there was some suppressed excitement, there was no indication that they were going to assert their freedom by abandoning the plantations." Indeed "they had not grasped their situation as freedmen . . ." he said.[13] A New York *Tribune* correspondent thought Florida freedmen "hardly knew what to do with themselves or with the boon of liberty." "The first and general anxiety was to do something on their own account," he added.

---

9 Long, *op. cit.*, 382; Ellen Call Long, History of Florida, 346.
10 Federal Writers Program, Florida Slave Interviews, 5-6.
11 N. Yulee to D. L. Yulee, June 8, 1865, in David L. Yulee Papers; S. A. Swann to R. Erwin, June 10, 1865, in Samuel A. Swann Papers.
12 W. E. B. DuBois, *Black Reconstruction* (Philadelphia, 1935), 122.
13 W. S. Simkins, "Why the Ku Klux," *The Alcalde*, IV (June 19, 1916), 735-48.

"They could think of nothing better than to go somewhere without asking leave or having a pass."[14]

After the first shock, the ex-slaves were inclined to test their new state. It was natural for a people who had been closely restricted to leave their former homes to demonstrate their freedom, and they began to wander. "The Negroes don't seem to feel free," a former slave owner wrote, "unless they leave their old home—just to make it sure they can go when and where they choose."[15] Soon "not less than a thousand of the dirty, ragged, jolly fellows" were in Jacksonville, Tallahassee, and Gainesville. Other towns also had an influx of Negroes.[16] A New York *Times* reporter noticed large numbers of Negroes at every railway station. "The large portion were females," he said, "decked in their gayest attire, and in a style that would throw the most ridiculous caricature in the shade."[17] Thomas W. Osborn, assistant commissioner of the Freedmen's Bureau in Florida, reported to his superior that "when the Negroes were first freed they exhibited a strong tendency to leave their homes and wander about the country," but the migratory spirit lasted only four to eight weeks. In his opinion the wandering of the freedman was due not to inclination alone, "but in a considerable degree to the disposition shown by his former owner and the unwillingness of the owner to adapt himself to the new conditions of the Negro."[18] The Gainesville *New Era* spoke of the "hundreds of colored women without husbands, roving about the country in penury and want . . . ," This disgraceful state, the editor said, was due to the "false impressions instilled into the Negro mind at his first reception of freedom by the false friends and crazy fanatics."[19]

Quick action was taken by military authorities to stop Negro migration. On June 13, 1865, a military patrol was established throughout the State to apprehend idlers and vagrants. "In case of Negroes found loitering about the country," the order read, "the cause of their absence will be inquired into, and if not satis-

[14] New York *Tribune*, June 20, 1865.

[15] E. Philips to J. J. Philips, January 21, 1866, in James J. Philips Papers.

[16] New York *Tribune*, June 20, 1865.

[17] New York *Times*, August 1, 1865.

[18] T. W. Osborn to O. O. Howard, November 1, 1865, in Bureau Records, Florida.

[19] Gainesville *New Era*, November 11, 1865.

factory, they will be returned to their homes." If such freedmen could not find employment they were to be sent under guard to the provost marshal, who was to turn them over to the superintendent of Negro affairs.[20] Colonel William Apthorp, commander at Jacksonville, received orders on June 18 to investigate the increase in the number of ex-slaves arriving in Jacksonville, and to cause all those unemployed to be sent out of town.[21] The Freedmen's Bureau also took steps to halt the roving freedmen. Assistant Commissioner Osborn ordered his subordinates to prevent as far as possible the congregation of Negroes about army posts and towns, and to disabuse them of the "impression they have that they will be fed. We must of course give some of them rations but I wish the number to be as small as consistency and humanity will permit."[22]

Not all of the freedmen wandered about the country after emancipation. A former slave, Louis Napoleon, said when the slaves on his plantation were notified of their freedom some of them left, but others remained deciding it was best to stay until the crops were harvested. These earnings helped them in their new venture in home seeking.[23] Another report stated that upon emancipation most of the "intelligent and those who had families almost immediately asked if they were compelled to leave." Those who had been well treated were eager to remain on the plantation.[24] The more intelligent Negroes, a white contemporary wrote, accepted freedom "with conscious sense of its responsibilities—while the more ignorant seemed awed and even fearful of a change. . . ."[25] Some of the ex-slaves seemed to have a vague idea of their independence but "little change in their relations to their old masters is perceptible," a traveler in Florida wrote. "In the back country they remain, as usual, on the little cracker plantations, and neither masters nor negroes succeeded in more than making a rude living."[26]

---

[20] General Orders No. 26, quoted in Gainesville *New Era*, November 11, 1865.

[21] S. L. McHenry to W. L. Apthorp, June 18, 1865, in U. S. Army Commands, Florida, National Archives.

[22] T. W. Osborn to D. P. Hancock, September 24, 1865, in Bureau Records, Florida.

[23] Federal Writers Program, Florida Slave Interviews, 5-6.

[24] Jacksonville *Florida Union*, May 27, 1865.

[25] Ellen Call Long, History of Florida, 347.

[26] Reid, *op. cit.*, 173.

Whether the freedmen roamed or remained at work their attitude toward their former masters was generally respectful. Even few native white Floridians complained of the Negroes' behavior. Indeed, the Negroes frequently retained affection for their former owners. One ex-slave, James Page, wrote the family of his former master several affectionate letters. One such epistle was headed "Miss Harriet My Dear Young Mistress," and closed with "ever your kind old servant and friend until death."[27] However, one Northerner traveling through Florida said, "the Negroes seemed deficient in love for the old masters, to whom we have been told that they were so much attached. . . ."[28] Even when they had no devotion to their former owners, the freedmen, whether through fear or respect, were usually inoffensive. Most of the disturbances between the races were initiated by whites.

The white reaction to emancipation was, of course, disapproval. It was difficult for many of them to comprehend, and some refused to give up the idea of slavery even after manumission was an existing fact. Floridians could not seem to believe the Negroes were really free, a native white wrote in later years. After the proclamation by local military officials such remarks were heard as " 'Negroes free? Free Negroes? I never heard of such a thing. I don't believe it.' "[29] General Vogdes reported in July that the whites were "as a body opposed to the freeing of their slaves, and many still have a lingering hope that some compensation will be awarded to them or that a system of apprenticeship will be established."[30]

The desire for slavery died hard, for in August the Gainesville *New Era* said,

> that there are quite a number of persons who seem to hope that the next Congress will reestablish slavery. Their hopes for future happiness and prosperity are wrapped up in this idea, instead of making up their minds to dismiss it at once and go to work manfully to make other arrangements for the future.

---

[27] James Page to Harriet Parkhill, January 9, February 17, March 23, 1866, in John Parkhill Papers, Southern Historical Collection, University of North Carolina, Chapel Hill, North Carolina.
[28] Reid, *op. cit.*, 162.
[29] Long, History of Florida, 346.
[30] I. Vogdes to O. O. Howard, July 31, 1865, in Bureau Records, Florida.

Major General John G. Foster, Commander of the Department of Florida, encountered the same idea. There were a large number of ex-slaveholders in Florida, he said in 1865, "who still hug the ghost of slavery, and hope that the State may get back into the Union with so loose guarantees upon that subject, that the institution may be revived by State laws at some future favorable opportunity." Whites in Florida "have so long and so selfishly regarded the Negro as created to be their slave—only that and nothing more—that their minds are cast in that mold." another observer reported.[31] A newspaper correspondent wrote:

> if Adam and Eve, when earning their bread by the sweat of their brows, had any deeper or sadder longing for a lost paradise than our planters have for a restoration of the institution of slavery, they must, indeed, have been unhappy and entitled to all the pity which misery could inspire.

These men did not look upon slavery as evil, but saw in it "nothing but personal ease and pleasure, political power and social position." In the absence of slavery they saw "poverty, lowliness, weakness, disgrace and ruin."[32] Florida whites in 1865 were already perpetuating the myth of the "good old days."

Some of the whites who accepted emancipation wanted, and in fact planned, to restore slavery under another name. One plan was to place a price upon labor without the consent of the laborer, and another was to authorize the employer to use the whip and other devices of the slave owner. Many planters discussed a scheme to enter into an agreement to employ only their own ex-slaves, thereby forcing the freedmen to remain on their old plantations and work on terms prescribed by their former masters.[33] Implementation of such designs was prevented by the Freedmen's Bureau, though the Bureau did frequently cooperate with the planter in forcing the freedmen to work at low wages.

Most whites apparently opposed emancipation, but their attitude toward their ex-slaves varied. That some of them retained

---

[31]Gainesville *New Era,* August 5, 1865; J. G. Foster to G. A. Forsyth, September 20, 1865, H. H. Moore to T. W. Osborn, February 25, 1866, in Bureau Records, Florida.

[32] New York *Tribune,* September 5, 1865.

[33] *Ibid.*

affection for their former chattels is demonstrated by an entry in the dairy of Susan Bradford of Tallahassee. "Nellie went away today," she wrote, "and the parting between her and Sister Mag was pitiful." Nellie had been Mag's nurse for years and the two girls had grown up together. When the former slave started to leave she "knelt on the floor and put her arms about sister, both were sobbing and both faces were wet with tears." Miss Bradford's younger brother was also "sorely distressed" at the parting, but "it is nothing as compared to his mother's grief. . . ."[34] Sometimes the whites' kind feeling for the Negroes was evidenced in an even more striking way. James Weldon Johnson, the Negro author, was born in Jacksonville in 1871. His mother was too ill to nurse him, and a white neighbor who heard of the unfortunate circumstances took the young Negro and nursed him "at her breast" until his mother had recovered. Thus, it appears in the land of black mammies at least one Negro boy had a white one.[35] Another white woman from Marion County wrote in her diary in February, 1867, that she went to some Negro houses and the church to attend the sick.[36]

According to many observers of the period the greatest hostility toward the Negro came from the poorer whites. General Vogdes wrote in July, 1865, that the "poor white" hated "the planters and the Negroes, envying the first and fearing the last." The white man's "hatred of 'yankees and niggers,' " a Union soldier stated, "seems to be in direct proportion to the depth of their ignorance, and the length of time that has elapsed since they last saw a newspaper." The feeling toward the freedmen "among the little planters, lawyers, . . . the cracker and other small fry" was "contemptible while the substantial planters" had "a degree of consideration for the former slaves that could hardly be expected," Assistant Commissioner Osborn reported in January, 1866.[37]

The antagonism between the freedmen and poor whites continued throughout Reconstruction and after. A Bureau agent in Holmes County, which had a small indigent population about one-

---

[34] Eppes, op. cit., 285-86.

[35] James Weldon Johnson, Along This Way (New York, 1933), 9.

[36] Maria Baker Taylor Diary, Typescript in P. K. Yonge Library of Florida History, Gainesville, Florida.

[37] I. Vogdes to O. O. Howard, July 31, 1865; T. W. Osborn to O. O. Howard, January 10, 1866, W. L. Apthorp to A. H. Jackson, September 10, 1867, in Bureau Records, Florida.

sixth Negro, made an acute observation. "In those isolated back-
woods counties the freedmen are still regarded as only 'niggers,'"
he wrote, "and the most worthless white man will persist in treat-
ing them as such, that they may have the satisfaction of thinking
themselves superior to at least some living creature. . . ." Human
nature in all its grades, he continued, "is ambitious of some sort
of superiority."[38] Unfortunately, even those who had affection
for the Negro exhibited it only as long as the freedmen kept
"their place." Miss Bradford, who was touched by the parting with
a former slave, tolerated no insolence. While sitting in her house
one day a group of Negro boys and girls passed singing "We'll
hang Jeff Davis to a sour apple tree." She seized a whip,
"and rushed into their midst and, laying the whip about me with
all the strength I could muster I soon had the whole crowd flying
toward the Quarters screaming as they went." It amused the
family to think that Miss Bradford was nineteen and had never
before struck a Negro.[39]

Whether white Floridians were fond of Negroes or detested
them they generally considered the Africans inherently inferior,
and intended to hold them in a subordinate position. The editor
of the Gainesville *New Era*, on June 8, 1865, announced his policy
as one of fairness and independence, but, he continued "'this is
a government of WHITE MEN,'" and "'inferiority of social and
political position for the Negro race, and superiority for the white
race, is the natural order of American Society.'"[40] Whites are bound
to treat the Negroes as free men, the editor said in August, 1865,
but "we are, and always will be the superior race."[41] Benjamin C.
Truman, a New York *Times* correspondent who was usually fair
to the South, discovered a class of people in Florida who pom-
pously claimed to be Caucasians and who disparaged every effort
made by the freedman. They raved about his being totally unfit
to care for himself, and insisted he was "but a few removes from
brute creation. . . ."[42]

The claim that the Negro was of a lower order appeared fre-

---

[38] W. J. Purman to A. H. Jackson, April 30, 1865, in Bureau Records,
Florida.

[39] Eppes, *op. cit.*, 280.

[40] Fritz W. Buchholz, *History of Alachua County Florida* (Saint Augustine,
1929), 130.

[41] Gainesville *New Era*, August 19, 1865.

[42] New York *Times*, December 25, 1865.

quently in the press and personal correspondence. A letter to the *New Era* from a seemingly educated man tried to demonstrate the reason for the Negroes' inferiority. The Moors, who were the "sons of Ham" went to Africa where their "minds became imbecile," he said. In Africa they had no human companions, but the baboon, ape, and orang-outang were suitable to their taste, "and long familiarity" brought about a resemblance between the animals and the descendants of the Moors. He suggested that the Moor interbred with the orang-outang, "the doctrine of the infecundity of hybrids" not being applicable in this instance. The Negro was "scarcely a whit" above the orang-outang in intelligence, he concluded.[43]

Such extravagant ideas were prevalent throughout the State. "The freed people are looked upon as an inferior and distinct race," a Bureau agent said, "and the difference, which is made is almost as great as in other parts of the civilized world, the difference between man and beast."[44] Even the clergy gave currency to such theories from the pulpit. A minister in Pensacola, in May, 1868, preached a discourse on the true gentlemen and lady. The sermon contained one undeniable thing, a member of the congregation said, "that a man of a certain cast could never be a true gentleman or *lady*."[45] The belief in the innate inferiority of the Negro was not restricted to the ignorant. An educated man from Florida, Emory F. Skinner, whose father was an abolitionist, believed the mulatto was a hybrid, "a cross which degenerates and devitalizes."[46] Florida newspapers approvingly quoted Dr. Josiah C. Nott, of Mobile, Alabama, who said the Negro had never shown any capacity for civilization or self government, and attained his nearest approach to civilization serving in a subordinate capacity. The brain of the African was inches smaller than the white, Nott added, and the large headed had always been the repository of true civilization. The Negro intellect could not be developed even by education continued through generations, and slavery was the

---

[43]Gainesville *New Era*, July 5, 1866.

[44] J. E. Quentin to C. Mundee, August 1, 1866, in Bureau Records, Florida.

[45] Warren Q. Dow Dairy, in P. K. Yonge Library of Florida History, Gainesville, Florida.

[46] Emory F. Skinner, *Reminescences* (Chicago, 1908), 282.

normal condition of the Negro, Nott believed. Indeed, servitude was advantageous to him.[47]

Many Floridians sincerely believed freedmen were of a lower order, but the theory was also used to rationalize unjust treatment. The privileges of voting and holding office were not considered "essential rights of freedom." The dark man was supposed to be incapable of exercising the right of suffrage.[48] Since the freedman was considered inferior, special laws were passed for his control. He did not receive the same treatment in courts of law, and his word was not good against a white man. The Negro, it was believed, should exist primarily to serve the whites. In the words of a Floridian, "no thinking man will doubt but that he will ever remain where he was intended, as the 'hewer of wood and drawer of water,' to the sons of Japhet."[49] Implicit obedience was to be rendered by the freedman. He was expected to "take the grossest insult with the calmness of a dumb brute," and the contradiction of the white man's word was "sufficient to warrant a blow."[50] In short, the Negro had been emancipated, but he was by no means equal, neither socially, politically, nor in the courts. White Floridians pretended to support such theories as the dignity of man, and the idea that all men were "endowed by their Creator with certain unalienable rights," among which were rights to "life, liberty, and the pursuit of happiness." But these rights for the most part were to apply only to themselves.

---

[47] Gainesville *New Era*, May 11, 1866; Weymouth T. Jordan, *Ante-Bellum Alabama Town and Country* (Tallahassee, 1957), 84-105; William S. Jenkins, *Pro-Slavery Thought in the Old South* (Chapel Hill, 1935), 242-284; Arthur Y. Lloyd, *The Slavery Controversy* (Chapel Hill, 1939), 228-242.
[48] Tallahassee *Semi-Weekly Floridian*, October 27, 1865; N. Yulee to D. L. Yulee, October 3, 1865, in David L. Yulee Papers.
[49] Gainesville *New Era*, October 28, 1865.
[50] J. E. Quentin to C. Mundee, August 1, 1866, in Bureau Records, Florida.

CHAPTER III

THE FREEDMEN'S BUREAU

It was obvious that the newly emancipated Negro needed help in adjusting to freedom. Suddenly the slave was free without the training and experience necessary to live successfully in a free society. Since the Negro was liberated by the United States government, a majority of congressmen believed it had a responsibility to supervise the transition from slavery to freedom. On March 3, 1865, after two years of congressional conflict, an act was passed creating the Bureau of Refugees, Freedmen, and Abandoned Lands. The new organization was placed under the War Department, and was to continue during the war of rebellion, and for one year thereafter.[1] The Bureau was authorized to supervise and manage all abandoned lands, and to control all subjects relative to freedmen and refugees in the Confederate States. The Bureau was placed under the management of a commissioner appointed by the president with the consent of the senate. An assistant commissioner could be placed in charge of each state declared to be in insurrection.[2]

The specific duties assigned the Bureau were few. The secretary of war was authorized to issue provisions, clothing, and fuel for the "immediate and temporary shelter and supply" of destitute freedmen and refugees. In addition, the commissioner was permitted to set apart abandoned and confiscated lands for the use of loyal refugees and Negroes. Every male freedman could be assigned a plot of land of not more than forty acres, on which he was to pay an annual rent not exceeding 6% of the value of the land as appraised by the State in 1860 for purposes of taxation. At the end of three years the land could be purchased by occupants on payment of the value from which the rent had been ascertained.[3] No provisions were made in the original act for Negro education,

---

[1] U. S. *Statutes at Large*, XIII, 507.
[2] *Ibid.*, 508.
[3] This clause of the act was partially responsible for the unfortunate forty acres and a mule myth. The freedmen came to believe that they would be given land and a mule, which caused some to be hesitant to go back to work for their former masters.

which was to be one of the more meritorious accomplishments of the Bureau. Authorization to supervise labor, organize Bureau courts, and establish freedmen's hospitals was not specifically given.[4] The responsibility of originating many of the policies necessary to protect and aid the freedmen devolved upon the commissioner.

The man selected to guide Bureau activities was General Oliver Otis Howard. Howard, a West Point graduate, became colonel of the 3rd Maine Regiment in June, 1861, and was soon promoted to brigadier general. He participated in the first battle of Bull Run and the Peninsular campaign, suffering the loss of his right arm at Fair Oaks. His personal bravery was undisputed and he gained a reputation as "a great Biblical soldier" and humanitarian. Howard's experience seemingly equipped him to handle the complex duties of supervising the freedmen, and "so far as good intentions, humanitarian passion, and religious enthusiasm were concerned," he was a good choice. Many observers, however, believed "Howard left much to be desired as an executive."[5] General Howard, appointed commissioner May 12, 1865, immediately assumed management of the Bureau, and soon had it in operation. The most pressing problems, he believed, were to rehabilitate labor, guarantee actual freedom for the Negro, secure justice for him in the courts, supervise labor contracts, aid benevolent societies as much as possible in their educational work, and raise revenue by rent on abandoned property to meet operating expenses.[6]

The Bureau was not at once organized in Florida. On June 13, 1865, Major General Rufus Saxton was made assistant commissioner of South Carolina, Georgia, and Florida, with headquarters at Beaufort, South Carolina.[7] During this time the Bureau accomplished little in Florida. The military still bore the primary responsibility of caring for the freedmen. The actual genesis of

---

[4] U. S. *Statutes at Large*, XIII, 507-509.

[5] *Dictionary of American Biography* (22 vols., New York, 1928-58), IX, 279-80.

[6] Oliver Otis Howard, *Autobiography* (2 vols., New York, 1907), II, 225.

[7] Florida had five assistant commissioners, but one of them, Rufus Saxton, never served in the State. The other four, Thomas W. Osborn, John G. Foster, John T. Sprague, and George W. Gile, were all respected by Florida whites. New York *Times*, June 25, 1866; U. S. Congress, *House Executive Documents*, 39th Cong., 1st Sess., No. 11, 46.

the Bureau in the State was marked by the appointment, in September, 1865, of Colonel Thomas W. Osborn as assistant commissioner.[8] Osborn was a native of New Jersey and a graduate of Madison University in New York. He gave up the study of law on the outbreak of the war to join the Union Army as an artillery officer, in which capacity he was seriously wounded several times.[9] Osborn served as Howard's Chief of Artillery at Gettysburg, and was described by his superior as "a quiet unobtrusive officer of quick decision and pure life."[10] He was familiar with conditions in Florida as he had campaigned in the State with the 24th Massachusetts Infantry.[11]

Osborn was a man of much energy and executive ability, and within three months he had the Bureau in reasonably effective operation, though he was greatly hampered by lack of assistance. In October, 1865, he lamented that he was absolutely alone, without even a clerk, and had a large accumulation of work on his hands.[12] By the end of 1865 only seven persons in Florida had Bureau work as their primary responsibility.[13] Osborn arranged to secure some part-time employees by issuing an order on September 30, 1865, directing all post commanders within the Department of Florida to report to him for duty in conducting Bureau affairs. The post commanders were not full-time agents. They were not excused from any of their military duties, and were not required to perform Bureau services if it in any way interfered with their activities as army officers.[14] On November 21, 1865, Osborn relieved the commanders of their responsibility to the Bureau, and made the judge of probate in each county a Bureau agent. In the absence of the judge the clerks of circuit court were ordered to act as agents for the Bureau and to "conduct its affairs within the limits of their civil jurisdiction."[15]

---

[8] *Ibid.*, 57.

[9] Rowland H. Rerick, *Memoirs of Florida* (2 vols., Atlanta, 1902), I, 306.

[10] Howard, *op. cit.*, II, 218.

[11] William Watson Davis, *The Civil War and Reconstruction in Florida* (New York, 1913), 380.

[12] T. W. Osborn to W. W. Maple, October 27, 1865, in Bureau Records, Florida.

[13] George R. Bentley, *A History of the Freedmen's Bureau* (Philadelphia, 1955), 73.

[14] T. W. Osborn to C. Mundee, September 30, 1865, in Bureau Records, Florida; General Order, No. 23, September 30, 1865, in U. S. Army Commands, Florida.

[15] Tallahassee *Semi-Weekly Floridian*, November 7, 1865; U. S. Congress, *House Executive Documents*, 39th Cong., 1st Sess., No. 70, 86-88.

Civil officers were advised by Provisional Governor William Marvin to comply with Osborn's request. Some of the civil agents did not seem to have the best interests of the freedmen in mind, but most of them accepted their duties in good faith. Though there were several complaints about the civil agents, Osborn reported in January, 1866, that they were generally attempting to deal justly with the ex-slaves. There were a few cases of partiality in dividing crops, but they were believed to be exceptions. The next month Osborn reported that he had been forced to remove some civil officials and countermand some of their orders. The service was unpopular, and those who attempted honestly to carry out their duties were frequently recipients of insults from native whites.[16]

In July, 1866, Congress overrode a presidential veto to extend the Bureau two more years. The new bill authorized Commissioner Howard to retain officers of the Veterans Reserve Corps already in the Bureau at the same compensation they received before being mustered out of the service. This made it possible to increase the number of Bureau employees, though the number of agents in Florida was always relatively small. By 1866, Bureau officials were scattered throughout the State. Local officials were titled sub-assistant commissioners and had jurisdiction over sub-districts composed of two to four counties.[17] In November, 1866, the Bureau in Florida employed twenty officers and five civilians.[18]

The act of 1866 which increased the personnel of the Bureau also extended its power. The sum of $6,994,450 was appropriated to be used for food, clothing, schools, and asylums for freedmen. In addition to the appropriation, the Bureau was authorized to use confiscated property for school houses.[19] The amount expended in Florida was never large. In 1866 the Bureau spent $15,-589.62 in the State. Expenditures increased to $27,435.09 in 1867,

---

16 *Ibid.*, 88, 275; U. S. Congress, *Senate Executive Documents*, 39th Cong., 2nd Sess., No. 6, 43; T. W. Osborn to O. O. Howard, January 10, 1866, February n.d., 1866, in Bureau Records, Florida.

17 *Senate Executive Documents*, 39th Cong., 2nd Sess., No. 6, 43; U. S. *Statutes at Large*, XIV, 174-77.

18 U. S. Congress, *House Executive Documents*, 39th Cong., 2nd Sess., No. 1, pt. 1, 753.

19 U. S. *Statutes at Large*, XIV, 174-77; Bentley, *op. cit.*, 134.

and to \$57,993.84 in 1868.[20] Aid rendered to the Negroes by the Bureau was not limited to money.

In July, 1868, the Bureau was again extended for one year. It could be discontinued in any State fully restored to the Union, except the educational division, which was not to be affected until the State had made adequate provision for Negro education.[21] In April, 1869, Commissioner Howard issued orders to assistant commissioners to discharge all agents and civil employees of the Bureau to take effect April 30, except the superintendent of education, one clerk, and agents who were helping Negro veterans collect their mustering out bounty.[22] By April 30, 1869, only George W. Gile, the superintendent of education, remained in Florida. By the end of 1870 the Bureau had been discontinued in the State.[23]

While the Bureau was in Florida it rendered significant assistance to the freedmen. The Bureau was a flexible organization which enabled it to adapt to and meet local needs. Therefore, its value in any locale depended to a large extent on the character and competency of the assistant commissioner and local agents. The Bureau officials in Florida were, in general, a creditable group and their accomplishments worthy of praise. A New York *Times* correspondent wrote in June, 1866, that both whites and Negroes spoke highly of Florida Assistant Commissioner Osborn. Not only was he an "upright and efficient officer," they said, but as a general thing his subordinates were men of "honor and respectability."[24] The Steedman-Fullerton investigation of early 1866, which was clearly intended to discredit the Bureau, gave Florida a favorable report.[25] The editor of the conservative Tallahassee *Floridian* wrote in May, 1866, "we doubt whether the duties of the Bureau could have been administered by anyone more acceptably, alike

---

20 J. G. Foster to O. O. Howard, October 1, 1866, J. T. Sprague to O. O. Howard, October 1, 1867, October n.d., 1868, in Bureau Records, Florida; *Senate Executive Documents*, 39th Cong., 2nd Sess., No. 6, 47.

21 U. S. *Statutes at Large*, XV, 83.

22 Circular letter issued April 13, 1869, by O. O. Howard, in Bureau Records, Florida.

23 Statement in Special Orders and Circulars, April 30, 1869, in Bureau Records, Florida; Tallahassee *Weekly Floridian*, November 19, 1870.

24 New York *Times*, June 25, 1866.

25 On April 11, 1866, at a time when congress was attempting to strengthen the Bureau, President Andrew Johnson sent two "carefully selected" men, Generals J. B. Steedman and J. S. Fullerton, to investigate Bureau activities. The investigation uncovered some abuses and corruption, but Florida received a favorable report. Bentley, *op. cit.*, 125-30.

to the blacks and whites, than they have been by Col. Osborn. . . .
Few could have done better—many might have done worse."[26]

Other agents received praise from native whites. When John
T. Sprague and John G. Foster were in charge of the Bureau they
usually maintained friendly relations with civil officials, and a
majority of the whites. Local agents were generally considered
fair also. When George B. Carse resigned as adjutant general in
1870, it was said that "when he had it in his power, as agent of
the Freedmen's Bureau, to deal harshly with us, he did not abuse
his privileges. On the contrary, his conduct was generally commended as just and fair."[27] In February, 1866, former Governor
Abraham K. Allison claimed the Bureau interfered "but very
little" in the affairs of citizens and he had not heard of a single
"instance of injustice" being done by it in the State.[28] Many of
the complaints about the Bureau were politically motivated and
came at a later date when it was no longer in existence.

All agents did not receive the approval of local whites. That
such an agency existed to aid and protect the freedmen was irritating to the many whites who claimed it was unnecessary.[29] In
protecting the Negroes, Bureau agents sometimes came in conflict
with whites, which caused unfriendly sentiments. In July, 1866,
a white physician wrote: "we are cursed with one of those pests
that remind us daily of our degradation," a Bureau agent. The
agent had encouraged the freedmen in such "reprehensible" activities as celebrating the anniversary of their emancipation.[30] Citizens of Marianna complained because the local agent, Captain
Charles Hamilton, had not accepted invitations to visit them. "He
seemed to prefer," they said, "the freedmen and certain white
men of no social standing, and kept himself aloof from the more
respectable portion of the community."[31] It was also disturbing
to white Floridians when Republican agents gave political instruction to freedmen.

---

26 Tallahassee *Semi-Weekly Floridian*, May 25, 1866.
27 *Ibid.*, June 8, 1866, April 30, 1867; Tallahassee *Weekly Floridian*, February 22, 1870.
28 A. K. Allison to D. L. Yulee, February 22, 1866, in David L. Yulee Papers.
29 W. Marvin to A. Johnson, February 20, 1866, in Andrew Johnson Papers, Library of Congress, Washington, D. C.
30 E. Philips to J. J. Philips, July 2, 1866, in James J. Philips Papers.
31 T. T. Flint to C. F. Larrabee, September 9, 1867, in Bureau Records, Florida.

Repeated attempts to discredit the Bureau with charges of corruption were unsuccessful. Agents were accused of selling rations that were supposed to be distributed to needy freedmen and refugees. Investigations always proved such accusations groundless, though rations were sometimes given to Negroes and refugees who could have cared for themselves.[32] Commissioner Howard, who was extremely sensitive to any accusation of corruption, exerted considerable energy in keeping his own house clean.[33] Agents in Jackson County did charge fees for drawing up labor contracts, until a War Department order in February, 1867, prohibited such charges.[34]

The Bureau, as will be seen, was able to provide freedmen much needed relief, education, a free labor system, and equal rights before the law for a short time. It created a small independent land-owning class of Negroes, and guided them politically. But what the freedmen really needed after their emancipation was something no federal agency could secure for them, a change in the attitude of the white South. The Bureau failed to solve the important, and perhaps impossible, problem of establishing good relations between whites and Negroes, but probably it did as well as any agency could have done in like circumstances.

---

[32] D. Boyd and G. Brown to J. T. Sprague, June 27, 1867, J. L. Husband to A. H. Jackson, September 16, 1867, in Bureau Records, Florida.

[33] O. O. Howard to T. W. Osborn, February 28, 1866, in Bureau Records, Florida.

[34] T. T. Flint to C. F. Larrabee, September 9, 1867, in Bureau Records, Florida.

CHAPTER IV

ADJUSTMENT TO FREEDOM

The newly freed slave had great adjustments to make to his new status. The transition from a life of dependency to one of independent responsibility required some aid. The rendering of such assistance fell to the Freedmen's Bureau. One of the first problems faced by the Bureau was feeding the destitute freedmen. Some of the Negroes left their homes after emancipation, and had no means of livelihood. Furthermore, some of the ex-slaves, including the old and disabled, were ejected from the plantations, and were facing starvation. The Bureau, at first, could see no way to feed indigent Negroes as it had no appropriations. But soon Commissioner Howard discovered a clause in the law establishing the government agency, which would permit the secretary of war to issue provisions and clothing to needy freedmen and refugees.[1] Secretary of War Edwin M. Stanton authorized the Commissary General of the Army, A. B. Eaton, to provide for destitute Negroes, as well as whites.[2] The Bureau began to issue rations in Florida in June, 1865. The more than 760,000 rations issued in Florida from June, 1865 to December, 1868, undoubtedly prevented starvation and extreme deprivation not only among Negroes, but among whites as well.[3]

Contrary to popular opinion, the Bureau in Florida did not support the Negro in idleness, though some of the freedmen, as well as whites, sought to take advantage of government provisions to avoid work. General Ulysses S. Grant reported in December, 1865, that "the freedman's mind does not seem to be disabused of the idea that a freedman has the right to live without care or provision for the future," and Assistant Commissioner Osborn wrote in November, 1865, that in some towns the drawing of rations was

---

[1] Howard, op. cit., II, 256.
[2] House Executive Documents, 39th Cong., 1st Sess., No. 11, 15.
[3] As late as 1867, it was reported that 500 whites were dependent on the Bureau at least six months out of the year. Monthly Reports of the Assistant Commissioner, July, 1866-December, 1868, in Bureau Records, Florida; House Executive Documents, 39th Cong., 1st Sess., No. 70, 276; Junius E. Dovell, Florida: Historic, Dramatic, Contemporary (4 vols., New York, 1952), II, 544.

becoming somewhat professional.[4] This was remedied by an order to Florida agents to inform Negroes that rations would not be distributed after December, 1865, even though such action would necessarily cause some suffering.[5] By 1867, the issue of provisions was limited almost wholly to those not only impecunious, but in hospitals and asylums. The Bureau believed it necessary to continue to give rations to this class of people, since the State was not caring for them.[6] The Bureau did relax its stringent rules against feeding the freedmen in 1868. That year Florida had an inferior cotton crop and many supplies were issued, but by 1869 most of the Negroes were on their own.[7] By intelligent issuing of rations the Bureau performed a laudatory service in preventing the Negro from starving until he could provide for himself, while at the same time convincing him that he must work if he intended to eat.

The question of health was another problem faced by the freedmen after emancipation. The breakup of the plantation system left the Negroes without proper medical attention. When in bondage, the freedmen had been cared for by their masters, but after emancipation the ex-owners no longer bore this responsibility, and the Negroes were often either unable or too ignorant to care for themselves. An ex-slave said the Negroes who had been associated with the "grannies" during slavery had learned how to cure all manner of ills, with herbs and roots, but such cures were sometimes more serious than the diseases.[8]

Moreover, the freedmen sometimes had little conception of proper sanitation, and diseases tended to assume epidemic proportions. Small pox, cholera, and chills and fever were ills suffered most frequently. In December, 1865, a few Negroes died of small pox in Marianna because of neglect, and at the same time

---

4 U. S. Congress, *Senate Executive Documents*, 39th Cong., 1st Sess., No. 2, 107; T. W. Osborn to O. O. Howard, November 30, 1865, in Bureau Records, Florida.

5 T. W. Osborn to O. O. Howard, November 30, 1865, in Bureau Records, Florida.

6 U. S. Congress, *House Executive Documents*, 40th Cong., 2nd Sess., No. 1, 677.

7 *House Executive Documents*, 40th Cong., 3rd Sess., No. 1, pt. 1, 1027.

8 Federal Writers Program, Florida Slave Interviews, 7; Weymouth T. Jordan (ed.), *Herbs, Hoecakes and Husbandry The Daybook of a Planter of the Old South* (Tallahassee, 1960), 72-114.

there were some small pox cases in Jacksonville.[9] This disease was controlled only by a sytematic campaign of vaccination by the Freedmen's Bureau. Thousands of Negroes received inoculations against this dread disease at vaccinating stations set up throughout the State.[10] Cholera also appeared among the Negroes in malignant form. On September 11, 1866, a Bureau agent reported twenty cases in Cedar Keys, mostly among the freedmen. Again this disease was controlled, but primarily by the Bureau. Citizens of the area were so panic stricken three white victims were left lying where they died, the agent said. He buried the deceased and encouraged sanitation.[11] The freedmen suffered more widely from malaria. Fully one-third of the population in northeast Florida, a Bureau agent wrote from Fernandina in September, 1867, had been prostrated with intermittent and congestive chills and fever. Some of the cases were fatal. Nothing seemed to prevent a recurrence of this illness except protracted rest, generous diet, and freedom from exposure. The Negroes, ignorant of hygienic laws and living in poverty, were "peculiarly disqualified for taking such care and precaution as is essential to restoration of health," the agent added.[12] Some of the freedmen suffered, not from any particular disease, but from malnutrition and neglect. There was among the freedmen, a Bureau agent wrote, "a great deal of suffering from want of proper food, and medical attention—some of them among the aged and infirm, who are not able to pay for medical attendance. . . ."[13] Largely because of this neglected class, the Freedmen's Bureau opened a hospital.

The Freedmen's Hospital was established on November 14, 1865, at Jacksonville with a capacity of fifty beds. The hospital was not intended for all freedmen, but for infirm Negroes and refugees, and those who could not secure medical treatment otherwise.[14]

---

[9] E. Philips to J. J. Philips, December 12, 1865, in James J. Philips Papers; Webster Merritt, *A Century of Medicine in Jacksonville and Duval County* (Gainesville, Florida, 1949), 64.

[10] William T. Cash, *History of the Democratic Party in Florida* (Tallahassee, 1936), 51.

[11] H. H. Kuhn to J. G. Foster, September 11, 1866, in Bureau Records, Florida.

[12] D. M. Hammond to J. T. Sprague, September 5, 1867, D. M. Hammond to A. H. Jackson, October 7, 1867, in Bureau Records, Florida.

[13] W. D. Dodge to C. L. Larrabee, May 31, 1867, in Bureau Records, Florida.

[14] J. W. Applegate to J. H. Lyman, October 28, 1866, in Bureau Records, Florida.

The medical staff in Florida was always small. In February, 1866, the State had only four medical officers, three regimental surgeons, and one acting assistant surgeon.[15] From the time the hospital was opened to June, 1869, 2,718 people were treated, 89 of whom died.[16] By the end of 1869 no Bureau physicians remained in Florida. Only a relatively small number had been treated in the Bureau Hospital, but it had rendered valuable service in providing for the aged, who had no one to care for them. The Bureau also helped support an orphanage for Negro children.

Adjustment to family life was another important problem encountered by the newly emancipated Negro. Through no fault of their own some of the freedmen had little conception of marital and family obligations. Slavery had "a degrading, dehumanising influence upon the slaves," and induced "a laxity in sexual relations" that carried over into freedom.[17] Generally speaking, "slave marriage did not exist as a legal institution, and chastity" was said to be "a rare virtue among the blacks."[18] The ex-slaves saw no particular reason for changing the practice by which they had always lived. However, whites, both Northern and Southern, decided that cohabitation among the Negroes should be legal since they were free, but there were complications in forcing the freedmen to go through legal ceremonies. Many of the ex-bondsmen had more than one mate while slaves, and a problem of selection arose. Furthermore, after emancipation some of the freedmen discarded husbands and wives selected for them by their masters, and chose their own. If they were to be forced to marry, which selection was the proper one?

To cope with the problem, General Saxton in August, 1865, sent down an elaborate directive naming those freedmen who could be married or divorced. Authorized by the Bureau to marry were those never before married who were of age, all those who could furnish acceptable evidence of divorce or death of all

---

[15] *House Executive Documents*, 39th Cong., 1st Sess., No. 70, 281.

[16] U. S. Congress, *House Executive Documents*, 39th Cong., 2nd Sess., No. 1, pt. 1, 720; 40th Cong., 2nd Sess., No. 1, pt. 1, 631; 40th Cong., 3rd Sess., No. 1, pt. 1, 1024; 41st Cong., 2nd Sess., No. 142, 1024.

[17] Alrutheus Ambush Taylor, *The Negro in the Reconstruction of Virginia* (Washington, D. C., 1926), 203.

[18] James G. Randall, *The Civil War and Reconstruction* (Boston, 1953), 66.

former spouses, and married persons who could prove they had been separated three years from their partners by slavery and had no evidence their former mates were alive, or if alive, would be restored to them. Ordained pastors and civil officers were authorized to grant marriage permits to all who met these qualifications. All persons whose marriage was only a mutual agreement without a ceremony were required to have their marriage confirmed by a minister, and to obtain some kind of wedding certificate.[19]

The freedmen did not immediately rush to ministers after General Saxton's directive. In October, 1865, the Gainesville *New Era* spoke of "the present immoral state of universal concubinage in which they were living. . . ."[20] It was difficult for some ex-slaves to understand why marriage was so important when one year earlier it had been of so little consequence. The Bureau promptly began to try to combat such attitudes. Bureau agents were instructed to inform their charges of the necessity of a legal ceremony, and in 1866 the State Legislature passed a law requiring marriage of those living together.[21] Freedmen were soon being married in large numbers. A newspaper reported in July, 1866, that the Negroes who had been living together as husband and wife were "coming forward promptly, and obeying the law upon the subject." Civil officials were marrying as many as twenty couples a day.[22] In June, 1866, Superintendent of Schools for Freedmen, The Reverend Mr. E. B. Duncan, visited a plantation at Waukeenah, where he married fifty-three couples, and married enough on a neighboring plantation to bring the number to one hundred. He formalized marriages, he said, in the fields or roads, anywhere, explaining the necessity of the solemn vows.[23] In accordance with state law, one man reputed to be one hundred and six years old and a woman eighty were married in Madison County. They had lived together many years during slavery, but had never been legally married.[24] In order to expedite marriages, mass weddings were sometimes held.

Florida Negroes were married by the hundreds, but still many of them had little conception of the obligations of the vows. "I

---

19 *House Executive Documents*, 39th Cong., 1st Sess., No. 70, 108-9.
20 Gainesville *New Era*, October 11, 1865.
21 J. H. Durkee to S. L. McHenry, July 1, 1866, in Bureau Records, Florida.
22 Gainesville *New Era*, July 13, 1866.
23 E. B. Duncan to T. W. Osborn, June 31, 1866, in Bureau Records, Florida.
24 Tallahassee *Sentinel*, September 11, 1866.

am sorry to represent," an observer wrote in August, 1867, "that the marriage relations between persons of color—is not properly understood nor regarded in its sanctity." He said that many of the Negroes had asked for permission to separate and marry again after only three months of marriage, and many men kept both wives and concubines.[25] Numerous observers commented that infidelity existed to a considerable degree. Many of the ex-slaves, it was said, thought it necessary only to "say quit" and they were at liberty to marry again.[26] Such a cavalier attitude toward marital vows was due to "the peculiar relations which they bore to one another before their emancipation."[27] There is little doubt that many of the marital problems of the freedmen had "their origin in the indiscriminate cohabitation which existed" during slavery.[28] The ex-slaves could hardly be expected immediately to become model husbands and wives.

The feeling of family responsibility did develop. As early as June, 1866, Duncan found the moral condition of the ex-slave improving daily.[29] Even if marriage relations were not what they should be, the Negroes soon began to appreciate their responsibility to law and society. The freedman had only recently been invested with the rights and responsibilities of marriage, and like his white neighbors did not measure up to professed white ideals. Though the freedman was not "fully up to the standard even of the class known as 'poor whites,'" an observer wrote in September, 1868, his "behavior thus far in the mixed condition incident to his 'previous relations' gives promise that he will soon rise far above their level." This progress was at least partially due to the churches. Religious societies, according to a contemporary, exercised "a constant scrutiny into the lives of their members; they punish with expulsion the profligate and unworthy, and cast much odium upon immorality and especially the absence

---

[25] A. B. Grumwell to A. H. Jackson, August 31, 1867, in Bureau Records, Florida.
[26] J. A. Remley to A. H. Jackson, July 31, 1867, J. T. Sprague to O. O. Howard, October 1, 1867, D. M. Hammond to A. H. Jackson, September 10, 1868, in Bureau Records, Florida.
[27] J. A. Remley to A. H. Jackson, May 31, 1867, in Bureau Records, Florida.
[28] J. A. Dickinson to A. H. Jackson, September 17, 1868, in Bureau Records, Florida.
[29] E. B. Duncan to T. W. Osborn, June 31, 1866, in Bureau Records, Florida.

of virtue."[30] In 1872, Harriet Beecher Stowe claimed many of
the Negroes were not legally married, but they were faithful in
family relations.[31] There were those who denied the reported improvement in the freedmen's morals. One minister wrote in 1871
that separations between Negroes were so frequent he had determined "to celebrate the Rites of Matrimony but seldom between
them."[32]

Infidelity was not the only problem marring family relations.
There were many reports of wife beating. Hardly a day passed,
wrote a transplanted Northerner, but that some freedman beat his
wife, "frequently laying her up for a day or two."[33] Bureau agents
also reported several complaints of wife beating, though one
thought it was no more common than among the lower class of
whites in the State.[34] The ex-slaves reputedly had so little feeling
of family responsibility it was deemed necessary by the Bureau to
define the responsibilities of the male to his wife and children.[35]
Infanticide was said to be high especially among young women, and
Negro mothers were accused of neglecting their children.[36] Some
of the negligence was due to ignorance rather than lack of affection,
because even when the relationship between husband and wife was
not understood, both mates seemed to want the children. The
Bureau had numerous requests to help locate children who had
been lost during slavery.[37]

Despite early shortcomings, the family relationship rapidly improved. The freedmen soon began to appreciate their responsibility for the "maintenance and proper training of their children."
"The industry of the freedman," wrote an observer in 1868, "ju-
diciously caring for themselves, together with a personal pride in
all that relates to his family, have been apparent this season far

30 J. A. Dickinson to A. H. Jackson, September 17, 1868, J. T. Sprague to
O. O. Howard, October 1, 1867, in Bureau Records, Florida.

31 Harriet Beecher Stowe, *Palmetto Leaves* (Boston, 1873), 291-92.

32 *Journal of the Proceedings of the Twenty-Eighth Annual Convention of
the Protestant Episcopal Church of the Diocese of Florida, 1871* (Tallahassee,
1871), 31.

33 A. B. Hart to Mary Hart, July 31, 1870, in Ambrose B. Hart Letters.

34 A. B. Grumwell to A. H. Jackson, July 31, 1867, September 14, 1868, in
Bureau Records, Florida.

35 *House Executive Documents*, 39th Cong., 1st Sess., No. 70, 110.

36 J. H. Durkee to A. H. Jackson, August 5, 1867, in Bureau Records,
Florida; Tampa *Florida Peninsular*, July 7, 1866.

37 F. E. Grossman to T. W. Osborn, October 1, 1866, in Bureau Records,
Florida; *The National Freedman*, I (September 15, 1865), 256.

more than at any former period" This change, he added, was the result of the churches and schools.[38] Even when the obligations of the family were understood, the women were not usually equipped to be housewives. Many of them had worked in the fields, and had no other training. Sewing schools were sometimes set up for women, and the teacher in one such school complained of the deplorable "ignorance of house and home life" among Negro women. "They have the simplest things to learn," she stated, and however rapidly they might acquire knowledge their early habits and associations would be difficult to overcome.[39] Moreover, most Negro families were further burdened with poverty.

Living conditions of the Negroes were not calculated to promote harmony even if misunderstandings did not exist. Most freedmen were poverty-stricken as evidenced by their quarters, apparel, and food. Rude huts, abandoned buildings, or any type of shelter was inhabited. In Jacksonville three-fourths of the Negro dwellings were reputedly worse than a respectable New England farmer "would consign a pig to. . . . Some contain only one room in which live a whole family, in dirt and misery." There were some neat cottages, but they were exceptions.[40] Everything resembling a "house, hut or hovel" was crowded to overflowing. In some families as many as five people slept in one bed. Every abandoned magazine in old fortifications in Jacksonville was said to be occupied by a family.[41] Some of the houses were without floors, furniture, and window panes. Many families were forced to build fires for cooking out of doors. A Florida citizen complaining about Negro housing in Tallahassee unkindly said, "you can tell how near you are to the city better by the smell than by the mile post."[42] Clothing and food were sometimes as pitiable as housing. Apparel was often not only coarse, but inadequate to provide protection from exposure. The primary diet was "hog and hominy"

---

[38] M. L. Stearns to A. H. Jackson, September 18, 1868, in Bureau Records, Florida; J. W. Alvord, *Fifth Semi-Annual Report on Schools for Freedmen* (Washington, 1868), 30.

[39] *The National Freedman*, I (July 15, 1868), 180-81.

[40] John Francis LeBaron Diary, in Jacksonville Public Library, Jacksonville, Florida.

[41] T. W. Osborn to O. O. Howard, February 19, 1866, in Bureau Records, Florida; Jacksonville *Florida Union*, September 16, 1865; E. Philips to J. J. Philips, October 27, 1865, in James J. Philips Papers.

[42] Tallahassee *Semi-Weekly Floridian*, November 7, 1865.

mixed with greens in season.[43] Roots and sweet potatoes were also eaten. The sweet potato became such a constant part of the Negro diet that in portions of Florida it was known as the "nigger choker."

Naturally, the freedmen did not live in such misery by choice, and conditions were altered as rapidly as possible. They were anxious to improve their condition, educate their children, provide homes for their family, and accumulate savings; and a few were successful, at least in a minor way. A few years after emancipation some Negroes had comfortable and neat, though rough, houses. As early as 1865, Whitelaw Reid saw in Key West dozens of new frame homes, built and inhabited by freedmen.[44] In 1874, the commissioner of lands and immigration in Florida reported that "the large body of our colored citizens have already acquired means enough to build houses, purchase property, and surround themselves with most of the comforts of home."[45]

Perhaps the commissioner's report was an optimistic picture, but the freedmen had made progress. They refuted those critics who claimed they would degenerate "into vicious and indolent vagabonds." They acquired habits of thrift and forethought equal to any other race of similar economic standing, and, indeed, they had made great strides in the acquisition of wealth within a decade of emancipation. They were not wealthy, a majority of them were not even in comfortable circumstances, but they had made remarkable gains considering their sudden independence and lack of training, their poverty, ignorance and continued oppression. Some of the freedmen were extravagant and squandered what small amount of money they acquired, but others were thrifty and thoughtful.

In 1874 a New York *Times* correspondent speaking of Florida freedmen said: "many of them have become well educated, and have given a good and proper direction to the sentiments of the lower class of Negroes. Starting out with mere instincts of liberty," he continued, "they have come to accept the conditions of law and order, and of mutual dependence, as essential to their own progress in the path which events have marked out for them."

---

43 Mrs. H. B. Greely to G. Whipple, March 1, 1865, in American Missionary Association Archives.

44Reid, *op. cit.*, 187.

45 *Sixth Annual Report of the Commissioner of Lands and Immigration of the State of Florida*, 1874 (Tallahassee, 1874), 17-18.

According to the census of 1870, Florida had 147 persons being supported at public expense. Only 62 of the 147 were Negroes. By this time there were many comments about the neat and orderly appearance of many of the freedmen. In July, 1871, a group of Negroes from Tallahassee made an excursion to Savannah. The Savannah *Republican* claimed to " 'have never seen a more decent, orderly and well dressed crowd of colored people' " and congratulated Tallahassee " 'upon the character of her colored citizens. . . .' "[46] By 1874 some of the ex-slaves were even in a position to aid the more unfortunate of their own race. Negro women in Ocala organized a benevolent society to attend the sick, hold sacred services for those with lingering illnesses, and inter those whose families were unable to provide decent burial.[47]

Despite their depressed condition, the freedmen were generally able to make the best of the situation, and enjoy themselves. Since the Negroes had not been accustomed to anything better they were not always fully aware of the depressed conditions in which they lived. Furthermore, they were able to adjust to existing circumstances in such a way as to permit them to get the most out of what they had. A former New Yorker, homesteading in Florida, wrote in 1867 that the Negroes laughed and sang from morning until night, and every evening they indulged in the "most constant string of stories and guffawes it is possible to imagine."[48] On Saturday the freedmen went to town in great numbers, where they visited the stores and each other. "They go marching about the streets," an observer said,

> orderly as a procession and file into the stores until there is scarcely standing-room, getting on very quietly until late in the day, when some of them, while under the influence of badly-adulterated whiskey, become noisy and obstreperous—thus ending their day's frolic in the lock-up.[49]

However, there was not much intemperance among the freedmen, according to commentators, at least in the first few years

---

[46] New York *Times*, October 29, 1875; *Ninth Census of the United States, 1870*, I, 568; Tallahassee *Weekly Floridian*, July 11, 1871.

[47] Tallahassee *Weekly Floridian*, July 21, 1874.

[48] A. B. Hart to Mother, January 23, 1867, A. B. Hart to Emily Hart, February 6, 1867, in Andrew B. Hart Letters.

[49] Abbie M. Brooks, *Petals Plucked From Sunny Climes* (2nd ed., Nashville, Tennessee, 1885), 330-31.

after emancipation. Although Negroes outnumbered whites three to one, an agent wrote from Monticello in September, 1868, few instances of intoxication were seen among them. This was not always because they did not drink, he said, but because they could not afford liquor. Other agents noticed little intemperance among the ex-slaves, though apparently it was on the increase by 1868, in part because of the freedmen's tendency to ape the whites.[50] Intoxication was reportedly no more frequent among Negroes than whites, but in order to combat the vice, and also to provide social organizations, many temperance societies were organized by the freedmen. Few towns of importance were without such a society, and reputedly they were effective. Whatever vicious habits may be attributed to Florida Negroes, one contemporary said, intemperance was not one of them.[51]

The freedmen engaged in organized social and recreational activities other than temperance societies. Baseball became popular, and games between neighboring towns were frequent. Volunteer fire companies served as social institutions as well as being a credit to the community. Parades, picnics, and barbecues were other popular pastimes.[52] Some of the freedmen were more ambitious. At least six Negro Masonic Lodges were organized in Florida as early as January, 1868. A general assembly was called in Jacksonville for January 17, 1870, to organize a Grand Lodge of Masons in the State.[53] The freedmen emulated whites in still other ways. In March, 1870, the Negroes of Tallahassee held a "grand tournament and gander pulling," complete with gallants and fair ladies. Mounted dusky knights attempted to spear rings with a lance, and pull the head off a greased gander.[54] There was considerable controversy in the papers over the pretensions of the Negro and the barbarous practice of gander pulling, the whites seemingly forgetting the Negroes learned both from them.

---

50 D. M. Hammond to A. H. Jackson, September 10, 1868, W. G. Vance to C. F. Larrabee, May 31, 1867, L. M. Shute to A. H. Jackson, July 8, 1867, A. B. Grumwell to A. H. Jackson, September 14, 1868, in Bureau Records, Florida.
51 J. T. Sprague to O. O. Howard, October 1, 1867, in Bureau Records, Florida.
52 J. A. Remley to A. H. Jackson, July 31, 1867, in Bureau Records, Florida.
53 The first three Grand Masters were Harry Thompson, 1870-72, Alonza Jones, 1872-73, and John R. Scott, 1873-79. *The Florida Sentinel.* Tenth Annual Number, 1880. Pensacola, Florida (a magazine published annually depicting Negro life in Florida).
54 Tallahassee *Floridian*, March 19, 1870.

Another important adjustment to be made by the Negro was his relation to the law. He had been ruled by his master, and when the owner's authority was terminated, he sometimes seemed to believe all restraint had been ended. The Negroes' relation to the law was further clouded the first two years after the war because it was used by whites to persecute him. Fairness to the freedmen did not seem to be a characteristic of Florida courts, with the result ex-slaves came to regard the law as an enemy. Many petty crimes were perpetrated by freedmen, stealing being the most common. The Negro had owned no property, and had little conception of proprietorship. Moreover, he was frequently hungry, and was inclined to satisfy his appetite wherever he could find food. Complaints of cattle and pig stealing were common. Nearly all of the Bureau agents received charges of Negro and poor white thievery. Hog killing became so widespread several farmers threatened to quit raising livestock.[55] A Bureau agent reported in October, 1868, that forty head of cattle had been killed on Amelia Island in the previous two years. About two weeks earlier, he continued, a Negro constable had attacked the problem, apprehending three of the perpetrators, whose confessions implicated a large number of freedmen.[56] The Bureau co-operated with civil authorities in attempting to stop the killing of livestock, and petty pilfering, with good effect. The Tallahassee *Floridian*, in October, 1868, noticed "with pleasure the generally good deportment of the colored people in this county." Few important cases, the editor added, had come up for trial. He believed Leon County would contrast favorably with any other in the State "for the observance of peace and good order."[57]

The most common Negro crimes were killing livestock and petty theft. An examination of court records for Florida reveals that most crimes of violence were committed by whites, but Negroes were sometimes guilty. When freedmen perpetrated such acts they were usually against other Negroes.[58] Assaults on whites by Negroes

55 D. S. Walker to D. L. Yulee, September 12, 1868, J. S. Perviance to D. L. Yulee, October 8, 1865, in David L. Yulee Papers; J. A. Remley to A. H. Jackson, October 31, 1867, T. W. Osborn to O. O. Howard, November 30, 1865, in Bureau Records, Florida; Tallahassee *Semi-Weekly Floridian*, February 1, 1867.

56 D. M. Hammond to A. H. Jackson, October 2, 1868, in Bureau Records, Florida.

57 Tallahassee *Floridian*, October 20, 1868.

58 J. T. Sprague to O. O. Howard, February 7, 1868, in Bureau Records, Florida.

were rare. On at least one occasion when a freedman allegedly committed a violent crime against a white person he was summarily dealt with by a lawless group of his own race. In July, 1868, a white woman was murdered near Ocala. Suspicion soon came to rest upon a Negro neighbor. The suspected man was apprehended by a number of freedmen, who whipped him until he confessed to the crime. The case was submitted to an impromptu jury of twelve men of his color, who adjudged him guilty and hanged him.[59] The Negro was killed by a lawless lynch mob in an area and time when lynching was considered a prerogative of the white to be used against freedmen. Whether the Negroes murdered the suspect because they were afraid he would escape justice, or in order to protect themselves against a white lynch mob is open to question. The crime for which the Negro was supposed to be most feared, rape of white women, was extremely rare in Florida, though a few Negro males broke a state law by living openly with white mates.[60]

Several cases of miscegenation were reported in Florida. According to a Bureau census of 1866 seven white women were living openly with Negro soldiers in Jacksonville.[61] In December, 1865, a traveler wrote of finding in central Florida "a rude, leaky, shanty with a white man, a big wench, and some half dozen Mulatto children for occupants."[62] Two white brothers in Madison County married Negro women. Fraternization between whites and freedmen sometimes led to disturbances. In June, 1872, a group of Negro men were fired upon by whites at Hawkinsville. The freedmen were accompanied by some "low white women" which supposedly caused the difficulty.[63] Miscegenation was illegal in Florida, but punishment for such offenses was usually meted out extra-legally. In 1874 a white man living with a Negro woman near Brooksville was forcibly taken from his home and hanged. Robert Crawford was taken from his home in March, 1876, and severely beaten evidently because he had married a Negro.[64] The law against

---

[59] J. T. Sprague to O. O. Howard, July 31, 1868, in Bureau Records, Florida.
[60] F. W. Webster to T. W. Osborn, February 7, 1866, in Bureau Records, Florida.
[61] Ibid.
[62] George F. Thompson Journal, December 12, 1865, in Bureau Records, Florida.
[63] Tallahassee Sentinel, June 22, 1872.
[64] Tallahassee Weekly Floridian, May 19, 1874, March 7, 1876; Jacksonville Daily Florida Union, March 8, 1876.

intermarriage was never strictly enforced. In 1875 a white woman married a Negro at Milton, and at least two Englishmen married Negro women in Florida.[65]

Despite their lack of preparation and considerable difficulties the Negroes as a whole adjusted rapidly to freedom. They quickly learned they had to work to live, they realized they had to obey laws, they learned the responsibilities involved in rearing a family, they strove to improve their economic condition, and attempted to improve their education. By the end of Reconstruction they were probably as good citizens as any race of similar economic standing.

[65] Tallahassee *Sentinel*, July 10, 1875; Tallahassee *Weekly Floridian*, August 11, 1874, May 16, 1876.

CHAPTER V

THE FREEDMEN'S BUREAU AND JUSTICE
FOR THE FLORIDA NEGRO

The miscarriage of justice in state courts was one of the most disgraceful aspects of Florida Reconstruction. Some white Floridians, believing the Negro to be inferior to the whites, advocated two standards of justice. When traveling in the State in late 1865, Commissioner Howard observed that the white majority did not treat the Negro fairly.[1] After the hanging of a white citizen for murder, and while the trial of another for shooting a Negro was pending, military authorities received letters from some Floridians saying they would not "live in a country where a man must be hung for resenting an insult with arms," and where "a man must be tried for his life for shooting a nigger." Some whites did leave the State for Texas and Brazil.[2] In June, 1865, a New York *Tribune* correspondent wrote of cases of shooting and violence, and said Negroes were still severely flogged with whip and paddle.[3]

Town and county officials were determined to make the Negro feel his inferiority, Colonel Sprague noted in 1866.[4] They accomplished their aim by arresting freedmen for petty offenses and by the imposition of large fines. Sprague feared this habitual injustice would call forth violence and retaliation from the ex-slaves.[5] An officer from Lake City gave an example of the Florida brand of justice. A Negro woman was convicted of assaulting another after she had discovered the latter in the act of committing adultery with her husband. The court fined her fifty dollars, which she could not pay; therefore she was hired out for the payment and had to work for one year. The woman had not been informed by the judge of her right to seek counsel.[6] Punishment for whites in civil courts was of a much different character. Ashley B. Hamilton was tried in the Marianna Circuit Court for whipping a Negro to death in December, 1865, and found not guilty. In April, 1866,

---

[1] *House Executive Documents*, 39th Cong., 1st Sess., No. 70, 355.
[2] *Ibid.*
[3] New York *Tribune*, June 20, 1865.
[4] *House Executive Documents*, 40th Cong., 2nd Sess., No. 57, 86.
[5] *Ibid.*, 87.
[6] *Ibid.*, 81.

James J. Denton was tried for the murder of a Negro man in Marion County. Denton was found guilty, fined $250 and sentenced to one minute imprisonment. Negroes were given larger fines for petty stealing.[7]

This extraordinary concept of justice provoked immediate interference in behalf of the Negro by the Freedmen's Bureau. On May 30, 1865, Commissioner Howard issued an order stating:

> in all places where there in an interruption of civil law, or in which local courts, by reason of old codes, in violation of the freedom guaranteed by the proclamation of the President and the laws of Congress, disregard the Negroes' rights to justice before the law in not allowing him to give testimony, the control of all subjects relating to the refugees and freedmen being committed to this Bureau, the Assistant Commissioners will adjudicate, either themselves or through officers of their appointment, all difficulties arising between Negroes and whites, or Indians, except those in military service so far as recognizable by military authority, and not taken cognizance of by other tribunals, civil or military, of the United States.[8]

Howard suggested the use of a court composed of three persons, a Bureau agent, a representative of the native whites, and a representative of the freedmen. Such courts were given authority to hear and determine civil cases between freedmen and whites not involving more than three hundred dollars. They could also try offenses committed by or against Negroes, provided the punishment imposed did not exceed a fine of one hundred dollars, or imprisonment at hard labor for thirty days.[9] These courts were used, but Florida agents frequently retained a single judge court supported by the military.[10] The white reaction to such courts was hostile. A citizen of Jacksonville after hearing of Howard's proposal wrote,

> a Negro court; one man of it to be selected by the whites, one by the Negroes, and one by the 'freedmen's bureau,' all of which out Negroes the Negro, all to pieces. That is to say, there will be in the court, two out-nigger Negroes, and one

[7] C. M. Hamilton to J. H. Lyman, October 24, 1866, in Bureau Records, Florida; Proceedings of the Union Republican Club of Jacksonville (1867), typescript in P. K. Yonge Library of Florida History, Gainesville, Florida.

[8] Howard, op. cit., II, 222-23.

[9] O. O. Howard to J. G. Foster, September 19, 1866, in Bureau Records, Florida.

[10] Bentley, op. cit., 153.

white man, they would say; (but I would say the blackest
Negro of all:)—Two to one. Howard's proposition! Two
to none, or one Negro alone, would be just as well; and just
as just and proper.[11]

Despite the opposition of native Floridians, the Bureau inter-
vened in behalf of the freedmen. In November, 1865, Assistant
Commissioner Osborn issued a directive forbidding discriminatory
penalties for Negroes guilty of vagrancy and other crimes. Negroes
were to be permitted to testify, and stripes and corporal punishment were to be abandoned with persons above fifteen, except by
authority of the courts. Since civil authorities were not trusted,
all cases of personal violence or murder were to be reported to
the nearest military commander. Floridians seemed to be especially incensed at the prevention of sentencing the freedmen to
whippings. The Gainesville *New Era* angrily accused the Bureau
of taking a strange position when it interfered "to prevent the
execution of the laws of the State, under some absurd and fanatical
principle that a black thief must not be whipped for robbery or
larceny, because forsooth, it smells of old slavery."[12]

The reorganization of the state government posed the question
of how Negroes would be treated in state courts. Provisional
Governor William Marvin saw no danger in permitting the Negro
to testify before the courts, even against white people, for a white
jury would determine the validity of the testimony.[13] The editor
of one of Florida's most important newspapers seemed to agree
that Negro testimony should be admissible though he felt the
freedman's affirmation would be unreliable.[14] There was a good
possibility the whites could rid the State of Bureau interference
with civil courts, if they passed laws guaranteeing the protection
of the ex-slaves.

The leadership of Governor Marvin, in regard to the Negro,
was not accepted by a majority of the legislature. On January 3,
1865, a law was passed authorizing freedmen to testify in cases
involving their own race, but they were not allowed to give

---

[11] O. M. Dorman, Dairy and Notes, Library of Congress, Washington, D. C.
[12] *House Executive Documents*, 39th Cong., 1st Sess., No. 70, 87; Gainesville
New Era, February 10, 1866.
[13] Tallahassee *Semi-Weekly Floridian*, October 27, 1865.
[14] *Ibid.*, October 24, 1865.

evidence against whites.[15] The lawmakers followed this same conservative trend when passing other statutes pertaining to Negroes[16] Over the protest of the assistant commissioner of the Freedmen's Bureau, laws popularly called black codes which frankly differentiated between the races were enacted. Special penalties were prescribed for the freedmen. In lieu of fine and imprisonment they could be sentenced to the pillory or whipping with thirty-nine stripes.[17] To imprison a delinquent Negro would mean his withdrawal from the plantation, but whipping meant a speedier return to work.[18] A death sentence was decreed for the rape of a white female, but no mention was made of punishment for the assault of a colored woman. It was unlawful for white women and Negro men to marry or live in adultery, but no amercement was decreed for sexual relations between the white male and the Negro female.[19] In addition, provisions were made for the segregation of freedmen at public assemblies and on public conveyances.[20] Laws were passed, applying special measures to the Negro in regard to vagrancy and labor contracts.[21] Freedmen were also forbidden to carry arms of any kind.

This legislation insured the intercession of the federal government. The Freedmen's Bureau took immediate action against the discriminatory laws. In early February, 1866, the commanding general of Florida, on behalf of the Bureau, announced that laws permitting the use of the pillory and whipping would not be tolerated.[22] This announcement was followed in a few days by an order to the same effect by Assistant Commissioner Osborn, who said there must be no difference in treatment before the law because of color.[23] The state attorney-general, upon protest of General Foster, declared unconstitutional the law forbidding the Negroes to carry arms.[24]

---

15 Florida, *Acts and Resolutions*, 1865-1866, 35-36.

16 T. W. Osborn to O. O. Howard, December 30, 1865, in Bureau Records, Florida; Abbey, *op. cit.*, 302.

17 Florida, *Acts and Resolutions*, 1865-1866, 23.

18 Davis, *op. cit.*, 421.

19 Florida, *Acts and Resolutions*, 1865-1866, 24-25, 30; Tallahassee *Semi-Weekly Floridian*, February 16, 1866.

20 Florida, *Acts and Resolutions*, 1865-1866, 25.

21 Abbey, *op. cit.*, 302.

22 Tallahassee *Semi-Weekly Floridian*, February 6, 1866.

23 Davis, *op. cit.*, 405.

24 U. S. Congress, *Senate Executive Documents*, 39th Cong., 2nd Sess., No. 6, 45.

The state criminal courts began operation in April, 1866, and the Bureau transferred cases previously taken before its courts to state tribunals. When in May, 1866, a Bureau agent reported some unjust decisions in his locality, Assistant Commissioner Osborn claimed inability to take official action in relation to sentences pronounced upon offenders convicted by county criminal courts.[25] In June, 1866, Osborn told Commissioner Howard he had "endeavored so far as practicable to transfer the control and protection of the rights of the Freedmen to the regularly authorized State Courts. . . ."[26]

In many instances state tribunals handed down fair decisions, but just as frequently they did not. In June, 1866, the judges in Alachua and Marion Counties sentenced a number of Negroes to receive lashes.[27] Later in the summer a seventeen year old freedman, Alfred Jefferson, was caught riding his employer's horse without permission. He was taken before the Bradford County Court and fined two hundred dollars and costs. He was unable to pay, so he was "sold at public outcry to Mr. Allen Thomas of Bradford County who became responsible for the fine and who now claims the services of Alfred Jefferson for three years."[28] The Bureau agent at Enterprise, Florida, noted that Milton Busby, Negro, was sold at auction for twelve months for assaulting his wife, and another Negro was sold for forty days for taking a drifting log out of the river and selling it.[29] Two Negroes at Lake City, convicted of stealing two boxes of goods from a railroad company, were fined five hundred dollars, which they could not pay. The system in Lake City, a Bureau agent said, was to sell the services of the freedman to the highest bidder when they could not pay their fines. There were a great many freed people serving such sentences throughout that part of the State.[30] An agent from Marion County indicated that Negroes usually had small chance of receiving justice in the civil courts. "I have very little faith in juries," he stated, "where Freedmen are concerned as against

[25] S. L. McHenry to W. G. Vance, May 8, 1866, in Bureau Records, Florida.
[26] T. W. Osborn to O. O. Howard, June 1, 1866, in Bureau Records, Florida.
[27] New York *Times*, July 4, 1866.
[28] F. E. Grossman to J. H. Lyman, October 19, 1866, in Bureau Records, Florida.
[29] W. S. Apthorp to T. W. Osborn, May 29, 1866, in Bureau Records, Florida.
[30] A. Mahoney to S. L. McHenry, May 1, 1866, in Bureau Records, Florida.

the white man in this community, and , I fear, it will be some time before the prejudices of the white people will be so eradicated" the Negro "will be able to receive justice at the hands of Florida juries."[31]

In addition to extreme sentences, the Florida freedmen suffered many injustices in state courts. Civil officers and justices of the peace usually demanded costs in advance from the Negro. This practice prevented the impecunious freedman from being able to procure justice. Even Governor David S. Walker believed some of the civil officials were charging more fees than the law permitted. "I should like to be informed of any such cases," he said, "so that I might have the officers prosecuted for extortion and put a stop to the practice."[32] In May, 1866, Florida's Attorney General, John B. Galbraith, after investigation at the request of the Bureau, declared that the practices of the officials were not based on any principles of justice, but "on the contrary it appears to me that such a practice would in many cases effect an absolute denial of justice and prevent the punishment of offenders."[33] Despite the attorney general's decision, the practice of demanding fees in advance continued, even in cases where the guilt of the white offender was obvious.[34]

While the Negro received harsh sentences for petty crimes and in many instances could not get his cases heard, white offenders were frequently not punished at all, if their offense was against a Negro. A woman wrote from Gainesville that a white man had knocked out the eye of an inoffensive Negro with a board, but the offender was excused on the ground of drunkenness. He was in town a day or two after the crime but was not arrested.[35] In July, 1866, a Negro from Alachua County brought suit against Elias Earle for assault and battery. The act was sworn to by several witnesses, but Earle denied committing the act and was found not guilty. At the same session three Negroes were charged with violation of contract, and were sentenced, in addition to forfeiture

---

31 J. A. Remley to S. L. McHenry, July 31, 1866, in Bureau Records, Florida.
32 Gov. D. S. Walker to T. W. Osborn, May 22, 1866, in Bureau Records, Florida.
33 Attorney General J. B. Galbraith to Gov. D. S. Walker, May, n.d., 1866, in Bureau Records, Florida.
34 A. B. Grumwell to C. Mundee, June 21, 1866, in Bureau Records, Florida.
35 Samuel Proctor, "Yankee 'Schoolmarms' in Post-War Florida," *The Journal of Negro History*, XLIV (July, 1959), 276-77.

of wages, to be publicly whipped and to pay court costs.[36] The county criminal court at Marianna, in March, 1866, tried John Bate and his son for assaulting a freedwoman, Lucinda Doges, who still had not recovered from her injuries at the time. The son was acquitted, but the father was found guilty and fined five cents.[37]

Sometimes county officials did not even trouble to try guilty whites. A Negro near Fernandina, who was living with a white woman, was shot at several times, wounded once, and finally killed. The murdereds were known to the citizens, but no action was taken for in their opinion any Negro who would live with a white woman deserved to be shot.[38] In Putnam County, in May, 1866, a freedman was murdered, stones were tied around his neck, and his body was thrown into a pond. The local agent said, "the parties that committed the act have never been arrested and no exertions, from all that I can learn, have ever been made by the authorities so to do."[39] Twelve Negroes had been murdered in his district by white men, Assistant Commissioner John G. Foster wrote in November, 1866, and despite undeniable evidence of guilt in some of the cases not one offender was convicted. However, a Quincy Negro killed the sheriff of Gadsden County, and he and three acquaintances were convicted and executed.[40]

Under such circumstances Bureau officials considered renewed intervention imperative. The federal agency at first simply appealed to Governor Walker for executive clemency in cases where it was believed Negroes received unjust sentences. Executive clemency was frequently granted. The Marion County Criminal Court convicted three Negroes for stealing cotton and sentenced them to $1,000 fines each. Upon complaint, Governor Walker reduced the abnormally high fines to $350 for one of the men and $250 for the others. The governor was generally sympathetic to the demands of the Bureau, and after its order against the use of whipping and the pillory, he recommended that Negroes sentenced to special punishment be turned over to military authorities. General Foster promised that freedmen turned over to him would

---

[36] J. H. Durkee to S. L. McHenry, July 20, 1866, in Bureau Records, Florida
[37] C. M. Hamilton to S. L. McHenry, March 31, 1866, in Bureau Records, Florida.
[38] T. Leddy to S. L. McHenry, August 1, 1866, in Bureau Records, Florida.
[39] J. A. Remley to J. G. Foster, August 31, 1866, in Bureau Records, Florida.
[40] J. G. Foster to O. O. Howard, November 7, 1866, in Bureau Records, Florida.

be punished by hard labor, one day for each stripe or for each two minutes pillory time. This was generally considered a just settlement, though the conservatives deprecated any interference with state criminal laws.[41]

Despite Governor Walker's good intentions, the Freedmen's Bureau found it necessary to take more positive action on behalf of the ex-slaves, for all white Floridians did not share the governor's views. In the spring of 1866, three white men murdered a Negro named Aaron. He had been shot in the leg, and then taken a distance from the house and shot twice through the head. The accused were brought before the court and acquitted for lack of evidence, even though one man ferried the three whites and the Negro across the river and later heard shots, and another testified that he had seen the men kill Aaron. In June, 1866, a white man, Frank Cheatham, killed a Negro, Simon, in the presence of several witnesses, when the freedman was too slow in carrying out an order. Cheatham had met Simon on the road and had commanded the latter to bring him a sharpened stick. When the Negro hesitated, the white man killed him. Cheatham was taken before civil authorities who refused to make an arrest.[42]

Several other Negroes were found murdered and verdicts of killed by person or persons unknown were rendered. General Foster, on June 9, 1866, declared martial law in Santa Rosa, Escambia, Levy, Madison, and Alachua Counties, because of several murders, attempted murders and other crimes against Negroes and soldiers. Civil authorities had failed to bring the criminals to justice.[43] At the same time civil officials were quick to arrest freedmen. One agent admitted that when freedmen were tried, they were in most cases guilty of violating some law, but whites were not punished for the same offenses. "To sentence a Negro to several dollars' fine for carrying a revolver concealed upon his person, is in accordance with an ordinance of the town," the agent said, "but still the question naturally arises to my mind, why is this poor fellow fined for an offense which is committed hourly by every other white man I meet in the streets." When the laws failed to define the punishment, but left it to the

---

[41] Bentley, op. cit., 155-57; Proclamation, February 12, 1866, in Records of the Department of State, Tallahassee, Florida.
[42] J. G. Foster to O. O. Howard, November 7, 1866, in Bureau Records, Florida.
[43] New York Times, July 4, 1866.

discretion of the courts, he added, the freedmen always received a more severe fine than did a white for the same offense. Juries appeared to act on the assumption the Negro was intrinsically wrong and did not deserve liberality.[44]

General Foster sent Governor Walker, in June, 1866, some examples of Florida justice. In Madison County, a Negro was tried for assaulting a white man. The freedman allegedly was innocent, the assault having in truth been made by the white upon the Negro in which attempt he was foiled by the latter, who took his gun and knife from him. Nevertheless, the court sentenced the freedman to thirty-nine stripes on the bare back, "which sentence was executed, with undue haste, in a building with barred doors," and against the protest of a Bureau agent. The court refused to try the charge of the Negro against the white man for assault with intent to kill. At the same session a white man was tried for beating a colored woman on the head with a club. He was adjudged guilty and fined one dollar. "Under the circumstances of the failure to obtain justice in the above cases," as in others, General Foster said, "I feel it is my duty to renew again the system of military arrests for the higher crimes. . . ." Prisoners so arrested would be held for trial before the United States District Court.[45]

Bureau interference did not deter state courts from handing down their usual decisions. After citing the acquittal of a man in Columbia County, who was clearly guilty of assault and battery, Assistant Commissioner Foster wrote to Governor Walker that,

> I bring this matter to your notice with regret, as being an instance in support of the charge, that many of the courts of the State cannot be relied on to administer justice in cases of white men against colored persons. The cases tend very much to strengthen the belief, especially among the colored people themselves, that the courts of justice are used as engines of oppression of their race, and to engender thoughts of combinations in their own defense against such injustices, instead of the harmonious feeling of dependence and promoting security which for the interest of all parties should prevail.[46]

---

44 *House Executive Documents*, 40th Cong., 2nd Sess., No. 57, 83.
45 J. G. Foster to Gov. D. S. Walker, June 12, 1866, in Bureau Records, Florida.
46 J. G. Foster to Gov. D. S. Walker, July 7, 1866, in U. S. Army Commands, Florida.

For a period the Bureau revived its extra-legal courts, and when civil officials refused to act, Bureau agents sometimes made arrests and acted as judges. In June, 1866, the assistant commissioner sent the agent of Madison County a detachment of troops to enable him to make arrests in cases where he considered unjust decisions had been rendered.[47] In Lake City, after the local tribunal had refused to act on an assault complaint, Bureau agent Captain F. E. Grossman convened a Bureau court to try the case. The court was composed of Grossman, a representative of the Negro, and a representative of the defendant. The defendant had two lawyers, while the Bureau agent acted as prosecutor as well as judge. After a three day trial the court found the defendant guilty and fined him seventy-five dollars.[48]

The Bureau courts, however, were to be used only in instances where the agent was convinced impartial justice could be rendered in no other way. More frequently the agents observed the trials in the county courts, and when they felt a decision to be unjust, it was appealed to the appellate court. If the verdict of the appellate court was considered unfair, the case could then be appealed to the United States District Court, which would be regarded as final.[49] Bureau courts were seldom used after 1866, and despite the close surveillance of civil courts by federal agents there was little intervention. The Bureau, as well as the military, interfered occasionally, but it acted with great caution.

It was unfortunate for the Negro that the federal agency stopped intervention, for the freedmen still failed to receive justice in Florida courts. The civil courts in the State were nothing but a mockery one agent wrote. Neither the Reconstruction laws, the Civil Rights Bill, nor the district commanders' orders were obeyed, he said.[50] In 1871 the sheriff of Madison County testified before a congressional committee that in the period of over three years he had been sheriff, thirty-seven murders had been perpetrated in his county and not one person had been convicted; a few had been prosecuted, but the jury had refused to convict them. Of the thirty-seven victims, thirty-four were Negroes.[51] According to estimates over one hundred and

47 C. Mundee to J. E. Quentin, June 12, 1866, in Bureau Records, Florida.
48 Copy of the proceedings of the Bureau Court, in Bureau Records, Florida.
49 C. Mundee to J. E. Quentin, June 12, 1866, in Bureau Records, Florida.
50 Bentley, op. cit., 166.
51 U. S. Congress, House Reports, 42nd Cong., 2nd Sess., No. 22, Pt. 13, 126.

fifty people were murdered in Jackson County alone in the years from 1868 to 1871. There were almost no convictions. A Bureau agent from Madison County wrote in August, 1868, that "assaults on freed people are as frequent as ever and four have been murdered within the last five or six weeks. . . ."[52]

In November of the same year a resident of Ocala cited a case of the murder of a Negro, adding that "these murders of freedmen are very common."[53] A Northern man in Jacksonville believed the courts had been "to a great extent, especially in jury trials, influenced by personal or local prejudices. There has been a general desire in the . . . courts to screen men of Southern sentiment from punishment." The decisions of the justices were apparently made in accordance with their own ideas of equality, he added.[54] One historian said, "the Conservative whites were determined to avoid punishing those whites accused of killing or maltreating Negroes or white Republicans. . . ."[55] There is no paucity of examples of injustice to the freedmen during Reconstruction in Florida.

Not all white Floridians favored the unjust treatment accorded the ex-slaves. Governor Walker's attitude has been cited, and undoubtedly other whites shared his views. According to an agent from Fernandina justice had been administered "with a loose hand" in his district, but with little partiality.[56] Most of the unfair decisions were in petty cases, Colonel Sprague thought, and when justice was not done the Negro he believed it was attributable "to combinations outside the court rather than illegal findings and rulings upon evidence."[57] An agent at Tallahassee asserted the freedmen in his district were fearful they would get *too much justice. It is just what they do not want. They ask mercy.*"[58] Even though some whites favored impartiality for the freedmen, the ex-slave in many cases did not receive equitable treatment in

---

[52] *Ibid.*, 221-23; J. E. Quentin to A. H. Jackson, August 1, 1868, in Bureau Records, Florida.

[53] J. A. Remley to G. W. Gile, November 30, 1868, in Bureau Records, Florida.

[54] J. H. Durkee to A. H. Jackson, September 24, 1868, in Bureau Records, Florida.

[55] Davis, *op. cit.*, 605.

[56] D. M. Hammond to A. H. Jackson, September 10, 1868, in Bureau Records, Florida.

[57] J. T. Sprague to O. O. Howard, October, n.d., 1868, in Bureau Records, Florida.

[58] M. Martin to A. H. Jackson, October 22, 1868, in Bureau Records, Florida.

Florida courts even after the organization of Republican government in 1868. Several counties in 1867 and 1868 were in a state of
virtual anarchy.[59]

The Freedmen's Bureau not only attempted to protect the Negro
from unfair Florida courts; it also volunteered its services to civil
authorities in catching and restraining delinquent freedmen. Many
were placed under guard of the military by officials of the Bureau,
while they were awaiting punishment. Agents also occasionally
punished Negroes for petty crimes without orders of the court.
Freedmen who indulged in violence were subject to reprimand by
federal agents. A Negro in Madison who sold liquor to his friends
and then tried to encourage a riot was sentenced to six months
hard labor by military authorities.[60]

In the process of securing justice for the Negro, the Bureau
sometimes treated the white man with something less than fairness. The "white man could expect nothing but oppression, and
the black man nothing but partiality," ran a popular saying in
Florida.[61] In communities where bitterness existed between Negroes and whites, the Quincy *Commonwealth* stated in late 1867, it
was frequently due to Bureau officers who discriminated "in favor
of one class to the detriment of another."[62] General George G.
Meade, Commander of Georgia, Florida, and Alabama, said some
of the agents, believing civil courts would not dispense justice,
refused to give them an opportunity.[63] Without doubt the Bureau
courts were sometimes partial to the Negro, but a close examination
of the Bureau Records for Florida indicate a majority of the agents
made every attempt to be fair to native whites. In fact, some of
them were openly prejudiced against the ex-slaves. Assistant Commissioner Sprague expressed the sentiments of many agents when
he wrote in 1867 that,

> without stringent laws, and these enforced with promptness
> and efficiency, the freedman will become a profligate bar-
> barian. His gross physique, degraded intellect, grovelling
> pursuits, habitual slothfulness, and licentious habits, tend

---

59 J. A. Remley to A. H. Jackson, October 1, 1868, in Bureau Records,
Florida.
60 E. S. Rigney to J. S. Rauson, September 14, 1865, in Bureau Records,
Florida.
61 Rerick, *op. cit.*, I, 299.
62 Quoted in Tallahassee *Semi-Weekly Floridian*, September 6, 1867.
63 Bentley, *op. cit.*, 166.

to make him a terror in society which can only be governed by stringent laws faithfully administered.[64]

The Bureau had only limited success in its attempt to secure justice for the Negro. Its courts were of great value in seeking to obtain equal rights for the freedmen in an area where two standards of justice were commonly practiced, but, the Bureau was able to extend protection to the ex-slaves only for the short time it was in existence, and left little permanent benefit. Yet the attempt was not wholly in vain. The federal agency had forced the termination of the use of the pillory and of whipping. Moreover, the threat of Bureau intervention probably encouraged civil courts to be fairer. But, most of the agents were aware, even before the Bureau left the South, they "had not gained for the Negro courtroom protection from the violence of white people."[65]

---

[64] J. T. Sprague to O. O. Howard, October 1, 1867, in Bureau Records, Florida.

[65] Bentley, *op. cit.*, 168.

CHAPTER VI

NEGRO LABOR AND OCCUPATION

One of the most pressing problems encountered in the post-war period was that of labor. The Negro had been the chief source of labor in Florida, as well as the rest of the South, and the breakdown of slavery necessitated the contrivance of a new system. Many white planters wanted to keep the freedmen on the plantation on terms similar to slavery.[1] Whites realized the Negro had ceased to be property, but many believed he still existed specifically to work for his "superiors."[2] General Vogdes wrote in July, 1865, that it would take "some time to eradicate the pernicious idea," that the labor of the freedmen belonged "to the community and not to himself," that he was chattel to be "bought, sold or whipped at the will of an irresponsible master."[3] The late masters in Florida had little conception of the Negro as anything other than a slave, it was reported in June, 1865, and severe beating had not completely disappeared.[4]

A "literary gentleman" of the State expressed his view of the ex-slaves as follows: "There is now nothing between me and the nigger but the dollar—the almighty dollar—and I shall make out of him the most I can at the least expense." This lingering desire for unrequited and poorly paid Negro labor was widespread.[5] The prevailing sentiment in the South was that freedmen would not work without physical compulsion. Florida planters were "generally irreconciled" to the new order of things, and believed it was "impossible to succeed by free labor."[6] Whites were handicapped by past experience and training. They were usually convinced without a trial that the Negro would not work.[7] Carl Schurz made a trip through the South and discovered that nineteen of every twenty men he spoke to insisted the ex-bondsmen would not

---

1 New York *Tribune*, September 5, 1865.
2 *Senate Executive Documents*, 39th Cong., 1st Sess., No. 2, 21.
3 I. Vogdes to O. O. Howard, July 31, 1865, in Bureau Records, Florida.
4 New York *Tribune*, September 5, 1865.
5 *Ibid.*
6 New York *Times*, August 1, 1865.
7 C. W. Tebeau. "Some Aspects of Planter-Freedmen Relations, 1865-1880," *The Journal of Negro History*, XXI (April, 1936), 135.

labor of their own will.[8] I have "little faith in the successful working of this free-labor for a long time," a Floridian wrote in July, 1866. "I am not planting this year," he added.[9] A white man at Key West told a traveler the freedmen were "saucy and worthless," would not work more than necessary; charged high prices for their labor; would rather steal than work; would "dance all night and be good for nothing" the next day; "were fearfully licentious"; and were, in short, "an unmitigated nuisance."[10]

The white Floridians' lack of faith in the Negro under a free labor system led to an attempt to secure immigrant white workers. A Marianna resident said he was "much inclined to white servants, Dutch or Irish," adding that those who knew the Negroes best did not expect them "ever to do much more work of any kind."[11] A majority of the planters around Gainesville reportedly were determined to go to New York in an endeavor to secure white labor. The Board of Immigration received many letters from the South requesting authorities to bring in immigrant labor, especially East Indian coolies.[12] Other Floridians suggested the Negro be given a chance to prove himself first, and if he was ineffective, then immigrant labor should be secured. A few planters believed the ex-slaves would work if handled properly. The whites had to induce the Negro to labor, where they had once forced him, a Jacksonville newspaper wrote. The freedmen required "kindness, guidance, and instruction" from the superior white race, the paper added.[13] The attempt to bring in immigrant labor met with little success.

The actions of the newly freed Negroes gave the planters some cause to be apprehensive about a free labor system. Many of them had an inaccurate conception of liberty. In writing about the Negro during Reconstruction, a Florida freedman, John Shuften, said, "in thousands of instances, it was their solemn belief that

---

8 *Senate Executive Documents*, 39th Cong., 1st Sess., No. 2, 16.
9 There were many comments in newspapers and correspondence indicating the planters lack of faith in free labor. W. G. Branch to Dear Sir, July 8, 1866, in Branch Family Papers, Southern Historical Collection, University of North Carolina, Chapel Hill, North Carolina; George F. Thompson Journal, in Bureau Records, Florida; Jacksonville *Florida Union*, May 27, September 30, 1865.
10 Reid, *op. cit.*, 186.
11 E. Philips to J. J. Philips, October 27, 1865, in James J. Philips Papers.
12 Tallahassee *Semi-Weekly Floridian*, December 1, 1865; *House Executive Documents*, 39th Cong., 1st Sess., No. 66, 6.
13 Jacksonville *Florida Union*, October 4, 1865.

freedom meant a total exemption from toil, the hardships of life and every kind of responsibility."[14] In addition to their peculiar concept of freedom, laziness was said to be a characteristic of ex-slaves. Schurz said many of them were lazy, but, he added, "the propensity to idleness seems to be rather strongly developed in the south generally, without being confined to any particular race."[15] Forced labor had done little to encourage industriousness among the Negroes, but with adequate rewards, they appeared to be no more or less lazy than any other race.

One reason why some freedmen were hesitant to go immediately back to the plantations was the false rumor that lands of their former masters would be divided among them. Schurz and General Grant made tours of the South in 1865, and both said the freedmen believed they would be given land.[16] The overseer on David L. Yulee's plantation reported that Yulee's former slaves had been led to think they could remain on the plantation "unmolested in possession" of some of the land as long as they pleased.[17] According to Assistant Commissioner Osborn, the rumor was propagated by soldiers when the State was occupied, and was given currency by Negro troops, who had come to Florida from the South Carolina coast where ex-slaves had been allowed to settle upon abandoned plantations. The Negroes thought the land distribution would be made after Christmas, 1865, and many of them were reluctant to make contracts providing paltry wages until after that time.[18] The myth of land distribution was so widespread the Bureau found it necessary to inform the freedmen to the contrary.[19]

By June, 1865, nine-tenths of the freedmen were at work on the plantations in spite of the unfortunate rumor they would be given land.[20] By May, 1865, "nearly all" planters in the vicinity of Tallahassee had made arrangements with the freedmen to remain on the plantations and cultivate the crops.[21] Many of the Negroes

[14] John T. Shuften, *A Colored Man's Exposition of the Acts and Doings of the Radical Party South From 1865-1876* (Jacksonville, Florida, 1877), 7.
[15] *Senate Executive Documents*, 39th Cong., 1st Sess., No. 2, 27-28.
[16] *Ibid.*, 31, 107.
[17] J. S. Perviance to D. L. Yulee, November 25, 1865, in David L. Yulee Papers.
[18] T. W. Osborn to O. O. Howard, November 1, 1865, in Bureau Records, Florida.
[19] *House Executive Documents*, 39th Cong., 1st Sess., No. 11, 12-13.
[20] New York *Tribune*, June 20, 1865; I. Vogdes to O. O. Howard, June 18, 1865, in U. S. Army Commands, Florida.
[21] Jacksonville *Florida Union*, May 27, 1865.

never left their former homes. Planters usually refused to promise to pay them wages, but some told the freedmen they would give them a share of the crops. The portion of the harvest the Negroes actually received ranged from nothing to one-half. Military officials encouraged the ex-slaves to work for shares, telling them their former owners were unable to pay wages.[22] Comments were frequently heard that the Negroes were doing "much better" than was expected.[23]

Those freedmen who were reluctant to labor on plantations were pressured to do so by military authorities and the Freedmen's Bureau. Upon emancipation freedmen were told they would be required to work. On June 3, 1865, General Vogdes again reminded the freedmen that "orderly and industrious habits" were "essential to the preservation of society" and that "idleness, vagrancy and all marauding pilfering" would be "promptly and severely punished."[24] Commanding officers of local posts were ordered, on June 10, 1865, to make frequent inspection of towns and to send patrols throughout the country to apprehend idlers. Ex-slaves who could not explain their absence from plantations were arrested and returned. A concession was made to the Negro when the order prohibited the use of firearms and cruel punishment to coerce laborers.[25] A later order stated that persons who remained idle would be sent to plantations and "compelled" to do the same amount of work required of other laborers.[26] A Tallahassee correspondent wrote in June, 1865, that the United States forces had taught freedmen that freedom was not synonymous with laziness.[27] Freedmen were forced to return to the fields, but at the same time military officials forbade any person to "expel from his premises" any Negro "formerly domiciled with him without due cause" and without military consent.[28]

---

22 E. Philips to J. J. Philips, August 2, 1865, in James J. Philips Papers; I. Vogdes to O. O. Howard, June 18, 1865, in U. S. Army Commands, Florida.

23 S. A. Swann to R. Erwin, June 10, 1865, in Samuel A. Swann Papers; N. Yulee to D. L. Yulee, June 8, 1865, in David L. Yulee Papers; I. Vogdes to O. O. Howard, July 31, 1865, in U. S. Army Commands, Florida; T. W. Osborn to O. O. Howard, November 1, 1865, in Bureau Records, Florida.

24 I. Vogdes to B. C. Tilghman, May 20, 1865, General Orders No. 24, June 3, 1865, in U. S. Army Commands, Florida.

25 Ibid.; General Orders No. 26, June 13, 1865.

26 Ibid.; General Orders No. 5, June 29, 1865.

27 Jacksonville Florida Union, June 24, 1865.

28 General Orders No. 9, July 3, 1865, in U. S. Army Commands, Florida.

The Freedmen's Bureau relieved military authorities of the burden of supervising Negro labor, in September, 1865, when Osborn was appointed assistant commissioner for Florida. The Bureau attempted to solve the labor question by removing the distrust between ex-slaves and ex-masters. Florida agents made many speeches in addition to sending out printed circulars to inspire mutual confidence. Agents insisted freedmen must be free to choose their own employers, and substitute slavery would not be tolerated; but at the same time they told the Negro he must fulfill his duties as a citizen, and must work and not be idle.[29] In his first instructions on labor, Commissioner Howard said no agent was to "tolerate compulsory unpaid labor," except for the legal punishment of crime.[30] In a circular of July, 1865, he ordered the negotiation of written agreements stating wages or interest in land or crops. The agreements were to be approved by a Bureau agent who would keep duplicate copies to make enforcement possible. No fixed wage was set by Howard, who left the matter to the discretion of individual agents.[31] Osborn believed the price of labor should be governed by supply and demand, so there was no set wage in the State.[32] According to Bureau orders contracts were to provide for a minimum of food, which should be no less than one peck of meal and four pounds of bacon a week for each worker. The head of the family could contract for all members of his family under twenty-one.[33]

The Bureau also revised some contracts already made with freedmen. Military officials had recommended the use of contracts, but in many cases the Negro had been swindled.[34] The freedmen generally were to receive four to fourteen dollars a month, or one-fifth to one-fourth of the crop, and in unusual cases one-half. But contracts were made to give the worker one-eighth and even less of the harvest. Commissioner Howard talked to a Florida freedman who was paid fifteen bushels of corn, one hundred pounds of pork and a few peas for one year's work. Others contracted for as little

---

[29] U. S. Congress, *House Reports*, 40th Cong., 2nd Sess., No. 30, 6.

[30] Howard, *op. cit.*, II, 225.

[31] Walter L. Fleming, *Documentary History of Reconstruction* (2 vols., Cleveland, 1906), I, 330-31.

[32] T. W. Osborn to O. O. Howard, February, n.d., 1866, in Bureau Records, Florida.

[33] Circular No. 9, November 15, 1865, in Bureau Records, Florida.

[34] General Orders No. 9, July 3, 1865, in U. S. Army Commands, Florida; New York *Times*, October 29, 1873.

as thirteen bushels of corn. A planter in Madison County delayed until his crop was harvested and then forced his laborers to leave with two to fifteen bushels of corn. Others were given nothing.[35] The Bureau revised some of the unfair contracts, and helped divide crops where no contracts had been made. ". . . We were greatly surprised to find the planters really received more than they had expected," one Floridian said.[36]

The introduction of the contract system did not prevent some idleness among the Negroes in 1865. Many of them still believed land would be distributed to them after Christmas, and others were hesitant to go back to the plantations which were so closely associated with slavery. In the face of continued slothfulness by some freedmen, Commissioner Howard urged the use of vagrancy laws that would be applicable to Negroes and whites alike. "A little wholesome constraint could not in many cases be avoided," Howard said later.[37] In keeping with the suggestion of his superior, Osborn, on November 15, 1865, ordered the use of the "usual remedies for vagrancy, breaking of contracts, and other crimes."[38] He had earlier decreased the number of rations issued to prevent the freedmen from gaining the impression the government would support them in inactivity.[39] In September, 1865, Osborn threatened to move forcibly some indolent Negroes from Jacksonville to Tallahassee to labor on plantations. No discrimination was made between male and female. All who were able to work were included in the order. According to a student of the Freedmen's Bureau, Florida and Georgia agents took more drastic measures than those in any other state to coerce the freedmen to labor.[40]

The Bureau policy of coercion was effective. A Northern observer reported in December, 1865, that "nowhere in this state is to be seen that staggering indolence and filth which is so pain-

[35] E. L. Rigney to T. W. Osborn, October 9, 1865, D. M. Hammond to T. W. Osborn, October 20, 1865, H. Stewart to T. W. Osborn, December 18, 1865, A. A. Gifford to T. W. Osborn, January 7, 1866, in Bureau Records, Florida; *House Executive Documents*, 39th Cong., 1st Sess., No. 70, 355; *House Reports*, 39th Cong., 1st Sess., Rept. 30, pt. 4, 8.

[36] Eppes, *op. cit.*, 305.

[37] Howard, *op. cit.*, II, 247.

[38] Circular No. 9, November 15, 1865, in Bureau Records, Florida; Tallahassee *Semi-Weekly Floridian*, November 21, 1865.

[39] T. W. Osborn to D. P. Hancock, September 24, 1865, in Bureau Records, Florida.

[40] Special Order No. 15, September 13, 1865, in Bureau Records, Florida; Bentley, *op. cit.*, 84.

fully noticeable in portions of Georgia and Alabama." On the contrary, he said, "there is a manifest disposition among the freedmen to work and to faithfully carry out their part of the terms of the contracts."[41] A visitor to Tampa in late 1865, found that Negroes devoted themselves to labor "with commendable assiduity."[42] Osborn, who toured the Gulf Coast from St. Marks to Key West in October, 1865, said the freedmen were "working well and receiving very little assistance from the Government" except in Hernando County. The Negroes were no more indolent than whites, Osborn concluded. In a report to congress in December, 1865, Florida, Tennessee, and Arkansas were singled out as having "an admirable condition of affairs," with freedmen "industriously" at work. The instances in which the cotton crop of a single planter would be as valuable as any previous year would not be rare, it was reported.[43]

There were dissenters to the optimistic reports of the success of free Negro labor. The workers frequently objected to being hurried or driven. Anything that smacked of slavery was resented. Some planters claimed they could not get "half work" out of the ex-slaves. An agent for Yulee wrote on November 5, 1865, that the freedmen had labored well the month before, but had not returned to the drudgery.[44] Ex-bondsmen were generally working well in 1865, but it was evident some of them had not yet adjusted to their recently attained status as free men.

There were complaints by the planters at the interference of the Freedmen's Bureau in their affairs, but the compulsory contract system was probably as beneficial to them as to the freedmen. The Bureau literally forced some of the freedmen to work on plantations, and the contracts approved by the agents often specified inadequate payment to the worker. The average wages in 1866 were about twelve dollars a month for first-class males, nine dollars for women, and five for children. Farm laborers frequently made less, and timber and railroad workers more. Many of the freedmen worked for a division of the crop, usually one-

---

[41] New York *Times*, December 25, 1865.

[42] Reid, *op. cit.*, 186-87; George F. Thompson Journal.

[43] T. W. Osborn to O. O. Howard, November 1, 1865, in Bureau Records, Florida; U. S. Congress, *Senate Executive Documents*, 39th Cong., 1st Sess., No. 43, 13.

[44] J. S. Perviance to D. L. Yulee, October 8, 1865, E. J. Lutterloh to D. L. Yulee, September 20, 1865, R. D. Meader to D. L. Yulee, November 5, 1865, in David L. Yulee Papers.

third. Their earnings were often paid in neither money nor a share of the harvest. Several of them were forced "to take the orders of their employers upon stores for such necessaries as they required." Full value was frequently not received when the workers secured their goods on the "order system."[45]

Bureau agents not only approved contracts stipulating low wages, but tolerated agreements worded in such a manner the Negro would get nothing in the event of a poor crop year. In a contract approved by the Bureau in Leon County the laborers agreed to mortgage the entire crop for security for the payment of rent on the land and any advance provisions. The workers pledged themselves to dispose of no part of the crop until four hundred pounds of lint cotton for each ten acres of land, and four hundred for each mule used had been given to the owners. Another contract signed in Leon County promised four and three pounds of pork per week to each man and woman respectively, and one peck of meal a week. The laborers were to receive one-fourth of the crop. They agreed to work diligently, paying for all lost time at the rate of forty cents a day, which together with all advances made by the employer would be taken out of their share of the crop. The workers agreed to comply with all orders and begin work not later than sunrise, taking no unnecessary time for meals.[46]

In addition to advance provisions, planters frequently deducted from the Negroes share of the crop such items as bagging, ropes, and the state poll tax. By the time the planters were through deducting, workers sometimes had just what they had as slaves, nothing.[47] Records from a plantation in Madison County for 1867 graphically demonstrate the inadequacy of some of the contracts.[48]

---

[45] *Senate Executive Documents*, 39th Cong., 2nd Sess., No. 6, 43-44; W. J. Purman to E. C. Woodruff, February 28, 1867, in Bureau Records, Florida.

[46] Records of Deeds, Leon County, Office of the Clerk of the Circuit Court, Leon County Court House, Tallahassee, Florida.

[47] Kathryn T. Abbey, "Documents Relating to El Destino and Chemonie Plantations, Middle Florida, 1828-1874," *Florida Quarterly Journal*, VIII (October, 1929), 84.

[48] J. E. Quentin to A. H. Jackson, January 1, 1868, in Bureau Records, Florida.

Name	Share in Crop	Accounts & Charges	In Debt to Planter	Due the Laborer
Fleming Green	36.28	83.61	47.34	_____
Susan Wheeler	27.21	48.72	21.51	_____
Lawrence Andrews (2 hands)	40.82	126.04	85.22	_____
Jerry Only (4 hands)	45.58	160.89	85.31	_____
Jim Holland (2 hands)	63.49	165.02	101.53	_____
Ben Wood	27.21	71.45	44.24	_____
Anthony Cobb (2 hands)	63.49	108.07	44.58	_____
Wesley Partlow (2 hands)	72.56	153.75	81.19	_____

Such contracts which left the freedmen in debt to the planter, and in his power tend to substantiate the report of Generals James B. Steedman and Joseph S. Fullerton, who said the contract system in the South was slavery in a modified form, enforced by the Freedmen's Bureau.[49]

The somewhat vicious share crop and crop lien systems were so disadvantageous to the freedmen, they were advised by the Bureau in 1868 to attempt to contract for a monthly wage. In 1867, the cotton crop was destroyed by the caterpillar, and not only did the freedmen have small harvests, but some planters showed a disposition to make up their own losses by cheating their croppers. "Many" planters who had been willing to make a fair settlement during good years, a Bureau agent reported, were turning out to be "perfect swindlers and rascals, unwilling to pay any debts whatever and generally making away with the crop."[50] Only a few freedmen realized anything beyond bare subsistence and a small amount of clothing. Some of the Negroes bore partial responsibility for ending the year in debt. In 1867 they sometimes purchased more than absolutely necessary. The cotton crop in 1868 was poor, but the misfortunes of the freedmen were lighter, because they had learned to be more frugal.[51]

[49] Tallahassee *Semi-Weekly Floridian*, August 27, 1866.

[50] J. E. Quentin to A. H. Jackson, December 16, 1867, W. G. Vance to A. H. Jackson, December 2, 1867, J. T. Sprague to O. O. Howard, October, n.d., 1868, in Bureau Records, Florida.

[51] A. B. Grumwell to A. H. Jackson, November 3, 1868, J. T. Sprague to O. O. Howard, February 7, 1869, in Bureau Records, Florida

Freedmen frequently suffered from unfair and inadequate contracts, but they would have fared even worse if the agreements had not been supervised by the Freedmen's Bureau. By 1866 the Bureau was becoming more unpopular with Florida whites, testified L. M. Hobbs, State Superintendent of Freedmen's Schools, because agents had been obliged to restrain whites from perpetrating injustice on the Negroes by "cheating them of their wages, and withholding remuneration from them."[52] Charles M. Hamilton, Commander of the Western District of Florida, forced the revision of some contracts in 1866 because he believed the existing ones were "outrageous."[53] Between 1865 and 1868 the Bureau supervised thousands of contracts in Florida. One agent said during the contract season his office was crowded from early morning until late at night, while another agent approved contracts involving 314 freedmen in one month in 1867.[54]

Not only did the Bureau supervise the making of contracts, but it forced planters to make settlements in accordance with the the terms of original agreements. An agent in Marianna once requested and received soldiers to force planters to make just payments to their employees.[55] Usually military force was unnecessary for settling labor disputes. Individual agents settled differences and decided cases involving division of crops. Generally the decision of the agent was acceptable to both laborer and employer.[56] In order to insure an equitable division of crops, Assistant Commissioner Sprague in January, 1867, directed that all labor contracts provide for a board of arbitration to settle disagreements between employers and employees. The board was to be composed of two citizens, one selected by each of the contracting parties, and a Bureau agent. The decision of the board was final.[57] In cases where freedmen worked without contract the Bureau could afford them little protection since such contingencies came under jurisdiction of civil courts. Court costs were required in advance, thus the freedmen were seldom able to begin a suit. When they did

---

[52] *House Reports*, 39th Cong., 1st Sess., No. 30, pt. 4, 8.

[53] *Ibid.*, 42nd Cong., 2nd Sess., No. 22, pt. 13, 281.

[54] Bentley, *op. cit.*, 137, 150; J. A. Remley to E. C. Woodruff, February 28, 1867, in Bureau Records, Florida.

[55] *Ibid.*, 149.

[56] A. B. Grumwell to J. H. Lyman, November 30, 1866, in Bureau Records, Florida.

[57] Circular No. 1, January 15, 1867, in Bureau Records, Florida.

get their cases before civil courts, the decision usually favored the employer.[58]

The Bureau found it necessary to force freedmen as well as planters to adhere to the terms of contracts. Some ex-slaves did not yet appreciate the necessity of keeping their agreements. In the opinion of Assistant Commissioner Foster, the contract system was necessary not to protect the Negroes, but to keep them from deserting their employers "at a critical time" and causing crops to fail. Another Florida agent said in May, 1866, that there were some "well-grounded complaints" made against the former slaves for breaking contracts, idleness, and disregard of the interests of their white employers.[59] One Floridian complained he used sixteen Negroes in a business which his predecessor, during slavery, had operated with nine, and his forerunner had been able to do twice as much work.[60] "Wages are very high. Common, poor, unreliable, lazy Negroes have to be paid $1 per day and *found*," wrote a New Yorker turned Florida lumberman, and "just about the time I can get a man thoroughly acquainted with his duties he wants to go home." The working man in Florida, white and Negro, reportedly refused to do more than was necessary to secure food and clothing.[61] There were many complaints about the refusal of Negro women to work in the field. Former Acting Governor Allison wrote in 1866 that the freedmen were making good progress but there were few women in the fields. They were, he said, "playing lady."[62]

As time passed, Negro labor became more efficient and responsible. When the ex-bondsmen did not work well the cause could frequently be traced to the oppression of the employer or inadequate wages. Negroes were opposed to working in gangs and having "drivers" as during slavery. They resented being cursed and threatened, and planters unable to adjust to a new

---

[58] R. C. Lowery to J. T. Sprague, May 1, 1867, in Bureau Records, Florida.

[59] *House Executive Documents*, 40th Cong., 2nd Sess., No. 57, 77.

[60] Tallahassee *Semi-Weekly Floridian*, March 12, 1867.

[61] Dovell, *op. cit.*, II, 545; A. B. Hart to Father, March 29, 1867, in Ambrose B. Hart Letters.

[62] In 1870 over 13,000 Negro women listed their occupation as housekeeper in their own home. Ninth Census of the United States, 1870, unpublished population schedules for Florida; A. K. Allison to D. L. Yulee, March 22, 1866, in David L. Yulee Papers; T. Leddy to S. L. McHenry, March 31, 1866, in Bureau Records, Florida; Gainesville *New Era*, April 27, 1866.

system discovered their laborers were often inefficient.[63]   Other employers expressed surprise at the industriousness of the freedmen. One planter raised as much cotton in 1866 with seventeen hands as he had with thirty-seven slaves. Another Floridian who was generally unfriendly toward Negroes asserted that indigent whites did not work as well as freedmen.[64] A settler from North Carolina wrote from Madison, Florida, in 1866, that he had twenty of the best hands he had ever seen, and had no trouble with them at all. One Negro, who a week before had never cut but two turpentine boxes in his life, cut 160 in one day.[65] Each year it was reported the freedmen worked better than ever before.[66]

When the Negroes did not work, the Bureau took vigorous action. If freedmen wilfully broke their contracts without cause, they were arrested and returned to their job. A Bureau agent in Monticello had a "contrary case" whom he put in jail on a diet of bread and water for six days after which time the laborer was "very willing to return" to the field. Incidents of contract breaking by Negroes were rare.[67] Penalties for contract violations were more serious for freedmen than planters. An employer was subject only to civil suit, but the Negro was faced with strict vagrancy laws which existed for the express purpose of controlling him as a laborer. One historian, writing of the earlier policies of the Bureau, stated that "on the whole its policies, both in the administration of

----

[63] *House Reports*, 39th Cong., 1st Sess., No. 30, pt. 4, 2; New York *Times*, June 11, 1866; Tallahassee *Semi-Weekly Floridian*, October 30, 1866; *The American Missionary*, X (February, 1866), 42; A. B. Grumwell to A. H. Jackson, December 31, 1867, in Bureau Records, Florida.

[64] E. Philips to J. J. Philips, September 5, 1866, in James J. Philips Papers; J. A. Remley to J. G. Foster, August 31, 1866, in Bureau Records, Florida; J. S. Perviance to D. L. Yulee, December 31, 1865, January 29, March 6, April 1, 1866, A. K. Allison to D. L. Yulee, February 22, 1866, in David L. Yulee Papers.

[65] Prior to 1901 the box method was usually employed for gathering turpentine. A cavity was chopped into the base of the tree for the purpose of receiving the resin which flowed from the scarred face of the trunk above it. D. H. Hamilton to wife, January 28, 1866, in the Ruffin-Roulhac-Hamilton Papers, Southern Historical Collection, University of North Carolina, Chapel Hill, North Carolina.

[66] Jacksonville *Florida Union*, June 29, 1867; Tallahassee *Semi-Weekly Floridian*, April 30, 1867; A. B. Hart to W. Hart, April 19, 1868, A. B. Hart to E. E. Hart, April 7, 1871, in Ambrose B. Hart Letters; Tallahassee *Weekly Floridian*, February 20, 1872; New York *Times*, October 29, 1873; Jacksonville *Tri-Weekly Florida Union*, May 5, 1874.

[67] A. B. Grumwell to A. H. Jackson, April 30, 1868, in Bureau Records, Florida.

relief and in the supervision of labor had been those that planters and other businessmen desired."[68]

The federal agency established to safeguard the Negroes extended considerable protection to the supposed oppressor at the expense of ex-slaves; nevertheless, the supervision of labor was valuable to the freedmen. Planters were forced to keep their contracts and to pay higher wages than they would have otherwise. Peonage would probably have been the freedman's destiny if the Bureau or some federal organization had not supervised his relations with Southern whites. As it was, in the long view, the foundation was laid for a free labor system.

The system of labor established under the Bureau was continued throughout Reconstruction and after. Sharecroppers, Negro and white, were exploited, the money by one means or another finding its way into the pocket of the landowner. The cropper frequently ended the year in debt and was forced to give the owner a lien on the next year's crop. When they were able, many of the freedmen turned to renting land, but even then they were dependent on landowners or merchants for advances, and compelled to pay interest rates of twenty to ninety percent.[69] Since the share cropper knew he would receive little or nothing in the settlement he often became something less than efficient.

Those who worked for wages fared better than the cropper. When the laborers were paid money wages, rather than a share in the crop, they, as well as the planter, seemed to be more satisfied, and the freedmen were usually more industrious.[70] Whatever system was used it was as effective as slave labor. The commissioner of lands and immigration reported in 1874 that in areas where they were still being raised, as much cotton and sugar were produced as before the war. In 1874 the corn crop in middle Florida was larger in area of land and growth than any previous season, and it was said the "cotton crop was never finer."[71] Practical experiments according to the commissioner, had demonstrated the

---

[68] Bentley, *op. cit.*, 86.
[69] Henderson H. Donald, *The Negro Freedman* (New York, 1952), 15-18; Ulrich B. Phillips and James D. Glunt (eds.), *Florida Plantation Records From the Papers of George Noble Jones* (St. Louis, 1927), 583-84.
[70] New York *Times*, October 29, 1873.
[71] *Sixth Annual Report of Commissioner of Lands and Immigration of the State of Florida for the Year Ending December 31, 1874* (Tallahassee, 1874), 143; Jacksonville *Tri-Weekly Florida Union*, May 5, 1874.

superiority of Negro labor. Immigrant white labor had rendered "more clear and incontestable," he said, the efficiency of the freedmen. The industry of the Negro had been proven and was constantly increasing.[72] By the end of Reconstruction the reliability of freedmen labor was firmly established.[73]

A semi-free labor system developed in Florida during Reconstruction, but a species of slave labor existed in the convict lease system. Under the constitution of 1865, the labor of Negro vagrants could be sold to pay fines and court costs, and later convicts in the state penitentiary were leased to the highest bidder. The first lease was made in 1869 when fifty inmates were contracted for three years. In August, 1870, fifteen convicts were leased to cut timber at $1.25 per day each. A work day for the inmates consisted of the time it took one man to chop down and trim two hundred "superficial feet" of timber.[74] In 1874 forty prisoners were leased for $12.50 each per month to work on a railroad. Their work consisted of ten hours a day, twenty-six days a month.[75] The convict lease system was retained and extended by the State after the end of Reconstruction, and became even more brutal. The state prison in Florida earned the title conferred upon it by a prison officer, "The American Siberia." The first law formally establishing a convict lease system in Florida was passed in 1877.[76]

Despite the large number of freedmen engaged on plantations, about 23,000, the Negroes followed many other occupations. Some of the freedmen were highly skilled as demonstrated by the following table, based on the census of 1870.[77]

----

[72] Ibid., 7, 45; Denis Egan, "Colored Labor," The Florida Agriculturist, X (January 3, 1874), 7.

[73] Tallahassee Sentinel, February 5, 1876.

[74] American Annual Cyclopedia and Register of Important Events for the Year 1869 (14 vols., New York, 1862-75), IX, 272; Minutes of the Board of Commissioners of Public Institutions, in Florida State Library, Tallahassee, Florida.

[75] Tallahassee Sentinel, May 2, 1874.

[76] Blake McKelvey, "Penal Slavery and Southern Reconstruction," The Journal of Negro History, XX (April, 1935), 159; Florida, Acts and Resolutions, 1877, 92.

[77] The table is based on an analysis of the Ninth Census of the United States, 1870, unpublished population schedules for Florida. The 1870 census contains many inaccuracies, but adequately shows that Negroes were important in many occupations other than farming.

Baker	12	Fisherman	30
Barber	27	Fruit Stand Keeper	1
Basket Maker	2	Gardener	21
Blacksmith	115[78]	Gardener (truck)	2
Boatman	25	Grist Mill Worker	31
Brickmaker	2	Grocer	12
Brickmason	37	Gunsmith	1
Butcher	19	Horse Collar Maker	1
Butler	1	Hospital Orderly	1
Cabinet Maker	6	Hostess	1
Cashier	1[79]	Hostler	14
Carpenter	365	Hotel Servant	30
Cemetery (supervisor and workers)	4	Housekeeper	13,060
Cigar Maker	19	Huckster	1[80]
Clerk (store)	13	Icecream Dealer	1
Cobbler	29	Icecream Maker	1
Cook	519	Jailor	7
Cooper	11	Janitor	2
County Officials	7	Justice of the Peace	3
Dairy Maid	3	Laborer	2,368
Distiller	1	Laundress	565
Drayman	95	Liquor Dealer	1
Driver	7	Liveryman	7
Engineer	14	Lumber Inspector	1
Farmer	1,730	Machinist	1
Farm Laborer	22,944	Mail Contractor	1
Ferryman	5	Mattress Maker	3
Fireman	17	Mechanic	1[81]

[78] On the basis of property holdings, the census indicates that blacksmiths were among the more affluent Florida Negroes.

[79] The bank cashier, William Stewart, was employed by the Freedmen's Saving Bank in Tallahassee. Tallahassee *Weekly Floridian*, July 11, 1871.

[80] According to travelers' reports there was more than the one huckster listed in the census. A visitor said in 1871 that at railroad stations one encountered hoardes "of tattered freedmen" selling food and other produce. New York *Times*, January 27, 1871; Frederick Trench Townshend, *Wild Life in Florida, With a Visit to Cuba* (London, 1875), 31.

[81] There was more than one mechanic in the State. As early as 1866 it was reported that there were "a number of excellent" Negro mechanics in Marianna who directed their own activities and were doing well. C. M. Hamilton to S. L. McHenry, June 30, 1866, in Bureau Records, Florida.

Merchant	7[82]	Sailor	55
Midwife	7	Seamstress	88[87]
Minister	59	Servant	2,161
Musician	1[83]	Shinglemaker	2
Nurse	166[84]	Shipbuilder	5
Painter	15	Spinner and Weaver	2
Penitentiary Guard	18	Steamboat Worker	22
Physician	1	Stevedore	20
Pilot	19	Steward	20[88]
Plasterer	1	Stocktender	7
Policeman	5	Stone Mason	7
Porter	16	Surveyor	3
Post Office Employee	5[85]	Tailor	7
Railroad Laborer	366	Tanner	1
Raftsman	1	Teamster	49
Restaurateur	3	Timber Worker	121
Root Doctor	1[86]	Turpentine Worker	83
Saddler	4	Typesetter	1
Saloon Keeper	6	Wagoner	3
Salt Maker	1	Waiter	28
Sawmill Worker	297	Watchman	5
Sawyer	2	Welldigger	10
School Teacher	38	Wheelwright	22

[82] Negro merchants apparently were usually successful. By 1870 a Suwannee County merchant had accumulated $1,700 of property, and a Jacksonville merchant had $1,000 personal property.

[83] Only one Negro was listed as a musician in the census but freedmen were frequently retained to perform for whites. A man who attended a masked ball in Fernandina in 1873 said that about nine o'clock three Negroes "started up the music on three fiddles and the fun commenced." George W. Parsons Diary, September 10, 1873, in P. K. Yonge Library of Florida History.

[84] Most of the Negroes classified as nurses were mere babysitters. Usually they were not trained to care for the ill.

[85] Two of the postoffice employees were post masters, one in Jefferson and one in Madison County.

[86] The root doctor was Jeff Martin, a 102 year old African born Negro living in Jefferson County.

[87] Some of the seamstresses were highly skilled. There were two families of seamstresses in Key West of whom it was said no New York or London tailor could equal "in making the linen shirts and white duck suits worn by the elegant gentlemen of the day." Jefferson B. Browne, *Key West: The Old and the New* (St. Augustine, 1912), 171.

[88] One was a stewardess fondly known as "Commodore Rose." Rose was a well-known character around the Jacksonville wharves for years. She reportedly had complete "charge of provisioning and running" the steamer *Darlington*, and no one "could get ahead of her in a bargain or resist her will in an arrangement." It was said that "nowhere in Florida" could one "sit at a more bountifully-furnished table" than that of "Commodore Rose." Stowe, *op. cit.*, 250; Edward King, *The Southern States of North America* (London, 1875), 385.

Negroes in Florida were engaged in occupations not listed in the 1870 census. The first Negro to practice law in Florida, Henry S. Harman, was admitted to the bar at a term of the Alachua Circuit Court in 1869. In 1873 two other Negroes, Josiah T. Walls, and Joseph H. Lee, were admitted to the bar.[89] The number of Negro lawyers remained small throughout Reconstruction. Florida even had a Negro inventor. In 1867 Elijah Williams received a patent on a boat propellor to be used on boats in streams previously innavigable by steam vessels. Williams had conceived his idea while a slave and began work on it as soon as he was freed. He completed his invention by March, 1867, and it was patented the next month.[90]

Most occupations paid more than plantation work. Harriet Beecher Stowe claimed her trained house servant left her, and secured a job as hotel cook for $40 a month. Servants usually made only $10 to $12 and board a month, but trained servants were at a premium, and the work was easier than in the field. An army lieutenant engaged four carpenters at $2.50 each per day when farm hands were making less than 50¢ a day even when they were paid.[91] A traveler had a Negro construct a boat for him, and was charged $26 for one weeks work. While using the boat the visitor met two Negro fishermen who claimed they sometimes made as much as $20 a day. He was surprised at the shrewdness of the freedmen.[92] The lumber industry paid about the highest wages in Florida, $20 to $40 a month. One lumberman in 1867 was paying his employees one dollar a day and board. Railroads and the turpentine industry paid almost as good wages as the lumber industry.[93]

A few of the Negroes, aware of the value of their labor, tried to improve their conditions by striking. Negro workers struck in eight sawmills in 1873 when their employer refused to reduce the

---

[89] Tampa *Florida Peninsular*, June 10, 1869; Tallahassee *Weekly Floridian*, April 15, 22, 1873.

[90] C. M. Hamilton to J. G. Foster, May 31, 1867, in Bureau Records, Florida; U. S. Congress, *House Executive Documents*, 40th Cong., 2nd Sess., No. 96, pt. 1, 768; *Ibid.*, pt. 2, 434.

[91] Stowe, *op. cit.*, 314; New York *Times*, October 29, 1873; W. L. Dodge to W. Logan, November 26, 1866, in U. S. Army Commands, Florida.

[92] John Francis LeBaron Diary, January 3, 7, 8, 1869, in Jacksonville Public Library.

[93] A. B. Hart to Mother, January 2, February 18, 1867, in Ambrose B. Hart Letters; A. Mahoney to T. W. Osborn, March 1, 1866, in Bureau Records, Florida.

work day to ten hours. Stevedores had earlier struck at Fernandina for higher pay. Both strikes failed. Public opinion in Florida, as well as the rest of the United States, had little tolerance for strikers during Reconstruction.[94]

In general Negro laborers were effective in postwar Florida, and were willing to work hard for adequate payment. About 33,000 freedmen were engaged in productive labor in 1870. Evidence indicates that the free labor system was a success. When the freedmen did not work satisfactorily it was usually because the system used was too much like slavery. Not only did the freedmen work, but they were as industrious as any other people. By 1870 they were purchasing their own homes and land, sending their children to schools, and saving money. Five years after emancipation they had accumulated about $521,000 of personal property, and over $355,000 real estate.[95] When the Freedmen's Savings and Trust Company failed in 1874, the Florida branch had 2,374 depositors, and deposits of $70,010.35.[96] Despite numerous obstacles, Negro laborers made significant progress during Reconstruction in Florida.

---

[94] D. M. Hammond to A. H. Jackson, October 2, 1868, in Bureau Records, Florida; Tallahassee *Weekly Floridian*, June 10, July 1, 1873.

[95] Ninth Census of the United States, 1870, unpublished population schedules of Florida.

[96] Davis, *op cit.*, 392.

CHAPTER VII

THE NEGRO FARMER

To possess land of their own, or at least to be independent farmers, was one of the strongest desires of the freedmen. Wage labor which remained closely supervised was too much like slavery, and financial rewards appeared to be greater for the independent farm operator. Many former bondsmen became sharecroppers thereby gaining more independent working conditions, but sharecropping sometimes turned into vicious exploitation. One Bureau agent predicted that many freedmen would be poorer than when they started, and in many cases he was correct.[1] Despite its shortcomings, the freedmen at first generally seemed more satisfied working for shares than for wages. Most observers thought the Negroes worked better when sharecropping, since there appeared to be a greater reward for initiative and industry. The freedmen soon learned, however, they often earned no more, and had little more freedom. Plantation owners seemed to prefer the sharecropping system for it was the method which "would produce the most constant supply of submissive labor at the lowest cost."[2]

A few former slaves were able to rent land outright, which was more satisfactory than sharecropping. In 1868, near Tallahassee, Simpson Coswell rented 175 acres, Peter Copeland 100 acres, and Ichabod Barrow 160 acres.[3] Most freedmen were not so fortunate, but many of them were able to rent and operate on their own. Occasionally a group of Negroes would co-operate to secure land. In 1868 four ex-slaves rented 120 acres of W. H. Branch's Live Oak Plantation, for twelve bales of cotton and twelve bushels of corn.[4] A Bureau agent who visited several of these plantations in June, 1868, reported that with few exceptions the freedmen were working well and their crops showed evidence of "careful and faithful toil." If the renters enjoyed a favorable season, he said, their crops would equal that of any previous year.[5]

---

[1] F. E. Grossman to S. L. McHenry, July 31, 1866, in Bureau Records, Florida.

[2] Fred A. Shannon, *The Farmer's Last Frontier: Agriculture 1860-1897* (New York, 1945), 87.

[3] Records of Rations Issued, in Bureau Records, Florida.

[4] Contract Made March 13, 1868, in Branch Family Papers, Southern Historical Collection, University of North Carolina.

[5] G. B. Carse to A. H. Jackson, June 1, 1868, in Bureau Records, Florida.

The number able to rent land was always small because the cost of rent, mules, equipment and seed was almost prohibitive. Some of the former slaves settled on abandoned lands. They were assisted in this endeavor by the United States government. On January 16, 1865, General William Tecumseh Sherman ordered certain lands between Charleston, South Carolina, and the St. John's River in Florida to be set aside for settlement of freedmen.[6] The directive included abandoned and confiscated lands. After the Freedmen's Bureau began operation such lands came under its control. The act of March 3, 1865, which created the Bureau authorized the commissioner to assign plots of not more than forty acres to the freedmen. They were to have an option to purchase within three years.[7] With the encouragement of various government agents the ex-slaves located on some of the land and planted crops. But, on May 29, 1865, President Andrew Johnson granted amnesty and pardon, with restoration of all property rights, except slaves and except where legal proceedings had been instituted by the government for confiscation. The Bureau was slow to implement the President's order to restore property, but finally in September, 1865, a circular was issued ordering confiscated property returned. The freedmen were to receive the benefit of their still unharvested crops.[8]

Other Negroes, without legal right, merely squatted on land abandoned at the moment. Confederate soldiers returned to find their vacated plantations occupied.[9] Railroad lands were also taken by squatters. Supposed friends of the Negroes in Fernandina advised the former bondsmen to settle on railroad lands, and tracts purchased by the government at tax sales. Local Bureau agents cautioned the settlers against costly improvements and erection of expensive buildings to no avail. When the land was restored to former owners and the railroad demanded their land be relinquished the freedmen were the losers.[10] A few Negroes were able to buy land but most of them had little or no money, and planters were not inclined to dispose of their land at prices ex-slaves could

---

6 *House Executive Documents*, 39th Cong., 1st Sess., No. 11, 10.
7 U. S. *Statutes at Large*, XIII, 508.
8 Circular No. 15, September 12, 1865, in Bureau Records, Florida.
9 New York *Tribune*, August 8, 1865.
10 A. A. Cole to A. H. Jackson, June 30, 1867, D. Richards to O. O. Howard, April 30, 1867, A. Mot to A. A. Cole, June 27, 1867, F. Suhrer to A. A. Cole, June 27, 1867, in Bureau Records, Florida.

pay. When they did manage to purchase land it was usually of an inferior quality.

More important to Negro farmers than abandoned and rented lands was the passage of a legislative act on June 21, 1866, which opened government owned lands in Arkansas, Mississippi, Alabama, Louisiana and Florida to homesteading. The fee at the time of patent issue was only five dollars. Discrimination on account of color was prohibited. All who had borne arms against the United States were forbidden to enter on public lands before January 1, 1867, which permitted freedmen time to secure farms before the "rebels" could legally homestead.[11] The Bureau made every effort to aid the freedmen. Locating agents assisted in finding the plots, and free transportation to the homestead and subsistence for one month was provided.[12] Negroes quickly began to take advantage of the Homestead Act. One agent reported that as a general thing the freedmen's "greatest ambition is to get a lot of ground for themselves."[13] The freedmen usually went in small groups to settle new lands. Meetings were held in churches to inform the congregation of the opportunity to own land to make plans for settlement.[14] The land office opened in Florida on August 25, 1866, and by October of the same year 32,000 acres of land had been entered, and it was reported the freedmen's interest in homesteads appeared to be increasing.[15] Between October 19 and November 1, 1866, a Bureau agent helped Negroes enter on 5,000 acres in Madison, Taylor and Lafayette Counties alone. By October, 1867, ex-slaves had secured 2,012 homesteads covering 160,960 acres, and within the next 60 days 419 more entries were made.[16]

These numerous entries by freedmen met with considerable opposition from whites. Negro homesteading was opposed for two primary reasons; the possible loss of labor, and the fear of some whites that the ex-slaves would become too independent and refuse to accept the role of second-class citizens. Some whites re-

---

11 U. S. *Statutes at Large*, XIV, 66-67.
12 O. O. Howard to J. G. Foster, August 22, 1866, in Bureau Records, Florida.
13 T. Leddy to S. L. McHenry, March 31, 1866, in Bureau Records, Florida.
14 Tallahassee *Semi-Weekly Floridian*, October 16, 1866.
15 J. G. Foster to O. O. Howard, October 1, 1866, in Bureau Records, Florida.
16 J. E. Quentin to J. G. Foster, November 1, 1866, J. T. Sprague to O. O. Howard, October 1, 1867, in Bureau Records, Florida.

fused to give their former slaves necessary information and freed-men were sometimes intentionally misguided. In a few instances Negroes were directed to private lands where they settled, cultivated the land, made improvements, and then were compelled to move or purchase at high prices. Where there was no open opposition by whites, Assistant Commissioner Sprague reported, there appeared to be a "silent compact" to retard Negro homesteaders.[17]

Attempts were made to intimidate ex-slaves from making settlements in some cases. A freedman, Thomas Hailey, and nine other Negroes left Tallahassee on September 3, 1866, to locate lands in Lafayette County. They were informed by a resident of the county that whites had organized to prevent homesteading. They went on, but encountered another white man "who kindly and in a friendly manner" told them he knew of twenty-five men who had signed an agreement to drive away any Negroes who came to settle, and he expected twenty-five more to sign the agreement that very day. The white resident advised the freedmen to go no further or they would be murdered. Bodies of three dead Negroes had been found in the Suwannee River recently, he added. Be-lieving the white man was advising them as a friend, the ex-bonds-men turned back.[18] Assistant Commissioner Foster wrote in October, 1866, that residents of some sections were opposed to Negro settlers, and had made threats, but the obstruction had de-creased "upon a proper representation of the futility of such an illegal course and of the consequences that must follow."[19]

Homesteaders also suffered from either fraud or incompetence at the hands of at least one land agent. Several complaints were lodged against Dr. A. B. Stonelake, Register of Public Lands at Tallahassee. Stonelake overcharged numerous freedmen, but after being questioned, insisted it was a mistake and the money would be returned. Some of those who paid their patent fees never re-ceived land, and a Bureau agent from Marion County, who sent money and applications to Stonelake for some Negroes, complained that over two months elapsed and no reply had been received. Stonelake claimed he never received the money. Bureau officials,

---

[17] J. T. Sprague to O. O. Howard, October 1, 1867, in Bureau Records, Florida.

[18] Statement sworn before Major J. L. Denniston, Tallahassee, September 17, 1866, by Thomas Hailey and four others, in Bureau Records, Florida.

[19] J. G. Foster to O. O. Howard, October 1, 1866, in Bureau Records, Florida.

as a result of complaints, began closer supervision of homestead entries.[20] Despite fraud, incompetence, and white opposition, nearly 3,000 Negroes, more than in any other state, eventually entered on homesteads in Florida.[21]

Not all of the homesteads were settled by Floridians or individuals. Approximately 19,000,000 acres of public lands in Florida were open for settlement and though much of it was of little value, Florida became something of a Mecca for Southern Negroes. Attempts were made to place Negro colonies on government lands in Florida. In 1867, General Ralph Ely arrived in Volusia County with about 1,000 freedmen from South Carolina. Ely settled at New Smyrna where difficulty was encountered from the beginning. Planning had been inadequate. The colony lacked subsistence, the homesteads had not been located, and the land was often poor. As soon as planters from the interior heard of the colony, they hastened there and hired away entire families. By the last of February only about 200 remained in the colony, and they had to be fed by the Freedmen's Bureau. Another attempt to colonize in Florida was made by the Florida Land and Lumber Company under the leadership of Dr. J. M. Hawks. This group located at Port Orange and was also a failure as a colony. Residents of the area described the plight of the freedmen as pitiful. They dwelt in palmetto huts, and lived on fish, oysters, and game. They were without bread, and occasionally begged corn to be ground with a handmill for meal from earlier settlers. Some of the Negroes went to work for white farmers, but several took homesteads near Port Orange, and were successful though the land was uncleared.[22]

Many other freedmen attracted by homesteads, migrated to Florida between 1865 and 1867. A majority of them came from Georgia and the Carolinas. In its last three trips the steamer *Dictator* had brought about 2,000 Negroes to Jacksonville, it was reported in January, 1867.[23] At about the same time, 117 mi-

20 A. H. Jackson to A. B. Stonelake, January 15, 1867, J. A. Remley to E. C. Woodruff, February 28, 1867, A. B. Stonelake to J. T. Sprague, March 11, 1867, in Bureau Records, Florida.

21 *House Reports*, 40th Cong., 2nd Sess., No. 30, 16.

22 J. T. Sprague to O. O. Howard, February 28, 1867, in Bureau Records, Florida; Pleasant Daniel Gold, *History of Volusia County Florida* (DeLand, Florida, 1927), 95-96.

23 Tallahassee *Semi-Weekly Floridian*, January 29, 1867.

grants reached Monticello where they were employed on a plantation. A man from Fernandina once counted twenty-seven wagons in one group containing immigrants and their household goods going to Marion County. All were from South Carolina. On January 4, 1867, a South Carolina paper told of 1,000 ex-slaves seen in one week on the way to Florida.[24] Assistant Commissioner Sprague estimated in October, 1867, that between 2,500 and 3,000 freedmen had arrived in Florida in the past year.[25] It is necessary only to glance at the unpublished census schedules of 1870 to see how many Negroes came from out of state. Most came to homestead, but many accepted jobs with Florida planters. A considerable decline in the number of Florida freedmen who were willing to work for wages had resulted from the Homestead Act. The influx of Negroes from other states prevented a serious labor shortage, as well as providing many homesteaders.[26]

Despite several outstanding successes, many of the homesteaders were destined to fail. The reasons for their failure are evident. The plan to place the freedmen on homesteads was more idealistic than realistic. When the Negroes first began locating on homesteads, Assistant Commissioner Foster said much of the land was of poor quality and questioned whether it would ever be of benefit to the freedmen financially. Many of the homesteads were located in inundated and swampy lands. Not more than a half dozen persons in his district, one agent reported, had procured land "fit to live upon."[27] Furthermore, much of the land was uncleared, and the freedmen needed money for purchase of implements and provisions for at least one year to be successful under such circumstances.

Whether or not the land was cleared, there were certain basic necessities for success on a homestead. Some kind of shelter, food, wagon, a horse or mule, fencing, and implements were needed. This added up to more than most Negroes could save in years working at the average wage of seven to twelve dollars a month. Some of the freedmen attempted to remain on their land by working for

---

[24] *Ibid.*, January 11, 1867.
[25] J. T. Sprague to O. O. Howard, October 1, 1867, in Bureau Records, Florida.
[26] J. A. Remley to A. H. Jackson, July 31, 1867, in Bureau Records, Florida.
[27] J. G. Foster to O. O. Howard, August 10, 1866, J. T. Sprague to O. O. Howard, February 7, 1868, A. B. Grumwell to A. H. Jackson, December 31, 1867, in Bureau Records, Florida.

neighboring planters during the day to earn subsistence, and culti-
vating their own land at night or at intervals. Often the father
worked for wages and the wife and children cared for the homestead.[28] Even with food, the homesteaders had a difficult time
for they usually lacked tools. A Bureau agent who inspected the
New Smyrna colony found the ex-bondsmen without implements
and mules. The ax and hoe were the primary farm tools. The
land was cleared with the ax, then holes were dug for the seed without plowing. Naturally such planting yielded small crops. Moreover, the acreage under cultivation was small, usually no more than
five to eight acres. It was difficult for them to reduce any larger
acreage from the "jungle of Hammock and palmetto" to a tillable
state with no help but the ax and hoe.[29] That some of the freedmen
strove mightily to succeed on their homestead under almost impossible conditions is illustrated by *The Florida Agriculturist*. Two
Negroes from Gadsden County, Handy Griffin and Ed Harris,
worked through the day for a planter, and on their own farm after
hours. They had no mule so one pulled the plow while the other
held, and where the ground was especially difficult, their wives were
called upon to fill the role of mules. In this manner five acres
of corn and four of cotton were planted, and were reported to be
as good as any in Gadsden County.[30] Unfortunately such methods
were less successful for others.

By 1868 it appeared that many freedmen would have to give
up their homesteads. In this crisis, the Freedmen's Bureau in
Florida attempted to assist by providing food. According to Circular No. 3, issued February 5, 1868, the Bureau would give rations
to Negroes who had within their control and were living upon ten
acres of fenced, tillable land.[31] This order did not apply solely to
homesteaders, but they were the primary beneficiaries. Many freedmen were able to remain on their homesteads, when otherwise they
would have been forced to work for wages to provide for their
families. Furthermore, others now found it possible for the first

---

[28] W. W. Armstrong to A. H. Jackson, June 30, 1868, in Bureau Records,
Florida.
[29] D. M. Hammond to A. H. Jackson, February 19, 1868, in Bureau Records,
Florida; Bentley, *op. cit.*, 145-46.
[30] *The Florida Agriculturist*, I (July 25, 1874), 237.
[31] Circular No. 3, Special Orders and Circulars, in Bureau Records, Florida.

time to locate on public lands.[32] There is little doubt the nearly 6,000 rations issued in 1868 at a cost of over $102,000 rendered considerable aid to Florida homesteaders.[33]

The issue of rations proved valuable to some homesteaders, but it was not enough to keep many of them from failing. Even with food they lacked proper agricultural implements. Inexperience as independent operators also injured the ex-slaves. Assistant Commissioner Sprague stated in 1867 that those who worked for themselves sometimes were less successful than the ones who worked under the supervision of a white man.[34] Furthermore, nature appeared to be against the struggling freedmen. In early 1868, there were many reports of fine crops being raised by freedmen, but 1868 proved to be a bad season as far as weather and the caterpillar were concerned. Fields that had looked good and had shown every evidence of a good crop were left with hardly a leaf, an agent reported in August, 1868.[35] The large number of failures can be demonstrated in Marion County. In 1868, 900 homesteads were entered by the freedmen in that county. According to the census of 1870 only 163 freedmen controlled land there. Nearly 3,000 homesteads were located by Negroes in Florida by 1868, but only about 1,000 owned land in 1870.[36] Approximately one third of the homesteads failed, which makes the Bureau's attempt to turn freedmen into independent farmers something less than a success. Many of the homesteaders who were able to stay on their lands failed to prove them. It was reported in November, 1874, that "either through carelessness or ignorance of the law" many farms were reverting to the government.[37] Others failed because of white opposition, and some were driven off their lands by white ruffians.[38]

---

[32] J. T. Sprague to O. O. Howard, March 31, May 31, 1868, J. W. Childs to A. H. Jackson, July 1, 1868, J. H. Durkee to A. H. Jackson, July 8, 1868, in Bureau Records, Florida.

[33] *House Executive Documents*, 40th Cong., 3rd Sess., No. 1, 1042; Monthly Reports of Assistant Commissioner, July, 1866-December, 1868, in Bureau Records, Florida.

[34] J. T. Sprague to O. O. Howard, March 31, 1867, in Bureau Records, Florida.

[35] M. Martin to A. H. Jackson, August 15, 1868, in Bureau Records, Florida.

[36] J. A. Remley to A. H. Jackson, October 1, 1868, in Bureau Records, Florida; Ninth Census of the United States, 1870, unpublished population schedules of Florida.

[37] *The Florida Agriculturist*, I (January 17, 1874), 20; Jacksonville *Tri Weekly Union*, January 8, 1874.

[38] Jacksonville *Daily Union*, February 8, 1876.

Though many Negroes lost their farms, the homestead movement should not be written off as a complete failure. Even though
only about one-third of the freedmen had retained their homesteads up to 1870, the existence of over 1,000 Negro land holders
demonstrated considerable progress since 1865 when none owned
land. In 1870 there were slightly over 10,000 farms in Florida, with
one-tenth of them owned by Negroes.[39] Many of the freedmen's
farms were marginal, but some ex-slave farmers were notably successful. Among the many pessimistic reports of Bureau agents in
regard to homesteaders were several favorable ones. By 1867
numerous ex-bondsmen had some land under cultivation, were
thriving, and had constructed "comfortable huts."[40] Even with
the poor cotton crop of 1867 some Negro homesteaders were
successful, more so than sharecroppers. Those who were more
industrious had a supply of corn and sweet potatoes, plus thriving
gardens of turnips, radishes, peas, and cabbage. The share-
cropper was more limited to cotton and one crop failure was
ruinous.

A large number of homesteaders, Assistant Commissioner
Sprague wrote in July, 1868, had ten to forty acres, well-plowed
and fenced, and were able to obtain a livelihood from year to year.
Though the cotton crop was not good in 1868, the state enjoyed a
sufficiency of such products as corn and sweet potatoes due in large
part to small Negro farmers.[41] S. F. Halliday, employed to locate
Negroes on public lands, gave some specific examples of successful
homesteaders in October, 1868. James McCartin, had settled a
homestead of 80 acres near Newnansville in 1866. By 1868 Mc-
Cartin had forty cultivable acres under good fence, a dwelling
house, stable, corncrib, and a well. McCartin produced in 1868,
an abundance of corn and potatoes, and two bales of sea-island
cotton. He was reported to be "comfortable and independent."
Charles Williams, who had a homestead near Archer, with the aid
of his son and daughter, produced 500 bushels of corn and 3 bales
of sea-island cotton in 1868. The cotton crop had been estimated

39 *Ninth Census of the United States*, 1870, III, 340.
40 S. C. Osborn to T. W. Osborn, June 1, 1866, J. T. Sprague to O. O.
Howard, July 31, 1867, J. E. Quentin to A. H. Jackson, November 2, 1867, in
Bureau Records, Florida.
41 J. T. Sprague to O. O. Howard, August 31, 1868, D. M. Hammond to
A. H. Jackson, August 31, 1868, in Bureau Records, Florida.

at six bales before being attacked by caterpillars. Halliday suggested that the industry of the Williams family should be an example for both white and colored Floridians.[42]

Other Negro homesteaders enjoyed similar achievements. In late 1869 a white homesteader described Negroes near Enterprise who had good cotton crops, and were "doing well."[43] Even the Tallahassee *Floridian*, which was never overly optimistic about the Negro, reported that most of the ex-slaves had "shown a commendable industry in acquiring property, especially land, mules, stock and farming utensils." By hard and continued work, the editor said, farms and homesteads had been secured.[44] Several homesteaders were successful enough by 1868 to employ freedmen as laborers.[45] In the 1870's the area under cultivation in Florida was increasing with a rapidity never before known in the State, and the freedmen deserved much of the credit.[46]

Other freedmen purchased farms outright. As early as 1865, a Negro, Sandy Cornish, was known as the best farmer on Key West. In the midst of surrounding waste land Cornish had a flourishing fruit grove, tobacco patches, and a garden. He was one of the wealthiest and most respected citizens of the area.[47] Other ex-bondsmen were eager to purchase land. If they could buy land it would in many cases already be cleared, which enabled them to raise full crops at the start. A teacher from St. Augustine wrote in 1866 that about six families were living in houses which they had purchased, and several others had saved enough money to buy land. Negro soldiers mustered out in Florida also invested their pay in small farms at a time when land was cheap.[48] July Thomas owned sufficient land in December, 1866, for a Monticello court

---

[42] S. F. Halliday to G. W. Gile, September 26, 1869, in Bureau Records, Florida.

[43] C. B. Chipman to G. W. Gile, September 26, 1869, in Bureau Records, Florida.

[44] Tallahassee *Weekly Floridian*, July 19, August 2, 1870.

[45] J. T. Sprague to O. O. Howard, January 10, 1868, J. A. Remley to J. T. Sprague, February 29, 1868, in Bureau Records, Florida.

[46] New York *Times*, October 29, 1873.

[47] Browne, *op. cit.*, 172; Reid, *op. cit.*, 183, 189.

[48] Mary M. Harris to T. W. Osborn, February 27, 1866, in Bureau Records, Florida; Eppes, *op. cit.*, 327.

to seize enough of it to satisfy a $200 debt. The court records mentioned goods and chattel, land and tenements.[49]

Some Negroes were able to compete favorably with white settlers. John Donaldson went to Pinellas County in 1868, where he worked for wages until 1871 at which time he had saved enough to purchase forty acres. Donaldson cleared the land, planted sugar cane, sweet potatoes, garden truck, and an orange grove, besides raising cattle and hogs. Within a few years, he was considered one of the wealthiest settlers, and was a man "universally respected and one who really kept pace with his white neighbors."[50] Apparently Cornish and Donaldson were not exceptions. "I wish all the people at the North," wrote a school teacher from Gainesville in 1870, "who doubt the ability . . . of the Freedmen to secure homes for their families, would visit . . . a colored family about a mile from here." The family had nine children, had kept six of them in school and had still saved enough money to purchase a house and a small plot of land after three years of wage working. All of their land was under cultivation, the teacher said. She claimed other families had experienced similar success.[51]

In 1872 the editor of the Palatka *Herald* told of a freedman who raised 9 bales of sea-island cotton and 150 bushels of corn. The Negro had purchased the land on credit, had paid for it, and was was enjoying "a handsome competency."[52] The editor of the Tallahassee *Floridian* wrote in February, 1872, of a "great many" freedmen who had rented land or otherwise farmed on their own responsibility, and by "close attention and economical management" had cleared from $600 to $1,000 a year.[53] Around 1870 Caesar Bryant had purchased twenty acres of "raw pine land" near Jacksonville with money saved from sharecropping. Some of the land was marshy so he ditched and drained it. By 1874 he had a "respectable cottage," barn, storehouse, a fine horse, and several cows, and pigs. He grew grapes, oranges, peaches, and vegetables for sale. His crops of corn, rice, and sugar cane were reported to be

---

[49] Records in Office of the Clerk of Circuit Court, Jefferson County Court House, Monticello, Florida.

[50] John A. Bethell, *Pinellas: A Brief History of the Lower Point* (St. Petersburg, Florida, 1914), 19-20; Karl H. Grismer, *The Story of St. Petersburg* (St. Petersburg, Florida, 1948), 188.

[51] *The American Missionary*, XIV (October, 1870), 121-22.

[52] Quoted in Tallahassee *Sentinel*, November 23, 1872.

[53] Tallahassee *Weekly Floridian*, February 23, 1872.

a credit to any farmer. In 1874 he employed several laborers to assist him at crop time. He had been offered $2,000 for his farm, but refused to sell.[54]

Bryant was not the only Negro with valuable property. According to the census of 1870, one Negro owned property valued at $8,000, and another held $7,000 worth of property, and others owned land appraised at $5,000, $4,000, and $3,000. Five freedmen had property valued at $2,000, eleven had land assessed at between $1,000 and $1,500, and eighteen held land worth $1,000. Many ex-slaves had land appraised at $600 to $1,000 for purposes of taxation.[55] The above figures indicate remarkable progress by Negro farmers in the five years after emancipation. Florida had a better record than most Southern states with independent Negro farm operators. In 1900, there were 5,607 Negro farm owners and 851 part owners in Florida.[56] There is little doubt that many of these farms came into the hands of Negroes during Reconstruction.

------

[54] *The Florida Agriculturist*, I (September 12, 1874), 292.

[55] Ninth Census of the United States, 1870, unpublished population schedules of Florida.

[56] *Twelfth Census of the United States*, 1900, V, pt. 1, 6.

CHAPTER VIII

NEGRO RELIGION

The establishment of independent churches for the freedmen was one of the most significant results of Reconstruction. Religious freedom was provided for the Negroes for the first time and such churches "opened up to Negro leadership at least one field of social endeavor."[1] The church became many things to the ex-bondsmen: a house of worship, a social center, the forum, the theater, and the gathering place of the Negro community. Of special importance, affiliation with an independent Negro church became a symbol of freedom. The church was one area in which the freedmen seemed to desire segregation. With their own organization, the Negroes would not be relegated to an inferior status, and it would provide a better opportunity for them to gratify ambitions to become ministers.[2] The Negro preacher became a man of considerable consequence as a social and political leader.

Church attendance was not new to the freedmen. As slaves they had attended services with their masters, and were usually of the same denomination. In the Tallahassee district of the Methodist Florida Conference the slave members outnumbered the whites, though they were not permitted in the church on an equal basis, and their individual services were closely supervised to prevent inflammatory statements by Negro preachers.[3] As a result, slave membership began to decline in 1863. In that year the Methodist church in Florida lost 987 slave members, in 1865 the loss was 560, and in 1866 it was 2,505. By 1871 the white Methodist Church had no Negro members.[4] Other white religious organizations underwent similar experiences The ex-members drifted into independent Negro churches.

---

[1] Francis Butler Simkins, *A History of the South* (New York, 1959), 307.

[2] Taylor, *op. cit.*, 206; Hunter D. Farish. *The Circuit Rider Dismounts: A Social History of Southern Methodism 1865-1900* (Richmond, Virginia, 1938), 171.

[3] Charles T. Thrift, Jr., *The Trail of the Florida Circuit Rider* (Lakeland, Florida, 1944), 95-96.

[4] *Ibid.*, 160.

Negro churches came into being even before the war ended, usually under the guidance of Northern whites. The Freedmen's Aid Society of Syracuse, New York, had established schools in Florida as early as 1862, and the schools were usually accompanied by Sabbath Schools, and religious services. The American Missionary Association had agents in Florida in 1864. By 1865 the Sunday Schools were thriving in areas occupied by the Union Army.[5] After the war, Southern whites also held services for the freedmen on the plantations. Formal organization of churches for the freedmen began in May, 1865, with the appointment of William G. Stewart as pastor of Florida, by the South Carolina Conference of the African Methodist Episcopal Church. He landed in Jacksonville, June 9, 1865, and on the following day organized a church at Midway, a few miles from Jacksonville, the first Negro church founded in Florida by an authorized pastor. Stewart soon organized churches at Quincy, Monticello, Aucilla, and Lake City. When he arrived in Tallahassee, a Negro, Robert Meacham, "famous in his day for building houses of worship," already had 116 members to be placed under the formal organization.[6]

The work of the African Methodist Episcopal Church seemed to be progressing satisfactorily, but Stewart was only a deacon, so in February, 1866, The Reverend Mr. Charles H. Pearce was sent to Florida. Pearce, described by a white contemporary as "a remarkably fine-looking, middle-aged, yellow-colored man, a good Christian minister, who would claim respect in any community," was a man of ability, and began work in earnest.[7] With the aid of F. A. Branch, white pastor of the Methodist Episcopal Church, South, Pearce founded a church in Jacksonville with sixty-four members. He then began to travel about Florida inspecting churches organized by Stewart, establishing new ones, and sometimes persuading members of the Methodist Episcopal Church, South, to affiliate with the African Methodist Church.[8]   The African Methodist Episcopal Church became the most important Negro religious organization in Florida, and Presiding Elder Pearce was

---

5 *The National Freedman*, I (April 1, 1865), 84; G. Greely to G. Whipple, November 8, 1864, in American Missionary Association Archives, Fisk University.

6 Charles Sumner Long, *History of the A. M. E. Church in Florida* (Philadelphia, 1939), 73, 195.

7 Tallahassee *Floridian*, February 20, 1868.

8 Long, *History of the A. M. E. Church*, 57-59.

the most potent force in its rapid growth. One colleague said all
things considered, it was doubtful if African Methodism had ever
produced a man superior to Pearce. Pearce, a former citizen of
Canada, later became a powerful political leader. The spread of
the African Methodist Church was so encouraging the Florida
conference was organized in Tallahassee in June, 1867, with 4,798
members.[9] It continued to grow rapidly. By March, 1868, it
boasted 8,000 members. In December, 1871, the organization had
25 traveling elders, 48 traveling deacons, 244 local preachers and
exhorters, and a membership of 11,582. The peak year of membership was 1874-1875 with 13,102.[10]

The African Methodist Episcopal Church was the most powerful religious organization for the freedmen, but by no means the
only one. Several churches were independent, and the Baptists
and other Methodist churches were strong. The Methodist Episcopal Church from the North penetrated the South during the
Civil War. It proposed to work among both Negroes and whites,
but was more successful with the freedmen. The work of this
church progressed so rapidly a Florida conference was organized in
1873. The Florida Conference was made up of both whites and
Negroes, and its mixed character posed no handicap at first.
But , after 1876 the situation changed and in 1884 the General
Conference authorized a division.[11] Another Methodist organization was an offshoot of the Methodist Episcopal Church, South. In
1870 this church began to use the name Colored Methodist Episcopal Church in America, for its Negro members.[12]

The Baptist Church was also important in Florida, but it was
organized locally, and records are scarce. The first Negro religious
organization in St. Augustine was a Baptist Church with 250 members.[13] There were several different kinds of Baptist churches, the
Missionary Baptist, the African Missionary Baptist, the Primitive

---

[9] Thrift, *op. cit.*, 108; Dorothy Dodd, "'Bishop Pearce' and the Reconstruction of Leon County," *Apalachee* (1946), 6; Benjamin W. Arnett (ed.)
*Proceedings of the Quarto-Centenial Conference of the African M. E. Church
of South Carolina, at Charleston, S. C., May 15, 16, and 17, 1889* (privately
published, 1890), 166-67.

[10] Arnett, *op. cit.*, 211.

[11] Thrift, *op. cit.*, 125-26.

[12] Charles Henry Phillips, *The History of the Colored Methodist Episcopal
Church in America* (Jackson, Tennessee, 1925), 27-35, 43, 94.

[13] A. B. Grumwell to E. C. Woodruff, December 31, 1866, J. H. Durkee to
A. H. Jackson, September 24, 1868, in Bureau Records, Florida.

Baptist, and the Baptist Institutional. One in Jacksonville was known as the Baptist "Praise House."[14] Still other churches were organized but with less success. The Union Congregational Church was established in Jacksonville with both whites and Negro members.[15] The Presbyterian Church reported twenty communicants in Jacksonville in 1870.[16] One of the most outstanding Negroes in the State, Jonathan C. Gibbs, was a Presbyterian minister, but the church was always small during Reconstruction. There were also a few Negro Catholics. It was estimated in 1867, that there were about 600 freedmen of the Catholic faith in St. Augustine, Jacksonville, Pensacola, and Key West. A majority of the freedmen in St. Augustine belonged to this faith.[17] The Episcopal Church also had a few members, but again the number was always small. The denominations that refused to permit the Negroes to have a separate organization enjoyed little success. The Episcopal Church belatedly recognized this fact, and in December, 1875, Bishop John Freeman Young organized the first Negro Parish in Florida. This was the beginning of St. Peter's Church, Key West, which for many years remained the largest congregation composed of Negroes in the Diocese.[18] The more emotional denominations remained dominant. The census of 1870 listed 88 Negro churches, 19 Baptist, 49 African Methodist Episcopal, and 18 Methodist of other varieties, with a property valuation of $29,950.[19]

The rapid growth of the Negro churches is not surprising as the Negroes seemed to have a propensity to religion or at least church services. The freedmen were "strictly, and peculiarly, a religious people," a Bureau agent wrote, and were faithful in

---

14 Jacksonville *Florida Union*, January 4, 1868.
15 *The American Missionary*, XXI (March, 1876), 56-57.
16 *Sixth Annual Report of the Presbyterian Committee of Missions for Freedmen, Presented May, 1871*, 13, 20.
17 St. Augustine *Examiner*, May 23, 1874; J. T. Sprague to O. O. Howard, October 1, 1867, in Bureau Records, Florida; J. W. Brinckerhoff to G. Whipple, November 23, 1864, in American Missionary Association Archives.
18 *Journal of the Proceedings of the Thirty-Fourth Annual Council of the Protestant Episcopal Church in the Diocese of Florida . . . 1877*, 41; Edgar L. Pennington, *Soldier and Servant: John Freeman Young, Second Bishop of Florida* (Hartford, 1939), 36-37; Joseph D. Cushman, "The Episcopal Church in Florida: 1821-1892" (unpublished Ph.D. dissertation, The Florida State University, 1962), 206-7.
19 Ninth Census of the United States, 1870, unpublished social statistic schedules of Florida.

attendance of services held in churches and brush arbors all over the country on Sundays and Wednesday evenings. Religious services were frequent and were held inside and outside depending on the weather.[20] If churches were not available, services were held in homes, old buildings and around campfires. Nearly all of the Bureau agents in Florida commented on the religious enthusiasm of the freedmen. In January, 1867, an agent from Lake City said, "there is an extraordinary interest manifested by the freedmen in religious matters," and in October, 1868, another reported that "religious societies engage much of the attention of the freed people." "Their faculty of veneration," he continued, "appears to be such that it is a hard matter to engage their minds in any other direction."[21] "The height of ambition with the colored children," a white Episcopalian declared, "is to possess a Bible and prayer-book and to know how to read them."[22]

The religious enthusiasm of the ex-bondsmen led to services that frequently started early and lasted late. This is indicated in the request of a white man for a cook. He wanted one, he said, without children if possible, and not partial to *all night prayer meetings.*"[23] The religious fervor of the freedmen led to a willingness to make great sacrifices to have a church. A congregation in Brooksville paid a white man $800 per year to preach for them. They donated their time and money to construct buildings, and support the church. Festivals to earn money for religious societies became popular. The Negro Methodist women in Tallahassee held a two day festival in March, 1866, and realized the handsome sum of $400.05. Lectures were held, and religious pictures displayed.[24]

Few contemporaries denied the religious zeal of Florida freedmen, but many were critical of the way in which the fervor was displayed. W. E. B. DuBois' description of the post Civil War Negro church as one of "intense emotionalism, trance, and weird

---

[20] C. M. Hamilton to J. G. Foster, May 31, 1867, M. L. Stearns to E. C. Woodruff, December 31, 1866, in Bureau Records, Florida.
[21] Jacob A. Remley to A. H. Jackson, October 1, 1868, J. P. Martin to E. C. Woodruff, January 11, 1867, in Bureau Records, Florida.
[22] *The Spirit of Missions,* XXXIII (February, 1868), 149-151.
[23] S. D. McConnell to E. M. L'Engle, December 1, 1869, in Edward M. L'Engle Papers.
[24] W. G. Vance to A. H. Jackson, September 25, 1867, in Bureau Records, Florida; Tallahassee *Semi-Weekly Floridian,* March 27, 1866, April 27, 1869.

singing,' with some African rites remaining." is applicable to
Florida.[25] A traveler in Florida referred to the Negro church as
"a full-developed institution, attended with its peculiarities and
noisy accompaniments, where the colored zealots could . . . give
vent to their religious enthusiasm by howling their emotional
feelings among others equally excited."[26] The freedmen seemed to
be a naturally devotional people, a Bureau agent said, but their
services were so mixed with barbarous forms the idea of worship
appeared to be lost. In St. Augustine and Jacksonville, a traveler
in 1870, saw "shocking mummeries, which belonged to the fetish
worship of savage Central Africa, and not of Christian America."
At least one missionary despaired of ever improving the old people
because of their superstitions, but had hope for the young.[27]

Harriet Beecher Stowe wrote a description of a Negro service
which she thought illustrated the African influence. The men
formed a ring outside the altar, she said, and the women began to
form into lines. To the rhythm of singing "the first sister in the
female procession shook hands with the first brother, singing the
chorus, and concluding with a short curtsy, and then passing to
the next repeated the same." In a short time, Mrs. Stowe added,
"there was a double file of men and women moving and singing,
and shaking hands and curtsying, all in the most exact time and
with the most solemn gravity." The songs were "wild and full of
spirit, the words simple and often repeated." Soon, she continued,
"there was a rhythmical column extending up one aisle, down the
other, and slowly moving out of the house at one end." The singing
and movement was continued until all were out of the church.
"When the fervor was at its height, the wild commingling of
voices, the rhythmical movement of turbaned heads, the sense of
time and tune that seemed to pervade the whole procession, was
quite wonderful." Mrs. Stowe reported.[28]

A transplanted Northerner in Florida, A. B. Hart, also recorded a Negro ceremony. The service, he said, began at sundown

25 Ruby F. Johnston, *The Development of Negro Religion* (New York, 1954), 32.

26 Brooks, *op. cit.*, 40.

27 J. H. Durkee to A. H. Jackson, October 1, 1867, in Bureau Records, Florida; G. W. Nichols, "Six Weeks in Florida," *Harpers Magazine*, XLI (October, 1870), 662-63; Mrs. H. B. Greely to M. Strieby, May 9, 1867, in American Missionary Association Archives.

28 Tallahassee *Semi-Weekly Floridian*, May 21, 1867.

one night, lasted until ten the next morning when it stopped long enough to take the Lord's Supper, and then resumed and was still going at eight that night. There were about twenty ministers present, and each wanted the floor for a time. In another service, Hart said the Negroes began "screeching, dancing, stamping and jumping. . . . They got to tearing around in a circle with two old preachers bobbing up and down in the center. . . . They broke the flooring all to pieces, cracked the sill" and finally the chimney began to show signs of crumbling before the demonstration was stopped. Hart believed religious services were held for recreation. On one occasion, "as a pretext for getting together and having a big time," a group of freedmen collected to repreach a funeral service for a child that had been "buried prayed for and preached over two months ago." That much of the Negro worship service was devoted to singing was corroborated by Hart's brother. "I have been hearing," he wrote one evening, "the wild deep-toned singing of the colored population who are holding a meeting over half a mile from here. Most of their service is in singing," he added, "and I hear them as plainly as though they were but a few rods off."[29] As late as 1873, one of Florida's most distinguished Negroes, Jonathan Gibbs, apologized for the freedmen, saying they "still preach and pray, sing and shout all night long in defiance of health, sound sense, or other considerations supposed to influence a reasonable being." He did say that "many of the things that shock good taste and good morals, which a few years ago were so prevalent, have passed away."[30]

Revival meetings occupied a large place in this emotional religion. Revivals were frequent and of long duration. In October, 1871, the Jacksonville *Courier* reported a meeting that continued for several weeks. The services had been unusually demonstrative, and since they went on all through the night some of the citizens were complaining.[31] The General Conference of the A. M. E. Church of 1872 noted that "great revivals" had been held in Florida and "thousands of souls were gathered into the church." In 1875 the annual camp meeting of the A. M. E. Church, held

---

[29] A. B. Hart to Father, June 15, 1869, A. B. Hart to Mary Hart, July 31, 1870, in Ambrose B. Hart Letters; W. N. Hart to Carrie Hart, March 27, 1867, in Walter N. Hart Letters.

[30] *The Florida Agriculturist*, I (January 17, 1874), 23.

[31] Quoted in Tallahassee *Weekly Floridian*, October 3, 1871.

near Jacksonville, ran for 11 days with over 100 professing "to find salvation in connection with the services."[32]

The preaching at revivals and other services was not always of the highest caliber. Many of the ministers were ignorant and bereft of any religious training. They frequently appeared to think if they did not preach loud and long they had no religion. Their sermons were not always instructive.[33] The following purports to be a correct copy of an original sermon delivered by a Negro minister in Jacksonville, on the subject "Lay up for yourselves treasure in heaven."

> My Dear Bredren:—De Lord is here to-day, goin' from de African to de white folks church, ridin' on a milk-white steed in de air. He knows all yer hearts and what your' thinkin' about. Ef yer hearts are not right, dey must all undergo a radical change until dey are made good. 'De Lord' taught his disciples on de lake of Genesis, and I'm now telling you all de way to do. I 'spec you all cum to de house of de Lord just kase yer friends are here. While yer preacher is tryin' to permulgate de gospel, you is lookin' down de street to see what is comin', and den you're thinking about what you will wear tonight when you come to preachin', payin' no attention to me, who is trying to save yer souls.
>
> O my bredren, dis is a fine new meetin'-house, but we should all seek a house whose builder and maker is de great Lord! Labor not for de perishin' spilin' meat!
>
> Last night was Saturday, and you have spent most of yer week's wages and earnin's, den put de rest in de Freedmen Savin' Bank, and you don't know as you'll ever see it any more in dis world! Somebody may get it, or you may die, and den you will leave it. How much did you bring here for de Lord? O my bredren when dem jerudic angels come you will be sorry you haven't done more for de Lord! When dey come, ef you hasn't dun nothin' for your blessed Jesus, den dey will not say, 'Come, ye blessed, home!'
>
> You must do nothin' wrong if yer want ter git up by dat great white throne among dem snowhite angels, and be one yourselves. You must never cuss or drink any whiskey. Paul told Timothy his son to drink some wine when he had de stumakake. My bredren, don't think yer sufferin' when

---

[32] Long, *History of the A. M. E. Church*, 102; Tallahassee *Sentinel*, September 11, 1875.
[33] *The American Missionary*, XIV (March, 1870), 54-55.

yer not, just for an excuse to git a dram. Old Master in heaven knows when yer sure enuff sick! Can't fool him about nothin![34]

This sermon is probably exaggerated, but other reports are similar. Mrs. Stowe thought the exhortations "seemed to consist in in a string of solemn-sounding words and phrases, images borrowed from Scriptures, scraps of hymns, and now and then a morsel that seemed like a Roman-Catholic tradition about the Virgin-Mary and Jesus." The most important image, according to Mrs. Stowe, was the angel and the blowing of the last trumpet. One of the phrases used by one of the preachers was, "and he will say, Gabriel, Gabriel, blow you trump: take it cool and easy, cool and easy Gabriel: dey's all bound for to come." But, as Mrs. Stowe wrote, who is to say whether or not they received something from this type of service? She thought they had. "It was at least an aspiration," she explained, "a reaching and longing for something above animal and physical good, a recognition of God and immortality, and a future beyond this earth, vague and indefinite though it were."[35]

Such demonstrations by Negro ministers are not surprising. Many of them had received neither education nor religious training. Some of them were unable to read and drew upon scraps of information gleaned by chance. Perhaps such ministers were more effective in reaching many of the freedmen than a better educated preacher would have been. Some of the Negroes were still ignorant and superstitious. Belief in evil spirits and conjuring was not unknown. A more intellectual appeal to such people might have been useless. A white missionary attended a Negro service in Jacksonville in 1868 in which the Negro minister "addressed his church so touchingly and eloquently," that she listened with tears in her eyes. "That gray haired African," she said, "ignorant though he was reached my heart in a manner that it could not be in listening to the most eloquent divines." Perhaps it should be added that emotionalism in religion was not unknown among white Floridians during Reconstruction. A resident of Jacksonville wrote of going by a white Methodist Church, and hearing shouts, groans, howling, bellowing, clapping, and stamping. Furthermore, not all Negro

---

[34] Brooks, *op.cit.*, 40-41.
[35] Stowe, *op. cit.*, 292-94.

services were of an extreme emotional character. A representative of the American Missionary Association wrote in September, 1865, of a church in St. Augustine, where the freedmen were not "noisy, as they are in many places, but are quite consistent in their manner of worship."[36]

Negro ministers in Florida were subject to considerable criticism during and after Reconstruction. A freedman, John Wallace, wrote that one of the greatest dangers to the ex-bondsmen was immorality, and he claimed it proceeded from the churches. "Numbers of immoral and ignorant men," he said, "have invaded the pulpits of our churches and are using the livery of Heaven to serve the devil in." Such men had been guilty of every wrong that could be committed against "innocence and virtue," he declared "and have violated every moral law and obligation."[37] At least one minister's wife apparently agreed with Wallace. The wife of a preacher in Gainesville "knocked her liege lord in the head with a mallet. . . . She was provoked thereto by the fact that he was too extremely polite to the *sisterin* generally."[38] Another newspaper in 1868 listed three Negro preachers as inmates in the Monticello jail.[39] Such ministers were peculiar neither to the Negroes nor the Reconstruction era.

Reports of other observers deal not so much with Negro immorality as with inability. Bishop Young claimed to have "an almost hopeless solicitude" for the Negro population because of their "decided and inflexible preference for attending upon the ministrations" of their own color. A majority of the ex-slave ministers, he asserted, were utterly ignorant and unfit. Another Episcopalian, William D. Scull of Midway, agreed. "The greatest obstacle in the way of improving, religiously and morally, the colored people," he wrote, "is their own ministry. The mischief which this effects is incalculably great." And, he added, "when we speak of it as fetish, fanatical, as stupid, exceeding stupidity, and even

---

36 O. M. Dorman, Diary and Notes; *The American Missionary*, X (January, 1866), 9; Mrs. E. W. Warner to E. P. Smith, September 3, 1868, in American Missionary Association Archives.

37 John Wallace, *Carpetbag Rule in Florida* (Jacksonville, Florida, 1888), 346.

38 Gainesville *New Era*, February 17, 1866.

39 Tallahassee *Weekly Floridian*, November 17, 1868.

diabolical, we do it no injustice."[40] Scull thought the freedmen should be placed under the guidance of the white man in all phases of their development, which may have colored his observation concerning Negro religious activities, but as late as 1875, an observer reported that preaching in Florida was of a very inferior character. He likened it to the blind leading the blind. Intelligent ministers were present in some of the towns, he admitted, but most of them had no education, and "were it not for the divine unction depended upon by the devout, degrading indeed would be the course advised and pursued."[41]

Not all of the Negro ministers were ignorant and incompetent. Even the critical John Wallace said many of them were intelligent and upstanding men. In 1869 a woman from the North wrote of encountering a Negro Baptist pastor in Monticello, who exhibited "more earnest good sense" than any she had met previously. "While his reading is defective," she stated, "he exhorts with a great degree of intelligence, and his prayers are fraught with not only pure, humble devotion, but clothed in language wholly unobjectionable." A white teacher attended the Annual Conference of the African Methodist Episcopal Church in 1874 and found that "many of the delegates were educated men, and all were interested in education."[42] "Some young men of deep and ardent piety, and gifts for public speaking" were commended by a white missionary. As early as 1870, a freedman, Joseph Robert Love, was admitted to the Holy Order of Deacons in the Episcopal Church. Love asked for no dispensations from the full requirement. He "sustained a protracted and searching examination on the full course of study, including the Latin and Greek languages." Love was a deacon in the church at Jacksonville, as well as minister to a Negro congregation.[43] There were other Negro ministers of ability, Jonathan Gibbs, a graduate of Dartmouth College, was one

---

[40] *Journal of the Proceedings of the Twenty-fifth Annual Convention of the Protestant Episcopal Church of the Diocese of Florida*, 26; *Ibid., Twenty-Sixth Convention*, 1869, 31; C. B. Wilder to E. P. Smith, August 28, 1867, in American Missionary Association Archives.

[41] *Eighth Annual Report of the Freedmen's Aid Society of the Methodist Episcopal Church* (Cincinati, 1875), 40.

[42] *The American Missionary*, XIII (February, 1869), 31.

[43] *Journal of the Proceedings of the Twenty-Eighth Annual Convention of the Protestant Episcopal Church of Florida*, 1871, 38; G. Greely to G. Whipple, September 10, 1865, C. D. Washburn to E. M. Cravath, January 20, 1875, in American Missionary Association Archives.

of the best-trained men in Florida; and Pearce, who was not as well educated as Gibbs, was certainly capable.[44] Robert Meacham, the son of his master, had been educated by his father, and was known as a fine preacher and a good pastor. Henry Call was described as "a decent colored man with some intelligence," and few would question the ability of Thomas W. Long, who became presiding Elder of the Jacksonville district of the A. M. E. Church in 1870. Several other Negro ministers were literate and reasonably able.[45]

Whether or not they were well trained and capable, the ministers of freedmen churches were men of power and consequence, both socially and politically. Bishop Young asserted that Negro ministers were "to their clans as chiefs to tribes," and the congregation followed their advice whether it was evil or good because they believed in their preachers completely.[46] The minister was the most important leader in the local community, and sometimes on a larger scale. The churches became involved in politics during Reconstruction, and Pearce, a major leader of the A. M. E. Church, was an influential political figure. Apparently Pearce used the pulpit for political purposes, and "was so firmly established" in Leon County it has been claimed he dictated the personnel of the county's delegation to the constitutional convention of 1868. Ministers charged with neglecting their churches for politics justified themselves on the ground that a minister had the duty to look after the political interests of his people.[47]

Negro preachers held several important political offices during Reconstruction. Gibbs was secretary of state and superintendent of public instruction. Pearce was sent to the state senate from Leon County, Meacham was registrar of Jefferson County in 1867, clerk of the circuit court in 1869, was appointed post master of Monticello in 1869, and was made superintendent of common schools for the county in the same year. He was also a state senator. Seven of the Negroes in the constitutional convention

---

44 Mifflin W. Gibbs, *Shadow and Light: An Autobiography* (Washington, D. C., 1902), 111.
45 Long, *History of the A. M. E. Church*, 75, 195; Federal Writers Program, *Negro History in Florida*, 9.
46 *The Spirit of Missions*, XXXIII (October, 1868), 788.
47 Thrift, *op. cit.*, 108-9; Dodd, *op. cit.*, 6; New York *Times*, October 29, 1873.

of 1868 were preachers.[48] At least five ministers of the A. M. E. Church, William Bradwell, Robert Meacham, C. H. Pearce, H. S. Harman, and Thomas W. Long, were members of the Florida Legislature. Several others held local offices.

Since the ex-slaves were sometimes charged with having little regard for either civil or moral law a question frequently asked during Reconstruction was, did the many Negro churches and ministers have any appreciable influence on the behavior of the freedmen. The church was considered by many to be the proper agency to provide the freedmen with the necessary training. There is considerable disagreement as to the efficacy of the churches. Bureau agents were frequently critical. One agent reported in November, 1867, that "while visiting churches and frequenting prayer-meetings nightly the colored people seem deficient in the true principles of religion." Another agent believed neither the freedmen nor the whites paid much attention to religion, while an observer in Lake City insisted that morally the freedmen had not improved. It was true, he said, they attended church frequently and sang and prayed to such an extent they disturbed the peace and quiet of the town, but the Negroes failed to show by their actions they understood Christianity. He was speaking specifically of the continued stealing and stock killing.[49] Similar observations were frequent. There seemed to be an "immoral piety" among the freedmen, The American Missionary reported in 1870, and religion and conversion sometimes had little correlation to good morals.[50]

Perhaps these critics expected too much too soon. The Negroes had been free only a few years. It is true, though, that the religion of the freedmen was sometimes little concerned with conduct. Services were sometimes more emotional than instructive. However, many contemporaries claimed to see an improvement in the ex-bondsmen based on religion. In October, 1866, George Greeley, a missionary to Florida, found "the moral condition of the people . . . perceptibly improved." "They showed increased intelligence in religion, higher ideas of right and wrong," he added, "and seem remarkably free from the vices solemnly imputed to them."[51] Colonel Sprague believed the churches were beneficial.

---

[48] Tallahassee Weekly Floridian, February 4, 1868.
[49] F. E. Grossman to A. H. Jackson, November 1, 1867, January 5, 1868, W. G. Vance to A. H. Jackson, December 2, 1867, in Bureau Records, Florida.
[50] The American Missionary, XIV (July, 1870), 160.
[51] Ibid., XI (January, 1867), 18-19.

He saw an improvement in morals and family relationships, which he thought was due to religion. Sprague claimed some of the churches were quick to punish members for immorality and profligacy.[52] The churches especially supported temperance. Congregations frequently pledged the abandonment of certain supposedly bad habits. These pledges sometimes had amusing aspects. Members of a Gainesville church agreed to give up smoking, drinking and profane language. Several of them were hesitant to sign because of the tobacco pledge, and one freedman would not sign because of the swearing, for as he said, he was "obliged to plow with some very ugly mules."[53] Religious services were probably as beneficial to the freedmen as to any group. There is evidence that even though changes were not immediate, the church improved morals. It also served as a gathering place, a social center and as a means of releasing tension for a people who lived a depressed life.

---

52 J. T. Sprague to O. O. Howard, January 31, 1867, September 9, 1867, October 7, 1867, October, n.d., 1868, in Bureau Records, Florida.
53 *The American Missionary*, XIII (July, 1869), 151-52.

CHAPTER IX

THE FREEDMEN'S BUREAU AND NEGRO
EDUCATION IN FLORIDA

The Negro mass which converged upon army camps and towns after emancipation was largely illiterate and ignorant. Life as a slave had provided little or no exposure to the rudiments of learning; and if the newly liberated freedman was to be responsible for his own livelihood and well-being it was evident he must be educated. Fortunately, a majority of the Negroes were very eager for the white man's knowledge. One historian has said, "the zeal with which the ex-slaves sought the benefits of literary education is unparalled in history. . . ."[1]

In many instances there was an almost sacred nature to the Negroes' attitude toward education. "In learning to read he was eating of the fruit so long forbidden to him, and he was entering a mystery which seemed almost holy."[2] The ex-slaves flocked to teachers who would provide them with "the magic of reading and writing." It is not surprising that freedmen had an ardent desire to learn. The feeling of inferiority forced upon them by slavery "fathered an intense desire to rise out of their condition by means of education."[3] Furthermore, the longing for knowledge is not peculiar to the white race. The yearning to explore the mysteries of the written word and the desire to increase one's store of learning is an inherent part of man, black or white. Throughout his lifetime the Negro had seen the power and influence of whites connected with education. If it could enhance the position of the white man, he reasoned, why could it not do the same for the Negro? The freedman also discerned the need for instruction to assist him in the practical business of life. Young and old alike crowded into the schools. In 1865 a school in St. Augustine had pupils ranging in age from twenty to seventy-five.[4]

---

[1] Francis B. Simkins, "New Viewpoints of Southern Reconstruction," *The Journal of Southern History*, V (February, 1939), 59.

[2] Bentley, *op. cit.*, 170.

[3] DuBois, *op. cit.*, 638.

[4] *House Executive Documents*, 39th Cong., 1st Sess., No. 70, 334; Mrs. H. B. Greely to G. Whipple, January 23, 1865, in American Missionary Association Archives.

One of the earliest sources of Negro instruction was the Union Army, which enlisted 1,044 Florida freedmen. While in the army the ex-slaves learned discipline, and many of them were taught the basic elements of reading and writing. As early as 1863 soldiers were operating informal schools for Negroes at Fort Barrancas. In 1866 a Florida teacher wrote that many of her Negro pupils had been in the army, and "I do not find one who has been a soldier unable to read."[5] The burden of taking education to Florida freedmen fell chiefly upon missionary and benevolent organizations. In 1862, the Freedmen's Aid Society of Syracuse, New York, organized schools in Fernandina and St. Augustine, under the leadership of Chloe Merrick.[6] It was Miss Merrick whom John Hay, while on a mission in Florida for President Lincoln in 1863, noticed "as one of those in charge of the high school in the little Florida town, leading light mulatto and white children together in a song about the wings of morning."[7] Esther Hawks, a representative of the Freedmen's Aid Society, wrote from Jacksonville in February, 1865, that she was conducting a school with an average attendance of one hundred and sixty, and it was in "a flourishing condition." In March, 1865, the school had four teachers, a local observer said, and the pupils of the school would compare favorably with the children in other institutions of learning. The National Freedmen's Relief Association probably sent the largest number of teachers to Florida. By 1865 it had twenty-four representatives teaching freedmen. Other societies also made worthy contributions. The American Missionary Association had fourteen commissioned teachers and missionaries in Florida by 1868.[8] These benevolent societies laid the base for the important work of the Freedmen's Bureau.

The act of congress creating the Freedmen's Bureau was destined to have a great influence on Negro education, but this influence was not immediately apparent, as the Bureau law made no provisions for Negro schools[9] The initial impetus given

---

5 *The Freedmen's Record*, III (February, 1867), 22; *Official Records*, III Series, V, 662; R. K. Diossy to L. Tappan, May 22, 1863, in American Missionary Association Archives.

6 Jonathan Daniels, *Prince of the Carpetbaggers* (New York, 1958), 84.

7 *Ibid.*, 83.

8 *The National Freedman*, I (December 15, 1865), 382-83; *The American Missionary*, XIV (June, 1870), 123; *The Freedmen's Record*, I (March, 1865), 39; Jacksonville *Florida Union*, March 25, 1865.

9 U. S. *Statutes At Large*, XIII, 507-09.

education for freedmen in Florida was due, not to the original Bureau bill, but to the industry of Commissioner Howard, who believed the only true relief for the ex-slave was education. Only education, he said, could relieve the Negro from "beggery and dependence."[10]

Aware that without appropriations the Bureau could do little to establish schools, Howard determined to co-operate with the benevolent societies in supporting the ones already in existence. When Thomas W. Osborn was named assistant commissioner for Florida in September, 1865, he worked closely with the benevolent organizations, as did H. H. Moore, who, in October, was made superintendent of instruction for the Bureau schools.[11] The Bureau accomplishments in co-ordinating and systematizing the activities of the various societies were notable, but, in addition, it contrived ways to contribute positive aid. School buildings, free transportation, and cheap rations for teachers, were provided. Another practice of the Bureau was to match all volunteer contributions by charitable organizations.[12] Moreover, Superintendent Moore requested army officers stationed at various points in Florida to open schools for the Negro children, and to detail educated soldiers as teachers. Five schools were opened in this manner.[13]

Florida's schools were flourishing, Osborn reported in December, 1865, despite some white opposition, and a shortage of teachers. Ten schools were being operated with 21 instructors and 1,918 pupils.[14] In addition, various Sunday and industrial schools were training children.[15] Esther Hawks wrote in early 1865 that she had "organized a sewing school—the children bringing such work as they have, and we teach them to mend, and patch, and the older ones to cut by patterns. . . ."[16] Most of the schools operated by the military were industrial.

The number of Negro schools continued to increase through 1866, especially on the plantations. Such schools were in demand

---

[10]Howard, *op. cit.*, II, 390.

[11] *House Executive Documents*, 39th Cong., 1st Sess., No. 70, 85.

[12] Howard, *op. cit.*, II, 271-75.

[13] H. H. Moore to S. L. McHenry, November 27, 1865, in Bureau Records, Florida.

[14] T. W. Osborn to O. O. Howard, January 10, 1866, in Bureau Records, Florida.

[15] *House Executive Documents*, 39th Cong., 1st Sess., No. 70, 276.

[16] *The Freedmen's Record*, I (March, 1865), 39.

not only by the freedmen, but by the planters who recognized the Negro would be more content if a school were available. Plantation schools could provide instruction, not only for the children but also for the adults when they were not working. One such school was organized in 1866 near Tallahassee on the plantation of William D. Bloxham, with a Negro, John Wallace, as instructor. The editor of a conservative Tallahassee paper expressed surprise at seeing "little children spelling and reading as though they had been accustomed to it all their lives." Perhaps too much significance should not be attached to the few plantation schools. The motives for such schools were selfish in that they were organized to insure a labor supply and to retain control of the freedmen. John B. Perviance wrote David L. Yulee in August, 1865, that "I believe the best way to manage the Negroes now is to educate them and increase as far as practicable their wants and dependence upon the white man. . . ."[17] Whatever the reason for plantation schools they did provide some learning to freedmen who otherwise would have been unable to receive instruction.

Native Floridians associated themselves with Negro education when the legislature in January, 1866, passed a law permitting the governor to appoint a superintendent of common schools for freedmen. The superintendent was to establish schools for the ex-slaves any time the number of children in a particular location so warranted. The schools were to be supported by a one dollar tax levied on all male freedmen between twenty-one and fifty-five; and by making the annual purchase of a five dollar license by all white teachers a prerequisite to teaching in Negro schools. The latter provision was more for the purpose of excluding Northern teachers than for raising revenue.[18]

The State law would have been of little value without the Freedmen's Bureau. The burden of supporting Negro schools rested upon the freedmen who had difficulty in paying the special tax. Furthermore, after being collected, sometimes forcibly, the school fund was not kept separate, and was absorbed by state liabilities, leaving little money for schools.[19] For all practical purposes the

---

17 J. S. Perviance to D. L. Yulee, August 6, 1865, in David L. Yulee Papers; Tallahassee *Semi-Weekly Floridian*, December 30, 1867; Tebeau, *op. cit.*, 138-39.
18 Florida, *Acts and Resolutions*, 1865, 37-38; *House Executive Documents*, 40th Cong., 2nd Sess., No. 1, 678.
19 G. Wall to J. T. Sprague, July 31, 1867, in Bureau Records, Florida; Tallahassee *Semi-Weekly Floridian*, July 14, 1867.

support of Negro education still rested with the Bureau and Northern societies. The Bureau even paid the salary of the state superintendent besides appointing him superintendent of Bureau schools in order to insure co-operation between the State and federal government.[20]

A law which proved to be more beneficial to Negro education was the congressional act of July, 1866, renewing and extending the Freedmen's Bureau. For the first time the federal agency was given formal appropriations for the support of schools for freedmen. Funds were provided for payment of school superintendents, and for repairs and rent on school houses. The Bureau was ordered to co-operate with benevolent associations and to furnish buildings any time the societies could "provide suitable teachers and means of instruction."[21] The law extended the life of the Bureau to July, 1868, which would permit the agents to get Negro education firmly established before leaving it in the hands of native whites.

Florida's educational system for freedmen continued to grow in 1866. E. B. Duncan, in charge of both state and Bureau schools, established, in the spring of 1866, twenty-four day schools taught by Negroes "of good moral character and limited education."[22] The average enrollment for 1866 was 2,726 as opposed to 1,900 in 1865.[23] But at times even greater numbers were under instruction. In November, 1866, Superintendent Duncan reported an attendance of 5,226 in 35 day schools, 30 night schools, and over 60 Sunday schools.[24] Attendance was always reduced during the planting and harvesting seasons, though one instructor had some students who "came just in time to recite, leaving as soon as the lesson was over to return to their labor in the field."[25]

Even though attendance was necessarily intermittent, Negro pupils showed remarkable improvement. A conservative correspondent from the North, who visited a Florida school in June,

20 Senate Executive Documents, 39th Cong., 2nd Sess., No. 6, 46; J. G. Foster to O. O. Howard, November 21, 1866, in U. S. Army Commands, Florida.

21 U. S. Statutes at Large, XIV, 176; Howard, op. cit., II, 331.

22 E. B. Duncan to J. G. Foster, October 31, 1866, in Bureau Records, Florida.

23 Thomas Everett Cochran, History of Public School Education in Florida (Tallahassee, 1921), 31.

24 Florida, House Journal, 1866, 28-29 in appendix.

25 The National Freedman, I (June 1, 1865), 148.

1866, observed that, "I witnessed the performance of one of the best classes in geography I have ever seen. Reading and spelling classes, I thought would compare favorably with those I have seen in our schools for white children." The whites, he believed, were ahead in mathematics and grammar, but on the whole he considered the Negro schools in Florida a great success. A large number of the children, he said, had "shown remarkable intellectual capacity in acquiring knowledge," and all had made surprising progress.[26] Another observer wrote: "it is astonishing how apt the little Negroes are to learn." "I may safely say," he added, "that the freedpeople, as a general thing, manifest greater interest in education than do the whites."[27]

Unbelieving whites frequently expressed surprise at the advancement of the ex-slaves. One woman, who had taught for twenty years, commented after witnessing a class of freedmen, "I could not have believed it possible that these people could have made such progress in the time. I am astonished at the improvement they have made."[28] A Northern teacher of a Negro school in Monticello received a visit from about fifteen white Floridians who expressed surprise at the efforts of the students. In late 1867 a white man attended a freedmen's school taught by William D. Scull in Gadsden County. The visitor witnessed recitations in reading, spelling, geography, and arithmetic. Students were required to name the capital of each state and describe its location, and to make "rather difficult" mental calculations. ". . . I must confess," the visitor stated, "that I listened to them with surprise, and involuntarily asked myself the question 'are these of that unfortunate race of whom it has been said, They cannot learn.'" Another observer averred that in February, 1866, he called upon a school, and saw children "read understandingly in the Second Reader and write a legible hand," who four months previous had not known one letter of the alphabet. Comments were also made on the excellent order and discipline in the Negro classroom.[29]

---

26 New York *Times,* June 11, 1866.
27 C. M. Hamilton to S. L. McHenry, March 31, 1866, in Bureau Records, Florida.
28 *The American Missionary,* X (January, 1866), 9; H. H. Moore to T. W. Osborn, February 25, 1866, in Bureau Records, Florida.
29 *The Spirit of Missions,* XXXIII (February, 1868), 449-51; *The American Missionary,* XIII (September, 1869), 197-98; H. H. Moore to T. W. Osborn, February 25, 1866, J. H. Durkee to A. H. Jackson, July 5, 1867, in Bureau Records, Florida.

One reason for the amazing progress of Negro students, was their intense interest. "You will be agreeably surprised" a teacher wrote, to see "a class so interested in having a good lesson, as to forego the pleasure of the usual recess, and remain engaged with their geography lesson."[30] Another instructor who had no school building convened classes around a big fire out of doors. "The Negroes, with their books and slates, and eager faces,—the elders on benches and the young ones squatting in the sand . . ." studied intently.[31] Even in 1867, when it was thought Negro eagerness had declined, Superintendent Duncan found the white Sunday schools poorly attended, but, "our colored Sabbath schools go ahead in numbers and interest. . . ." The colored children learn more rapidly, he added; "they have a mind to learn."[32]

Unfortunately, despite some outstanding success, progress in general, was slow. Not the least of the reasons was the necessary use of ill prepared teachers. Some of the Negro instructors were so far from being adequately qualified they were hardly less illiterate than their pupils. Therefore, only the most elementary subjects were taught, and those sometimes ineffectively. Zeal and sincerity could not completely compensate for lack of training. Thirty-three of the reported forty-one teachers in December, 1866, were freedmen.[33]

Not all of the Negroes were unqualified. Some of the native freedmen were able, and several well trained Negroes were sent from the North to teach in Florida schools. Mary Still, who went to Jacksonville in 1866, was born in Philadelphia and had taught for several years in her native state and in New Jersey. Susan L. Waterman was born, educated, and had taught in New Jersey before coming to Florida soon after the war. Other Negro women, including Mrs. M. E. C. Smith, Mrs. Martha Sickles, and Josephine Jones, had been educated in the North and were competent women. Bureau agents commented on the ability and efficiency of these Negro ladies, especially Miss Waterman and Mrs. Sickles. An ex-slave reported the freedmen were happy to welcome these "yankee niggers" in their midst since they were interested in

---

[30] *The National Freedman,* I (July 15, 1865), 185.
[31] *The Freedmen's Record,* III (February, 1867), 22.
[32] E. B. Duncan to J. T. Sprague, March 21, 1867, in Bureau Records, Florida.
[33] Consolidated Monthly School Report, December, 1866, in Bureau Records, Florida.

elevating the Negro standard of living, as well as educating them.[34]

White teachers from the North were better trained than their Negro cohorts, but they were more disliked by Florida whites. In 1866 the state superintendent of education reported that, "in no case have the people shown a willingness to render us any assistance. . . ." The whites, he said, held a deadly hatred toward the training and elevation of the Negro. "Every respectable family shrinks from the idea of boarding our teachers, as from a pestilence." "Not one in a thousand," he continued, "has the moral courage to brook the odium which would be vested upon them by their neighbors in such a case."[35] By refusing to board teachers, and closing all buildings to schools, the whites could and sometimes did keep teachers out altogether. In Gainesville, "an old shell of an unfinished dilapidated church, without door or windows," was the only place that could be procured for a school house. No private family would board the teachers, and only "with the greatest difficulty" could board be obtained at a public house at $30 per month.[36] Teachers were "recipients of many taunts and sneers," and were occasionally threatened by mobs. A teacher in Marianna was confronted with revolvers, and threats of shooting if he did not close his school, while another left Monticello after a "midnight assault" and the previous burning of her provisions. The assault consisted of firing six shots through the door of her dwelling, "some of them while the lady was standing in the doorway."[37]

Petty harassment of Negro schools was frequent. Stones were thrown through schoolroom windows, sometimes aimed at instructors. In Gainesville a disturbance was created in 1866, when the students at a white school objected to the singing of "Rally Around the Flag Boys," by Negro pupils. The Bureau agent advised the teachers to do nothing that would excite animosity, but

---

[34] Long, *History of the A. M. E. Church*, 187-192; E. B. Duncan to J. T. Sprague, March 21, 1867, A. B. Grumwell to A. H. Jackson, April 1, 1867, in Bureau Records, Florida; Federal Writers Program, Florida Slave Interviews, 4-5.

[35] *The National Freedman*, II (January 15, 1866); 3; Henry L. Swint, *The Northern Teacher in the South* (Nashville, 1941), 117.

[36] H. H. Moore to T. W. Osborn, February 25, 1866, in Bureau Records, Florida.

[37] A. Mahony to T. W. Osborn, February 23, 1866, C. M. Hamilton to S. L. McHenry, April 30, 1866, A. B. Grumwell to A. H. Jackson, September 14, 1868, in Bureau Records, Florida.

they claimed the right to sing patriotic songs. After another disturbance the agent was a little more firm. Opposition to freedmen schools was so widespread in Jackson County in 1866 an agent insisted they could not be established in areas too isolated to be protected by the Bureau. Even as late as 1869 when white antagonism had supposedly declined, a school house was burned at Port Orange when a white teacher arrived, and a Bureau agent asked for Negro teachers for Florida because whites might be molested.[38]

White Floridians were ready to believe the worst of the Northern teachers. When some dead infants were found in a river near Jacksonville, one bitter resident remarked that it was "probably the spawn" of some of the "hell-born, time serving, sycophantic" female teachers, who had gone to Florida "under their pretended sanctimonious . . . to practice their infamy, where they were not known." The statement of another Floridian is a commentary on the shortcomings of Florida's educational system for whites as well as on the misunderstanding of Northern teachers. A young lady wrote in May, 1868, that "the Nortan womas that comes out to take charge of the Negro schools have married Negro men what a disgrace but tha send the loest of the low. . . ." Even the Floridians who sympathized with efforts to educate the Negro, H. H. Moore reported, were "suspicious and nervous" in regard to the influence of Northern educators. The whites preferred, he added, ignorant freedmen to the "most accomplished whites from the North.[39]

Perhaps the white teachers gave the Floridians some cause for their fears. They tended to foster racial and social equality in an area where the Negro was considered not only socially subordinate, but inherently inferior in intelligence.[40] Carl Schurz said he heard hundreds of times, while on tour in the South, that "learning will spoil the nigger for work," and "negro education will be the ruin

---

[38] J. H. Durkee to T. W. Osborn, May 1, 1866, W. J. Purman to C. M. Hamilton, May 31, 1866, in Bureau Records, Florida; *The Freedmen's Record*, V (February, 1869), 67; J. W. Alvord, *Seventh Semi-Annual Report on Schools for Freedmen* (Washington, 1869), 24.

[39] O. M. Dorman, Diary and Notes; Eliza Horn Diary, Typescript in Florida State Library, Tallahassee, Florida; H. H. Moore to T. W. Osborn, February 25, 1866, in Bureau Records, Florida.

[40] "The Problem of the Black Races," *Debows Review*, I (January, 1866), 266-283.

of the South." Education might teach the freedmen to demand better wages and working conditions. Moreover, there existed the feeling that freedmen could be elevated only with the accompanying degradation of the Southern whites. Poor whites feared the economic competition of freedmen, and education would make it impossible to hold them at menial tasks. The more ignorant the white Floridians, the more they resented "the black's mad search after the alphabet."[41] Furthermore, the instructors usually aligned themselves with the Republican party, and were ready to find fault with the South at the slightest provocation. A white teacher from Gainesville claimed to tremble when she thought of Democrats assuming power. She depended on the Lord to prevent such a catastrophe, she said. A Bureau inspector once described the teachers as "a band of missionaries who have come from Christian homes of the land—following the example of their divine Master—going about doing good."[42] Such a pious and condescending attitude did not endear the Northern teachers to the proud and defeated South. Besides, the antagonism was not always toward Negro education *per se*, but toward the type provided by Yankee instructors. Some of the whites, however, simply opposed Negro education. As a Bureau agent said, Florida and the South had looked upon the education of their white masses with "criminal indifference" and they could not be expected suddenly to look with "pleasure and generosity" upon the education of their former slaves.[43] The conflict between Northern teachers and Southern whites tended to retard the growth of Negro schools, and adversely influenced the quality of instruction.

The year 1867 was an eventful one for Negro schools. The Bureau now had appropriations and could give more vigorous support to the education of the ex-slaves. Furthermore, the white attitude toward freedmen's schools was improving in some quarters. There was still opposition, but many Floridians were beginning to see the necessity and value of educating their former chattels. One agent noted "a decided change" in the feelings of the whites

41 *Senate Executive Documents,* 39th Cong., 1st Sess., No. 2, 25; Davis, *op. cit.,* 390; Howard K. Beale, *A History of Freedom of Teaching in American Schools* (New York, 1941), 175.

42 Swint, *op. cit.,* 43, 59; E. B. Eveleth to E. M. Cravath, October 29, 1872, in American Missionary Association Archives.

43 W. J. Purman to A. H. Jackson, September 9, 1867, in Bureau Records, Florida.

toward Negro training. There had been "intense hostility" toward all such enterprises, but opposition was declining. Indeed, many planters were making arrangements to have their laborers taught to read and write. The Bureau readily cooperated with the planters. Assistant Commissioner Sprague reported that instead of erecting expensive school building in towns, it was his intention "to dot the State . . . with cheap log cabins in the vicinity of large plantations" to permit parents to send their children to near-by schools with little expense. It was thought such a plan would enable Florida to be "among the first of the Southern states to establish and sustain a public school system for all children."[44]

White opposition to Negro education had declined since 1865, but the freedmen's feverish desire for learning had not. Negro interest was not only failing to disappear as some had predicted, but was actually appearing in new forms. Children were now teaching, and old men and women were among the students. Schools filled up as soon as they were opened. Moreover, there were many signs of student improvement. By 1867 a sufficient number of pupils had advanced in their studies to make it feasible to divide them into four grades in at least six different schools.[45]

Since the freedman's interest in learning continued unabated, and white opposition had declined, conditions existed which permitted the educational work in Florida to move forward. The Bureau continued to supervise, encourage, and provide all possible funds for construction and rental of buildings. The freedmen themselves displayed "remarkable zeal and self-denial" in "all things pertaining to education, in several instances constructing school houses at their own expense . . . and afterwards contributing from their limited funds for the support of a teacher." In March, 1867, former bondsmen in Ocala subscribed $370 for erection of a school house. Quincy freedmen raised $300 in 1867, and Negroes in Marianna purchased a lot and contributed $340 toward a building.

---

[44] J. H. Durkee to A. H. Jackson, January 1, 1867, J. T. Sprague to O. O. Howard, September 9, 1867, in Bureau Records, Florida.
[45] J. W. Alvord, *Fourth Semi-Annual Report on Schools for Freedmen* (Washington, 1867), 36-40.

Three hundred dollars was a sizable sum to be collected from freedmen.[46]

Despite these advances, there remained the problem of securing competent teachers for the many schools. An attempt was made to obtain teachers for Negro schools from the ranks of white Floridians. Duncan took "a decided position" that the educational work should be done by Southerners. He made an appeal in newspapers for white teachers saying, "I love the distinction that stands aloof from the vulgar and vicious, but I ignore that false distinction that would isolate men from humanity. . . ." The appeal was not successful. When a few whites did venture to instruct in Negro schools, they were sometimes treated cooly by their neighbors. A Negro, Robert Meacham, said three young white men, born in Florida, taught in schools for freedmen in Jefferson County, and other whites would hardly speak to them. Though Florida had some schools that would rank with the best in any state, a majority of them were taught by instructors capable of imparting only the most basic elements of learning.[47]

In spite of this difficulty, the schools were of such caliber the State Convention of Florida Teachers in May, 1867, complained that Negroes had an excellent system of instruction, but white schools were inadequate.[48] As a result, some whites attended Negro schools. There was no well developed system of schools for whites before 1869, and if parents did not have the funds to send their children to private schools, the only alternative frequently was to send them to Negro schools operated by the Bureau. A school at Port Orange had twenty-five students, eight of whom were white. No discord had occurred. The children played together "as harmoniously as kittens," the teacher said. At least ten other Negro schools reported white attendance, with Mt. Pleasant having 31 whites out of an average attendance of 99. Some Floridians were willing even to permit Negroes to attend white schools. A white man in a community near Jacksonville assisted in organizing a school. When asked if the whites would admit Negro children

---

46 J. T. Sprague to O. O. Howard, October 1, 1867, J. A. Remley to E. C. Woodruff, March 31, 1867, J. M. Sanno to J. T. Sprague, September 29, 1867, in Bureau Records, Florida; Tallahassee *Semi-Weekly Floridian*, March 8, 1867.
47 Alvord, *Fourth Report,* 37; Tallahassee *Semi-Weekly Floridian*, March 13, 1866; Kennedy. *op. cit.*, 95.
48 Tallahassee *Semi-Weekly Floridian*, May 28, 1867.

if they wished to attend, he said, "Admit them! Of course we would.' " He had three children and he would have no objections, and he believed the others would not if they could only get a school. The teaching staff was integrated in several schools even when the students were segregated.[49]

It soon became apparent that some method was needed to prepare Negro instructors. Florida had a few advanced schools, but no institution for training teachers. A school had been organized in Jacksonville in late 1865 to prepare as teachers girls between sixteen and twenty-five. It was considered a success, but only the most basic subjects were taught, and it ceased operation after a year.[50] Therefore, in 1868 in Jacksonville, the Bureau began construction of the "largest and finest school edifice in the State," and on April 10, 1869, the $16,000 building was dedicated as the Stanton Normal School. By 1869 Stanton boasted 348 students taught by six instructors. It offered higher education to all, but only one white attended.[51] The organization of the normal school did not immediately alleviate the teacher shortage. Florida now had some capable Negro teachers, but the majority remained unqualified. However, student advancement continued. Statistics for 1868 indicate that the number of pupils in advanced reading, writing, geography, and higher branches had increased appreciably.[52]

Two important events occurred in 1868. In July the Bureau was extended for one year, with the stipulation that the educational division was not to be affected, until the Southern states had made suitable provision for the education of freedmen.[53] Another development of some consequence was a scheme devised by Commissioner Howard to help pay the salaries of the teachers. The Bureau heretofore had not been permitted to pay instructors and by 1868 there was an urgent need for teachers. Howard, therefore,

---

[49] *The Freedmen's Record*, III (December, 1867), 190; Teachers Monthly School Reports, 1867-1868, in Bureau Records, Florida; *The American Missionary*, XI (October, 1867), 223-24.

[50] S. L. McHenry to H. H. Moore, November 13, 1865, H. H. Moore to T. W. Osborn, February 25, 1866, in Bureau Records, Florida.

[51] Florida, *Senate Journal*, 1870, 65 in appendix. Bill, *op. cit.*, 85; Howard, *op. cit.*, II, 412; Teachers Monthly School Report, November, 1869, in Bureau Records, Florida.

[52] Cochran, *op. cit.*, 31.

[53] U. S. *Statutes at Large*, XV, 83.

authorized the societies to charge the Bureau rent for buildings they owned. Money collected in this manner could then be applied to the payment of teachers. The Bureau even transferred titles of government structures to the schools and then paid for their use. In this roundabout manner, the federal government was able to help support Negro schools through a critical period when benevolent agencies were being forced to curtail expenditures. In 1869 the Bureau paid rent sufficient to support 40 instructors, in addition to constructing twenty school buildings, in 1868-1869 at a cost of $52,600. Beginning in 1869 the Bureau erected buildings only if a lot were deeded to a board of trustees to be held for school purposes for the benefit of all citizens of the county; thus insuring the building's continued utilization for educational purposes.[54]

Contrary to many predictions, the Negroes' interest in education did not diminish. In late 1868, Assistant Commissioner Sprague wrote: "there is no abatement in the desire shown by the freedmen for their own education and that of their children." They continued to support the schools to the extent their impoverished condition permitted. In many instances they contributed all the labor required in constructing school houses with the Bureau furnishing the materials.[55] Attendance increased in 1868 with 3,328 pupils regularly reported, and decreased slightly in 1869 to 2,769.[56] The reduction was probably among the adults who found it very difficult to attend school and work at the same time.

In the meantime the Florida Legislature, dominated by Republicans, had approved, in January, 1869, a school law, which promised to establish and maintain "a uniform system of public instruction, free to all the youth residing in the State between the age of six and twenty-one years."[57] The new law did not end Bureau activities. It constructed many buildings in 1869-1870,

---

[54] Florida, *Senate Journal*, 1870, 65 in appendix; "Report of the Superintendent of Public Instruction on the Organization of the Department of Public Instruction," in School Reports of Florida, 1868-94, in Office of Superintendent of Public Instruction, Tallahassee, Florida; Circular No. 2, May 19, 1869, in Special Orders and Circulars, Bureau Records, Florida.

[55] J. T. Sprague to O. O. Howard, October n.d., 1868, in Bureau Records, Florida.

[56] J. W. Alvord, *Sixth Semi-Annual Report on Schools for Freedmen* (Washington, 1868), 30; U. S. Congress, *House Executive Documents*, 41st Cong., 2nd Sess., No. 142, 24.

[57] Florida, *Acts and Resolutions*, 1869, 7.

supplied books, and paid teachers. In 1869 the Bureau spent even more money for education in Florida than did the State itself.[58] The growth of Florida schools in 1869 was said to have exceeded that of any other state. In late 1869 Florida had 153 schools, with 157 teachers, and 6,992 pupils.[59]

Even though the state school system got off to a slow start, the Bureau soon became less important. In late 1870 the last of the Bureau school officials left Florida, but not before valuable contributions had been made to Negro education. According to the census of 1870, 15.9% of Florida Negroes over ten were literate. Furthermore, an age group widely reached by the Bureau, six to ten, was not counted in the census, which leads to the conclusion that the federal agency's educational work was highly successful.[60] Moreover, the Bureau helped lay the base for a public school system in Florida. The introduction of schools for Negroes in the South in the years immediately following the Civil War was without question one of the truly significant accomplishments of Reconstruction. Florida, as well as all the states of the South, and of the Nation, gained from this accomplishment.

---

[58] Cochran, op. cit., 55.
[59] J. W. Alvord, Ninth Semi-Annual Report on Schools for Freedmen (Washington, 1870), 31.
[60] Ninth Census of the United States, 1870, I, 19, 405.

CHAPTER X

EDUCATION UNDER "CARPETBAG" RULE

The government established in Florida under President Johnson's plan of Reconstruction gave almost no support to public education, but delegates to the constitutional convention of 1868 recognized the needs, and provided for a system of public schools. According to Article VII, section 1, of the constitution it was "the paramount duty of the State to make ample provision for the education of all the children residing within its borders, without distinction or preference." The State was to create a system of common schools and a university in which instruction would be free. A superintendent of public instruction was to be appointed to exercise general supervision over the educational interests of the State. Public schools were to be supported by the following: the common school fund, the proceeds of United States government land granted for educational purposes, private donations, state appropriations, proceeds of property that accrued to the State by forfeiture or escheat, proceeds of property granted to the State when no other purpose had been specified, funds paid as exemption from military service, fines collected under penal laws, a portion of the per capita taxes specified by law, and twenty-five percent of the proceeds of public lands owned by the State. In addition, a special tax of not less than one mill on the dollar on taxable property was to be levied.[1]

Funds collected by the State were to be distributed among the counties in proportion to the number of resident children between four and twenty-one. In order to receive appropriations for education the counties were required to raise by taxation a sum not less

---

[1] In 1894 an historian of education in Florida said the Walker government had made no provision for public schools because it was feared that the "odious doctrine of co-education of the races" would be forced upon the State by the federal government. *Bi-ennial Report of the Superintendent of Public Instruction of the State of Florida for the Two Years Ending June 30, 1894* (Tallahassee, 1895), 9; Florida *Constitution of the State of Florida, Framed at A Convention of The People, Begun and Held at the City of Tallahassee on the 20th Day of January, A.D., 1868, Together with the Ordinances Adopted by Said Convention* (Jacksonville, Florida, 1868), 17.

than one-half of the amount provided by the State.[2] State taxation to support public schools, as decreed by the constitution, was an innovation in Florida. There had been no previous state-wide taxation for educational purposes with the exception of the one-dollar tax levied on Negro males for education of Negro children. The principle of direct taxation was an important Republican contribution to the public school movement in the South and in Florida.[3]

C. Thurston Chase was appointed first superintendent of public instruction in July, 1868, but could do little until the legislature passed a law implementing the educational provisions of the constitution. In the meantime he traveled about the country investigating various school systems and wrote the law that was eventually enacted. A later Democratic superintendent claimed that "Mr. Chase planned well; he began a great work, and gratitude and honor are due him."[4] Several representatives, including Negroes, exerted considerable energy to pass a school law in the session of 1868, but their endeavors were defeated, in part, by Charles H. Pearce, Negro chairman of the committee on education.[5] Pearce was genuinely interested in education, but opposed the proposed law of 1868 because of an amendment which prohibited integrated schools. He would rather have no schools at all, he stoutly announced, than to support a bill requiring segregation of the races.[6] A school law could not be passed in the 1868 session over the opposition of Pearce, but one was approved January 30, 1869, which permitted, but did not compel segregation. The law provided for segregated schools by empowering local boards of education to establish "separate schools for the different classes in such manner as will secure the largest attendance of pupils, pro-

2 Florida, *Constitution of the State of Florida*, 1868, 18.

3 In 1852 Tallahassee supported a public school by city taxation, DuBois, *op. cit.*, 663-64; Nita Katharine Pyburn, *The History of the Development of a Single System of Education in Florida, 1822-1903* (Tallahassee, 1954), 85.

4 The Superintendent of Public Instruction and dates of appointment were as follows: C. Thurston Chase, July, 1868; Charles Beecher, March 18, 1871; Jonathan C. Gibbs, January 23, 1873; Samuel B. McLin (acting Superintendent of Public Instruction), August 17, 1874; William Watkin Hicks, March 1, 1875. Cochran, *op. cit.*, 49; *Bi-ennial Report, 1894*, 12.

5 John Wallace singled out two educated Negro representatives H. S. Harman and Richard H. Black, for special praise for their energetic support of a school law for the education of all Floridians. Wallace, *op. cit.*, 84.

6 Dodd, *op. cit.*, 8.

mote harmony and advancement of the school, when required by the patrons."[7]

The school law of 1869 provided for a board of education, composed of the superintendent of public instruction, the attorney general, and the secretary of state, to have general supervision over education. Other officers of the department of public instruction included a county superintendent and a county board of public instruction. The county superintendents were appointed by the governor, and members of the boards of public instruction were appointed by the state board of education on the nomination of the superintendent of public instruction and the recommendations of county representatives. Each county was constituted a school district under the supervision of county superintendents and county boards. The county board in turn appointed, on the recommendation of patrons, at least one and not more than five trustees to take charge of one or more schools. Teachers were employed by the local trustees.[8] Schools were to be kept in operation at least three months out of the year.

The present public school system in Florida may be said to have had its origin in the constitution of 1868, and the laws passed by the legislature in the following year.[9] The new school legislation was not easily implemented. Since no appropriations were made immediately, the Freedmen's Bureau still bore the primary burden of support of education in 1869. For the year ending June 30, 1870, the Bureau expended $20,346 for construction of 16 school houses, plus paying $750 rent on buildings for teachers' salaries.[10] Unfortunately, the educational efforts of the Bureau came to an end in July, 1870, but some important aid came from another source outside the State. The trustees of the Peabody Fund had begun rendering aid to Florida in 1869. In that year the Fund made available to Florida $1,850 in addition to 2,000 volumes of school books to be distributed to pupils whose parents were

---

[7] A civil rights act passed in 1873 prohibited compulsory segregation in public schools. Florida, *Acts and Resolutions*, 1869, 12; 1873, 25.

[8] Ibid., 1869, 7-11.

[9] Boyce F. Ezell, *The Development of Secondary Education in Florida* (DeLand, 1932), 19; *Bi-ennial Report, 1894*, 9.

[10] G. W. Gile to E. Whittlesey, July 6, 1870, in Bureau Records, Florida; U. S. Commissioner of Education, *Report for the Year 1870* (Washington, 1870), 106.

impoverished.[11] Assistance from the Peabody Fund increased to $6,950 in 1870 and in 1874 reached a peak of $9,900. Between 1869 and 1876 Florida received $41,950 from the Peabody Fund.[12] Other benevolent societies were still rendering some assistance also.

Though the State gave inconsequential financial support to education in 1869 there was an attempt to organize the proposed new system of schools. By the end of 1869 boards of public instruction had been organized and schools opened in twenty-six counties.[13] There was much work to be done with an 84.1% illiteracy rate among the Negroes, and with 27.6% of the whites illiterate in Florida,[14] but the superintendent of public instruction and local boards encountered many problems. By 1870 fifteen of the counties still had not levied taxes to support schools.[15] Many of the schools did not even have adequate physical facilities. In Alachua County some of the buildings did not have a desk and chair for the teacher. Twenty of the school houses in the county had a water bucket and drinking cup, but only nine were "comfortably seated for pupils."[16] The county board estimated that about 600 youths were not attending school for lack of accommodations. The most serious obstacles in the way of public education in Alachua County, according to the board, were apathy of the patrons, lack of suitable books, lack of suitable buildings, and an insufficient number of instructors. One Negro school in Gainesville had 170 students with only two teachers. Educators in Levy County encountered a "hostile spirit" toward public education, which became "more virulent" with the collection of taxes.[17] Other counties experienced similar financial problems. Most of the school houses in Volusia County were built

---

[11] Jabez L. M. Curry, *Peabody Education Fund: A Brief Sketch of George M. Peabody and a History of the Peabody Education Fund through Thirty Years* (Cambridge, 1898), 147; G. W. Gile to E. Whittlesey, June 30, 1869, in Bureau Records, Florida.

[12] Curry, *op. cit.*, 147.

[13] School Reports of Florida 1869-1894, in Office of the Superintendent of Public Instruction, Tallahassee, Florida; U. S. Commissioner of Education, *Report for the Year 1870*, 105.

[14] *Ninth Census of the United States*, I, 19, 405.

[15] By 1871 all but four counties had levied a school tax. U. S. Commissioner of Education, *Report for the Year 1870*, 106; Florida, *House Journal*, 1872, 57 in appendix.

[16] School Reports.

[17] *Ibid.*

of logs, while none of the schools in Taylor County had toilet facilities.[18]

In a report in September, 1871, the Superintendent of Public Instruction, Charles Beecher, a brother of the famous Henry Ward Beecher, admitted the educational movement in Florida had not fulfilled expectations. Beecher assigned several causes for the retardation of the public school movement. There had been an apparent estrangement between Governor Harrison Reed and Superintendent Chase. In addition, the legislative action of 1869 limiting the amount of taxation in the counties for school purposes to one mill was detrimental, Beecher thought. The maximum was later raised to five mills. Furthermore, the superintendent testified, the legislature had not paid the interest on the school fund in currency, and there had been irregularities in the assessment and collection of school taxes in some counties. Still, Beecher claimed, the checks and discouragements were less serious and "disastrous than might have been anticipated." In the same report he pointed out that the number of children in Florida between 4 and 21 was 62,869, of which only about 14,000, white and Negro, were being reached by the schools. Approximately four-fifths of the children considered to be of school age were not in attendance. Moreover, the average school term for those attending was only four and two-thirds months.

"Education encounters fearful obstacles," the United States Commissioner of Education wrote of Florida in 1871. The state system had made little progress, the commissioner said, "notwithstanding the ability and utmost endeavors of the newly appointed Superintendent," Beecher.[19] Nevertheless, Florida had some good schools in 1870. Trustees of the Peabody Fund reported in early 1871 that Ocala had an "excellent" Negro school for over 100 students operating 10 months out of the year. Apalachicola, the report continued, had a "good school of 100 pupils," and Key West and Gainesville had adequate schools for freedmen with enrollments of 172 and 200 respectively. Even the pessimistic report of the United States Commissioner of Education admitted that St.

---

18 *Ibid.*
19 Some of the counties ignored the law and levied taxes up to two and one-half mills. *Ibid.*; Florida, *Acts and Resolutions*, 1869, 13; 1874, 102; U. S. Commission of Education, *Report for the Year 1871* (Washington, 1872), 12, 119; Florida, *House Journal*, 1872, 56-57 in appendix.

Augustine, under the stimulus of Peabody funds, had "shown a disposition to adopt a system of free public schools."[20]

Most of the better schools for Negroes continued to have large enrollments. The school at Gainesville had so many students the instructors hoped in vain for a decrease in 1870.[21] A resident of Jacksonville visited an evening school for Negroes in January, 1873, and saw students, young, middle-aged and with grey hair. Among the pupils were masons and carpenters from forty to fifty years of age who were regular and hard working students, the instructors said.[22] The superintendent of Hernando County wrote in April, 1872, that the Negro school in Brooksville was the "largest and best attended school in the county."[23] In the same year S. F. Halliday, superintendent of Alachua County, said the interest manifested by the freedmen in education was "not a little remarkable. . . ." The ex-slaves were still demonstrating a "great willingness to build school houses and make other sacrifices for the education of their children," Halliday insisted. In Liberty County there was a larger ratio of Negroes than whites attending school, though this might have been because the freedmen tended to live in the more settled areas.[24]

Harriet Beecher Stowe distributed spelling books among some Negroes in 1873, which, she asserted, "they eagerly accepted, and treasured with a sort of superstitious veneration." The recipients of the spellers, she added, would appear after work and on Sundays begging to be taught. The superintendent of Marion County reported sixteen large Negro schools, and maintained that the interest in schools and education evidenced by freedmen was on the increase. In Hernando County the demand for schools increased in 1873-1874 on the part of both whites and Negroes. In 1872 the county had 15 schools, and the demand was so great the number was increased to 17 in 1873 and to 22 in 1874. As late as 1878 the superintendent of Jefferson County wrote that the deep

---

[20] Ibid.; Peabody Education Fund, *Proceedings of the Trustees at their Annual Meeting, February, 1871* (Cambridge, 1871), 32-34; E. B. Eveleth to E. M. Cravath, February 1, 1872, in American Missionary Association Archives.
[21] *The American Missionary*, XIV (May, 1870), 103-4; U. S. Congress, *House Executive Documents*, 41st Cong., 3rd Sess., No. 1, pt. 2, 316.
[22] S. L. Smith to J. V. Richardson, January 29, 1873, in Miscellaneous Collection, P. K. Yonge Library of Florida History, Gainesville, Florida.
[23] School Reports.
[24] Ibid.; Florida, *Senate Journal*, 1873, 29 in appendix.

interest manifested by Negroes "at their emancipation in the cause of education . . . has not abated, but grows, and on the part of many has become an all absorbing passion to have their children educated."[25] The charge of declining interest in education on the part of the freedmen does not seem to have been widely applicable in Florida.

By 1873 the public school system in Florida appears to have been extensively organized. In that year county superintendents reported from all counties in Florida except Brevard, Holmes, and Dade, and the three counties combined had a Negro population of only 169 including adults.[26] In August, 1873, Superintendent of Public Instruction, Jonathan C. Gibbs, in a speech to the National Education Association, said Florida had 18,000 pupils in school at a cost of $101,820. The year 1873-1874 witnessed an enrollment of 21,196 and expenditures of $139,870.60. In 1874-1875 enrollment climbed to 32,371 with total receipts from school taxes amounting to $188,952. Receipts for 1875-1876 fell to $94,104 and expenditures declined to $158,846.36.[27]

Organization of public schools in Florida was of more immediate benefit to whites than Negroes since the latter already had schools operated by the Bureau and benevolent societies. But, the freedmen, despite problems such as the accidental burning of the largest Negro school in Leon County, and difficulties in collecting school taxes, profited greatly and continued their earlier progress. Freedmen retained their interest in learning and continued to amaze skeptical whites. In April, 1872, T. S. Coogler, a former slave-owner, attended an examination of pupils in a Negro school at Brooksville. His former belief of the "mental incapacity" of the freedmen "underwent a complete change," he admitted. Coogler

---

25 *Ibid.*; Stowe, *op. cit.*, 296-97; *The Florida Agriculturist*, I (February 21, 1874), 61.

26 School Reports; *Ninth Census of the United States*, 1870, I, 19.

27 In 1894 the Superintendent of Public Instruction, William N. Sheats reported that Gibbs enjoyed "the distinction of being the only Superintendent of Public Instruction of the State that has ever been assigned a place" on the program of the National Education Association. "It is a matter of rumor" Sheats added, "that no representative from the South has ever received so great an ovation at the hands of that body." U. S. Commissioner of Education, *Report for the Year 1874* (Washington, 1875), 61, 532-33; *Report for the Year 1875*, 65; *Report for the Year 1876*, 61; "Education in the South," read by Gibbs at Elmira, New York, August 7, 1873, in School Reports; Florida, *House Journal*, 1874, 62-72 in appendix; *Bi-ennial Report, 1894*, 15; Davis, *op. cit.*, 684.

professed to be convinced that all the ex-slaves needed was "half of an opportunity" and they would develop as much "mental calibre as any other race." A report from Madison County in November, 1871, pronounced the progress of Negro pupils as "truly wonderful."[28] The rapid progress of the students, the informant said, was probably due to their competent teachers.

William Cullen Bryant, after visiting a Negro school in March, 1873, said the students seemed to be progressing satisfactorily. The teacher informed Bryant that the scholars of whom they were most proud had gone away to college in Atlanta. They had, the teacher continued, become experts in algebra, had made a beginning in Latin, and were so well trained that professors from Northern colleges who had visited the school in the previous winter had "expressed their astonishment at their proficiency." Many of the Florida Negroes who went away to college met with considerable success. James Chestnut went to Atlanta College from Gainesville and was considered by the college faculty as "one of their jewels." "He was ahead in all his studies, and is the leader in a Latin class of forty boys," they reported. Except for the young, Bryant believed education had made little impression upon the ignorance of Negroes.[29] On the other hand, a New York *Times* correspondent wrote in October, 1873, that many of the freedmen "have become quite well educated, and have given a good tone and proper direction to the sentiment of the lower class of Negroes."[30] Superintendent of Public Instruction, W. Watkin Hicks agreed. The freedman's "advancement in the ordinary curriculum of the common branches" was "as sure and as rapid as that of his more favored white brother," he said in 1876. In the higher branches, such as arithmetic and writing, Hicks added, a comparison of grades in white and Negro schools showed the Negro youth was little if any behind the white in the same grade.[31]

The continued advancement of Negro pupils was due in part to increasingly competent teachers. Freedmen themselves were more competent to teach, white Floridians gradually began to accept

---

28 School Reports; Florida, *Senate Journal*, 1873, 34-35, 37, in appendix.
29 Charles I. Glicksberg, (ed.) "Letters from William Cullen Bryant From Florida," *Florida Historical Society Quarterly*, XIV (April, 1936), 264-66; E. V. Eveleth to E. M. Cravath, April 29, 1873, in American Missionary Association Archives.
30 New York *Times*, October 29, 1873.
31 School Reports.

positions in Negro schools, and instructors were still being imported
from the North. Furthermore, white opposition toward education
for freedmen appeared to be gradually declining. The altered
attitude of whites was demonstrated, Madison County Superintendent Dennis Egan said in November, 1873, when six Northern
ladies teaching in Negro schools outside of Madison were able to
secure rooms with the "best of families."[32] Nevertheless, there was
still some resistance to Negro education. An attempt to establish
a school at Ellaville in 1873, "met with every opposition" from
local whites. In the same year "enemies to the advancement" of
Negro children in Jackson County were reported. Southerners
admit Negroes have made "very great improvement" since we
started teaching, a Northern teacher wrote from Gainesville in
April, 1873, but they still refused to associate with Northern
teachers "because they say—we affiliate with the nigger in sewing school and bible class." As late as 1876, Superintendent
Hicks declared it would be "folly to disguise" the continued strong
prejudice of some whites. Indeed, he added, it was liable to increase.[33] Even so, white Floridians were gradually accepting Negro
education and in some cases giving their active support.

Most of the schools were primary, but Florida did have a few
secondary schools. Eight white and three Negro schools would
probably be classified as high schools in 1874. The three Negro
schools were Stanton Institute in Jacksonville, Lincoln Academy
in Tallahassee, and Douglas High School in Key West.[34] The most
important of the three schools probably was Stanton. The com-
modious building housing the Lincoln Academy was accidentally
burned in 1872, causing a decline in that school, and Douglas was
slow getting started, though by late 1876 it had an enrollment of
about 300.[35] By 1872 Stanton had nearly 400 students and seven
teachers, and was expecting an increase.[36] It offered courses in
Latin and algebra, besides all other subjects commonly taught in
Northern public schools.[37] A Jacksonville reporter who visited the

---

32 *The Florida Agriculturist*, I (March 7, 1874), 79.
33 *Ibid.*; School Reports; E. V. Eveleth to E. M. Cravath, May 29, 1873, in
American Missionary Association Archives.
34 U. S. Commissioner of Education, *Report for the Year 1875*, 65.
35 School Reports.
36 *Ibid.*; Pyburn, *op. cit.*, 113; C. E. Williams to E. M. Cravath, January 22,
1874, in American Missionary Association Archives.
37 *The American Missionary*, XIX (February, 1875), 37.

school in 1874 was eloquent in his praise. Stanton was, he said, one of the first Negro schools of any importance in the State, and was the most successful. The "self-sacrificing" ladies from Massachusetts, especially Miss C. E. Williams and her sister, he said, had done a work for Negroes of Jacksonville, and the State at large, "which for the influence on the present and future," had "no parallel in any line of effort for their advancement." Stanton, the article continued, clearly demonstrated the capacity of freedmen to learn "by the same methods" as white children and with "like ease." The reporter was impressed with the "order pervading the school" and the methodical precision and accuracy with which each student performed his work. "Therefore it is no panegyric no mere useless words of compliment." the witness added, "but the sober truth to say that the most valuable work" yet done for the Negroes of Jacksonville was "the four years of hard, earnest labor of the Misses Williams and their able assistants in the Stanton Normal Institute." The Negro pupils were reading well and spelling better than many white adults, he continued.[38]

Florida also had a Negro institution of higher learning, Cookman Institute, located at Jacksonville. Cookman was founded in 1872 by The Reverend Dr. S. B. Darnell under the auspices of the Freedmen's Aid Society, and named after The Reverend Mr. Alfred Cookman, a Methodist minister who donated money for construction of the first building.[39] It was the first, and for several years, the only such institution in the State. In 1875 the Freedmen's Aid Society reported two teachers and fifty students. There were more applicants, but they could not be accommodated. The purpose of the school was to prepare young men for the ministry, and to prepare teachers of both sexes.[40] In July, 1923, Cookman Institute was merged with the Daytona Normal and Industrial Institute to become the co-educational Bethune-Cookman College.[41]

Two other attempts were made during Reconstruction to

---

[38] *Ibid.*, XVIII (January, 1874), 8-9.

[39] J. S. Stowell, *Methodist Adventures in Negro Education* (New York, 1922), 77.

[40] *Eighth Annual Report of the Freedmen's Aid Society of the Methodist Episcopal Church* (Cincinnati, 1875), 40.

[41] Mary McLeod Bethune, *An Upward Climb* (Daytona Beach, [Pamphlet], n.d.), 3.

establish Negro institutions of higher learning. On February 18, 1870, a law was approved providing for the creation of the Florida State Agricultural College, but lack of funds delayed its establishment. In the same month the legislature chartered the Brown Theological Institute. The school was organized by the A. M. E. Church, with C. H. Pearce the outstanding leader. Pearce went about the State making speeches and collecting money. In May, 1872, it was reported the school was progressing satisfactorily. Buildings were completed by 1873, and the name changed to Brown University, but the white man who supervised the work and finances kept the money rather than paying the builders. The construction workers sued the board of trustees and won their case. The land and buildings were sold at auction in 1874, ending the attempt to establish a second advanced school for Negroes in Florida.[42]

Despite numerous problems, including white opposition and difficulty in securing sufficient funds, the organization of a public school system in Florida had met with considerable success by 1876. In 1874-1875 Florida had 32,371 students enrolled, many of them Negro. Obvious proof of the success of the public school system can be seen in census figures. In 1890, 49.5% of the Negroes in Florida were literate, the highest literacy rate enjoyed by any of the eleven former Confederate states.[43] Floridians contended the literacy rate would be higher if it were not for the tide of "ignorant" Negro immigrants from other states.[44] There is no doubt the so-called "Radical Republicans" rendered a valuable service to Florida in organizing and supporting a public school system. By 1876 the idea of public schools seemed to be too firmly entrenched to permit abandonment.

Unfortunately the education system was seriously crippled by the retrenchment policy of Florida Democrats.[45] An important Democratic leader, Charles E. Dyke, boasted in 1880 that despite increased population, Florida schools were operating with reduced

---

[42] Long, *History of the A. M. E. Church*, 83-84; Tallahassee *Sentinel*, May 11, July 6, 1872; School Reports; Florida *Acts and Resolutions*, 1870, 45-49; 1872, 68.

[43] Bureau of Census, *Negro Population 1790-1915* (Washington, 1918), 415.

[44] *The Florida Agriculturist*, I (February 21, 1874), 68.

[45] C. Vann Woodward, *Origins of the New South 1877-1913* (Baton Rouge, 1950), 61; Hodding Carter, *The Angry Scar* (Garden City, 1959), 190.

revenue.[46] In 1879 the legislature reduced the maximum that counties could tax for school purposes from five to two and one-half mills.[47] School officials commented, sometimes bitterly, on the legislative action. In December, 1880, J. V. Harris, superintendent of Monroe County, wrote that "the reduction of the school tax by the last Legislature was a serious blow at the cause of education." It had caused "much embarrassment" in operating existing schools and precluded the establishment of contemplated new ones, he said.

In the same month the superintendent of Nassau County said a sufficient fund to operate all the schools in the county successfully could not be raised with a tax of two and one-half mills. He, along with the superintendent of Madison County, thought the maximum should be at least five mills, or the legislature should leave the matter of assessing a school tax to the county. Henry N. Felkel, superintendent of Leon County, in 1880 claimed "the reduction of the school tax by the last General Assembly has had the effect of embarrassing, to a most hurtful extent, the operation of the schools of this county." Several other county superintendents reacted adversely to the reduction of school funds. Some counties were forced to reduce the length of the term of their schools to three months.[48] These complaints were not made by disgruntled Republicans, but by white Florida Democrats.

Money saved on education by Democratic regimes was at the expense of Negroes. The proportion of total expenditures going to Negro schools declined rapidly. By 1896 the highest monthly salary paid a white male was $187.50. The highest paid Negro teacher received $80. The highest salaried white female made $100 monthly, while the Negro female received $50. The same variation existed in facilities. In 1896 the value of Negro school buildings was $71,560, while for the whites it was $352,873. Each Negro pupil in daily attendance cost the State $5.45, but $11.13 was spent for each white student. The per-centage of each race enrolled in school was about the same, but the average number of days schooling given to each white child was fifty-two. The average

---

[46] Speech made September 6, 1880. Copy in P. K. Yonge Library of Florida History.
[47] Florida, *Acts and Resolutions*, 1874, 102; 1879, 39.
[48] School Reports.

number of days for Negroes was thirty-three. The average student load per teacher in 1901 was thirty-nine for white, and seventy-nine for Negro teachers.[49] In spite of Democratic retrenchment—some even suggested that public education be limited to primary grades— the public school system in Florida had been too well organized and too widely accepted to permit its destruction.

---

[49] *Bi-ennial Report of the Superintendent of Public Instruction of the State of Florida for the Two Years Ending June 30, 1902* (Tallahassee, 1903), 4-5, 7, 9, 11.

CHAPTER XI

MILITARY RULE AND THE PROVISIONAL GOVERNMENT

The first government encountered by the freedmen after emancipation was military rule, and tradition to the contrary, the army generally did not pamper the ex-slave. Freedmen were recognized by the military as free men, but were still closely regulated. In May, 1865, an order of General Vogdes declared that Negroes were to be recognized as free, but "in no case" were they "to be allowed to remain in idleness at the expense of the Government." Local commanders were ordered to acquaint the late slaves with their acquired rights, but to urge them to work for planters near their homes.[1] On the same day local commanders were told to instruct the freedmen that the government would protect them in their rights under the law, but it was expected that they would "remain" as far as possible at their old homes and await the "peaceable adjustment of such rights." The order had been issued after the commander learned freedmen were assembling in crowds at various places. Commanders were ordered to make a proper disposition of their men in such a way as to preserve order.[2] As late as September, 1865, patrolling parties visited plantations to insure order among the former bondsmen. One of the strangest orders of the military was issued on December 1, 1865, in St. Augustine. It commanded all Negroes, whether soldier or civilian, when meeting white people to give them the inside of the street or walk. When questioned about the order, the local commander said it was issued to avoid trouble.[3]

Many Union soldiers had a low opinion of the freedmen. One Florida Negro claimed ex-slaves were maltreated by the army.[4]

---

[1] General Orders No. 22, May 24, 1865, in U. S. Army Commands, Florida.

[2] S. L. McHenry to E. Kellog, May 24, 1865, in U. S. Army Commands, Florida.

[3] General Orders, No. 30, September 21, 1865, in U. S. Army Commands, Florida; H. H. Moore to T. W. Osborn, January 4, 1866, in Bureau Records, Florida.

[4] Wallace, *op. cit.*, 37.

This charge was not widely applicable, but some antagonism did develop between freedmen and white soldiers. Negroes in Jacksonville complained about the behavior of soldiers, and an altercation occurred between white Union soldiers and freedmen in 1869. On the evening of February 22, a patrol was fired upon by a group of armed Negroes, and one soldier was wounded. The soldiers then reputedly "made a determined war upon all" Negro males on the night of February 26. For an hour volleys could be heard all over town, and the streets were bare of freedmen the rest of the night and next day. One Negro was found dead, but the soldiers denied knowledge of it. They had been firing blanks, they said, and were only frightening the freedmen.[5]

Soldiers were not brutal toward the freedmen as a rule, and they did guard their rights and protected them from violence of whites; but that the general policy of the military toward freedmen was strict is demonstrated by the reaction of Southerners. Union soldiers were not always unpopular with white citizens, as they were ordinarily considered fair to them. The commander of troops in Ocala, a local white wrote, was a West Point officer who appeared to be quite a gentleman, and who "properly" appreciated the character of the Negro. Proper appreciation of Negro character meant he agreed with native whites.[6] Guards were even furnished for weddings and parties.[7] Though there was considerable denunciation of army occupation after the troops were gone, Floridians were frequently complimentary while soldiers were still in the State. In April, 1866, the Quincy Commonwealth said probably no officer in command of a department in the South had "pursued a more just and liberal conduct, in the performance of official duties" than had General John G. Foster, Commander of the Department of Florida. He was generally popular throughout the State, the paper continued, and citizens had "no apprehension of a harsh administration of any of the orders from the war department."[8] Colonel John T. Sprague, the St. Augustine Examiner maintained in 1867,

5 Thomas F. Davis, History of Jacksonville Florida (Jacksonville, 1911), 151; C. C. Gilbert to Asst. Adjt. General, no name, February 24, 1869, in U. S. Army Commands, Florida.
6 E. J. Lutterloh to D. L. Yulee, September 20, 1865, in David L. Yulee Papers; R. Bullock to E. M. L'Engle, December 5, 1965, in Edward M. L'Engle Papers.
7 Eppes, op. cit., 304.
8 Quoted in Gainesville New Era, April 13, 1866.

had the "approval of all Right Minded men." Florida had been fortunate in military appointments, according to the *Examiner* and "if we live under a military despotism we have scarcely felt its iron heel."[9]

Florida was the last state to request the establishment of a civil government, and then it was advised to do so by military authorities. A New York *Tribune* correspondent explained such a development by saying that martial law was administered so "mildly and wisely" "the people had no occasion to complain."[10] Florida experienced fewer disturbances than other Southern states, and the wise policy pursued by military commanders was reputed to be the reason. A lady from Jackson County who was quick to defend the Klan in its violence against freedmen and white Republicans, expressed the opinion that trouble had been caused by carpetbaggers, but not by the military. "All the officers sent among us in command of troops," she said, "have conducted themselves in a gentlemanly manner," and have borne with "amazing patience the irritating speeches and conduct of many of our people."[11]

It is not surprising the military was not widely hated in Florida. The State suffered little material hardship from Union occupation.[12] Furthermore, though freedmen were protected, military policy was not far out of line with ideas of the whites. In addition, the soldiers engaged very little in politics, which was the major complaint against most Northerners. Most of the complaints about occupation were not that the army was so brutal or unfair, but that it was there at all.

There were a few incidents between military and civil officials, some of them amusing. Francis Eppes, Intendant of Tallahassee, arrested soldiers for fast riding, and fined them, even when they were discharging their duty. The first arrests were made for galloping, then for loping, then for fast trotting, General Foster reported, and he was informed that all would be arrested who trotted their horses, either fast or slow. Eppes claimed it was not the gait, it was the speed that was important. The difficulty

---

9 St. Augustine *Examiner*, August 31, 1867.

10 New York *Tribune*, August 8, 1865; Jacksonville *Florida Union*, August 19 1865.

11 F. B. Chapman, Unpublished Account of Jackson County Affairs, in Call Papers, Florida Historical Society Collection, University of South Florida, Tampa, Florida.

12 Davis, *op. cit.*, 465.

was settled when Foster informed Eppes that martial law was still supreme.[13]

Floridians were less complimentary of Negro than white soldiers. In 1866 the general assembly commended the military by asking that the Freedmen's Bureau be operated by the army, but at the same time it requested Governor David S. Walker to exert himself to secure the removal of Negro soldiers. The request was made, according to the resolution, because Negro troops were "exerting an injurious influence on the blacks and causing insubordination."[14] The whites were afraid the freedmen would neglect their work by assembling at Negro camps, and the example of a Negro in authority would cause the ex-slaves to be rebellious.[15] Negro troops did occasionally side with freedmen in disputes between Negroes and whites, but the military itself prevented the ex-slaves from congregating around the camps.[16]

Fear that the freedmen would not work and would be insubordinate was not the only objection to Negro troops. The presence of ex-slaves in positions of power was annoying and frightening to former slave owners. A disturbance occurred in Lake City in November, 1865, between whites and Negro soldiers. The original cause of the irritation arose when Negroes were posted in the public square in what seemed to be a supervisory capacity over the conduct of citizens on election day. This angered the whites and when a civilian freedman was attacked by them, the soldiers threatened revenge. Colonel Sprague removed the troops, as he ordinarily did when a disturbance occurred between citizens and Negro soldiers.[17] Placing Negro troops in charge of whites was correct, but unwise.

Naturally former slave owners resented having former slaves garrisoning their state, but all whites were not opposed to Negro soldiers. The Negro troops were sometimes disorderly as were white soldiers, but usually they were well-behaved. Several observers com-

---

[13] D. S. Walker to F. Eppes, September 15, 1866, in Bureau Records, Florida.

[14] Florida, *Acts and Resolutions*, 1865, 102, 113.

[15] Eppes, *op. cit.*, 273; Wallace, *op. cit.*, 19-20.

[16] W. G. Vance to T. W. Osborn, March 27, 1866, in Bureau Records, Florida.

[17] J. T. Sprague to C. Mundee, December 3, 5, 1865, in U. S. Army Commands, Florida.

mented on their good conduct.[18] On at least one occasion, white Floridians requested their return. After a company of the 99th U. S. Colored Troops was ordered out of Hamilton County at the request of Provisional Governor William Marvin, lawlessness became so widespread that white citizens joined in a petition to have the company returned.[19] Even though the soldiers were generally orderly and well-behaved, a majority of whites were pleased, when in September, 1866, the last Negro troops were withdrawn from the State.[20]

In keeping with his plan to turn the government of the Southern states over to civil officials as rapidly as possible, President Andrew Johnson, on July 13, 1865, appointed William Marvin provisional governor of Florida,[21] a selection which gave general satisfaction in the State. Marvin had been a territorial judge, judge of the district court for the South District, and was known for his impartiality in making decisions. He had been a Unionist during the war.[22] Marvin immediately began a series of speeches to disclose the president's plan of Reconstruction. Delegates to a state convention would be selected as soon as the citizens were enabled to qualify themselves. All who had taken the oath of amnesty set forth by the president on May 29, 1865, and were qualified to vote by the state constitution prior to secession were eligible to vote for delegates to the convention.[23] According to a Florida paper few Floridians were excluded by the amnesty oath.[24] October 10 was set as the day for election of delegates to the convention. Thirty-nine counties were authorized to send representatives.

Since the freedmen were going to be placed under the control of civil officials, the attitude of Florida whites toward their late slaves was of special importance. It was evident from the first

---

[18] Jacksonville *Florida Union*, August 19, 1865; New York *Tribune*, August 8, 1865; Pleasant Daniel Gold, *History of Duval County Including Early History of East Florida* (St. Augustine, 1929), 155; James W. Covington, *The Story of Southwestern Florida* (2 vols., New York, 1957), I, 147.

[19] J. G. Foster to Adjt. General, no name, December 11, 1865, in U. S. Army Commands, Florida.

[20] Tallahassee *Semi-Weekly Floridian*, September 4, 1866.

[21] *The American Annual Cyclopedia and Register of Important Events* 1865, V, 359; Wallace, *op. cit.*, 6.

[22] Jacksonville *Florida Union*, July 29, 1865; Davis, *op. cit.*, 357; John E. Johns, *Florida During the Civil War* (Gainesville, 1963), 155.

[23] *The American Annual Cyclopedia and Register of Important Events*, 1865, V, 360.

[24] Jacksonville *Florida Union*, June 24, 1865.

that Negroes could not expect equal treatment and privileges. Governor Marvin traveled about the State making speeches to freedmen, and his speeches apparently reflected the sentiment of a majority of whites. Marvin told the Negroes they were recognized as free men, but cautioned them to be respectful and avoid insolence, because whites were still their superiors. The ex-slaves were as free as white people, Marvin said, but they must not think they were equals of the whites. The Negro had to "do a great many things" before he could "begin to be as great as whites," Marvin added. "You must work in the fields," Marvin told the former bondsmen, and "conduct yourself precisely as you formerly did." The freedmen were also warned against pretensions of social equality.[25]

Assistant Commissioner Osborn wrote in November, 1865, that his experience in Florida had by no means convinced him control of the freedmen should be turned over to civil authority so soon. If military authority were removed, Osborn contended, the partially subdued bitterness of whites would be vented on the freedmen. The whites were not prepared to govern themselves, much less legislate justly for the Negro, he continued.[26] Other reports tend to substantiate Osborn's view. In July, 1865, the Jacksonville *Florida Union* declared the whites were the dominant race and would remain so, in political power, wealth, intellect, energy, ambition, education, self-possession, and self-dependence.[27] L. M. Hobbs, Superintendent of Bureau Schools, heard threats in 1866 that if the military withdrew, "there would be plenty of dead niggers lying around in the woods." The same people who made the threats claimed they should have full control of the freedmen since they understood them better than United States government officials.[28] A white teacher in Florida heard a former slave-owner say the freedmen would still be slaves "in some way." The whites, she believed, were just waiting for a chance to crush the Negro.[29] Not all whites wanted to murder Negroes, and reinstitute slavery, but the outlook for freedmen was bleak.

---

[25] *Ibid.*, September 30, 1865; Tallahassee *Semi-Weekly Floridian*, September 26, 1865.

[26] T. W. Osborn to O. O. Howard, November 30, 1865, in Bureau Records, Florida.

[27] Jacksonville *Florida Union*, July 22, 1865.

[28] *House Reports*, 39th Cong., 1st Sess., No. 30, pt. 4, 9-10.

[29] *The National Freedman*, I (July 15, 1865), 182-83.

The whites were especially adamant in their opposition to Negro enfranchisement. Floridians were reported to "perfectly abhor" Negro suffrage.[30] Many who were willing to grant rights in the courts to freedmen opposed suffrage. David L. Yulee's wife believed the ex-slaves should have the protection of the State, but considered them "shiftless, improvident, idle," and unfitted for voting.[31] Any Southerner "who advocates *immediate universal* suffrage," the Tallahassee *Floridian* declared, "must be either incapable of understanding the true theory of government, or else is sacrificing for dubious ends . . . those lofty principles which should guide the patriot and statesman."[32] The editor of the *Florida Union* maintained that advocates of Negro suffrage were falling into the ruts of fire-eaters who had caused the Civil War.[33] Some whites objected to Negro voters because they sincerely believed the freedmen were unqualified for suffrage. Others feared the privilege of voting would be the first step to increased power. If the Negro could vote, the Gainesville *New Era* explained, he would soon be entitled to hold office, and would be "a successful aspirant for political honors" in areas where there was a Negro majority. If freedmen had the right to hold office, the *New Era* continued, the question of equality of races would be "settled forever, and the *unnatural* doctrine of miscegenation would be firmly established and fully practiced in our land." Besides, the editor added, Caucasians were regarded as superior by all other races, and governed the world.[34] By the time the convention met on October 24, 1865, it was certain that Negroes would not be granted political privileges.

Citizens at large demonstrated little interest in the election of delegates to the constitutional convention, which resulted in control by ex-slaveholders.[35] The convention was organized with E. D. Tracy of Nassau County as president. In a message to the convention, Marvin reminded the delegates that the Negro was free and should be so recognized by the constitution. The rights

---

[30] *House Reports*, 39th Cong., 1st Sess., No. 30, pt. 4, 4.
[31] Reid, *op. cit.*, 164-65; N. Yulee to D. L. Yulee, October 3, 1865, F. C. Barrett to D. L. Yulee, October 5, 1865, in David L. Yulee Papers.
[32] Tallahassee *Semi-Weekly Floridian*, September 26, 1865.
[33] Jacksonville *Florida Union*, July 29, 1865.
[34] Gainesville *New Era*, September 30, 1865.
[35] Davis, *op. cit.*, 365; E. J .Lutterloh to D. L. Yulee, September 20, 1865, in David L. Yulee Papers.

of freedmen should be defined as closely as possible, he said. Rights of the late slaves, Marvin continued, would probably consist of protection in enjoyment of life, in acquisition of property, possessions and transmission to heirs, rights to improve one's intellectual and moral condition, and to pursue happiness according to one's own ideas as long as it did not interfere with others. Freedom did not necessarily include participation in government, or privileges of voting, right to hold office, or sit on juries, Marvin added.[36]

Congress would not refuse to admit representatives and senators from Florida just because freedmen were not permitted to vote, the provisional governor thought, if the convention abolished slavery and guaranteed the protection and security of former bondsmen. Marvin claimed only a few Negroes even desired suffrage, though some Florida freedmen had sent a statement to the United States Senate requesting that no state be allowed to pass an amendment to the Constitution which would disfranchise anyone because of race or color.[37] The provisional governor's ideas appeared to be in keeping with those of President Johnson. Johnson had not given explicit instruction to the convention, but he had informed David S. Walker that he was a friend of the South and wanted the states back in the Union with their rights. Johnson said readmission of the states was a critical question, Walker wrote to Yulee, and the president "hoped we would not by our action or non-action give any unnecessary advantage to our opponents."[38]

A majority of delegates to the convention were ex-Confederates who yielded to the pressure of the new era only as much as necessary. They drew up a constitution that definitely provided for a white man's government.[39] Only whites could be elected to the state legislature, freedmen were not permitted to vote, the state militia was to be white only, and freedmen were not permitted to testify except in cases involving their own race. In apportionment for representation for the legislature the freedman was counted as

---

[36] *The American Annual Cyclopedia and Register of Important Events 1865*, V, 362.
[37] U. S. Congress, *Senate Miscellaneous Documents*, 39th Cong., 1st Sess., No. 56, 1; Wallace, *op. cit.*, 15; Tallahassee *Semi-Weekly Floridian*, October 27, 1865.
[38] D. S. Walker to D. L. Yulee, September 12, 1865, in David L. Yulee Papers.
[39] Abbey, *op. cit.*, 296.

three-fifths of a white man as during the days of slavery.[40] A
vagrancy ordinance passed by the convention was described as
placing freedmen in a position of semi-peonage.[41] Slavery was
abolished, and freedmen were to enjoy the rights of person and
property without distinction.[42] The convention also annulled the secession ordinance. The constitution was not submitted to the
people for ratification.

November 29 was set as the day for the election of a governor
and legislature. David S. Walker, a former Whig and an opponent
of secession who had followed Florida out of the Union, was the
only candidate for governor. General apathy surrounded the election. Of the 8,000 registered voters, only about one-half cast their
ballot. The legislature was composed primarily of ex-slaveholders
and Confederate veterans.[43] After the two houses organized, they
met in joint session and declared that Walker had been elected
governor, but President Johnson did not order Marvin to relinquish
the direction of the government until January 18, 1866.

Walker's inaugural address was largely devoted to the question
of the Negro. The governor assumed a paternalistic attitude
toward the ex-slaves. The State, he said, was "bound by every
consideration of duty, gratitude, and interest," to make the freedmen "as enlightened, prosperous and happy," as their new situation would permit. The freedmen had been "faithful, contented
and happy slaves" for generations, Walker said. They had remained at home during the war, provided for the army, and had
even gone to war with their masters. It was not the freedman's
fault he was no longer a slave, Walker declared, indeed, some had
even been "anxious to take up arms" for the Southern cause.[44] But
since the Negroes were free, and were "no longer contented and
happy slaves," and no longer had "the intelligence of a superior
race" to look out for them it was the duty of whites to prevent
their "suffering and ultimate extinction." Walker suggested that
Negroes be protected from white immigrant labor, even though

---

[40] Copy of Constitution of 1865, in U. S. Congress, *House Miscellaneous
Documents*, 59th Cong., 2nd Sess., No. 357, pt. 2, 686, 690-91, 695-98, 702.
[41] Abbey, *op. cit.*, 296; Davis, *op. cit.*, 364-65.
[42] *House Miscellaneous Documents*, 59th Cong., 2nd Sess., No. 357, Pt. 2, 702.
[43] Jacksonville *Florida Union*, November 18, 1865; Abbey, *op. cit.*, 297;
Davis, *op. cit.*, 365.
[44] Florida, *House Journal*, 1865, 32-34.

white labor was cheaper, and Negro workers were inefficient. "I trust," Walker added, "that we are not yet so far degraded as to consult interest alone."

After pointing out to the legislature that Negroes were an inferior race, for whom the whites should feel sympathy, Walker said the freedmen should be protected in their rights of person and property as fully as whites. Since the ex-slaves were so ignorant, the governor added, written contracts should be made for labor, and violations of the contract by the freedmen should be a misdemeanor. When the Negroes were dismissed without good cause they should be permitted to collect damages.[45] The freedmen should be protected, but were not to have political power. Florida could never give in to the demand for Negro suffrage, Walker maintained. "Much as I have worshipped the Union," he said, "and as much as I would rejoice to see my state once more a recognized member" it would be better, "a thousand times better, that she should remain out of the Union, even as one of her subjugated provinces" than to return " 'eviscerated of her manhood,' despoiled of her honor, recreant of her duty," and without her self-respect, which would result from acceptance of Negro suffrage.[46] The governor's speech set the tone of the legislative session. It was expressions such as Walker's that convinced Senator Charles Sumner the people of Florida in late 1865 were more hostile than they had been during the war.[47]

On December 22, 1865, Governor Walker laid before the general assembly a report which further indicated that freedmen were to occupy an inferior status. Marvin, at the request of delegates to the constitutional convention, had appointed a committee to investigate the changes, amendments, and additions to existing statutes required to cause the statutes to conform to the constitution with special reference to the altered position of the Negro.[48] The committee first recommended the establishment of county criminal courts to aid in handling the increase in crime caused by emancipation. The county courts were necessary, according to the committee, because the household tribunal that had previously

---

[45] *Ibid.*, 34-46.
[46] *Ibid.*, 41.
[47] U. S., *Congressional Globe*, 39th Cong., 1st Sess., pt. 1, 313.
[48] The committee consisted of C. H. DuPont, A. J. Peeler, and M. D. Papy. Florida, *House Journal*, 1865, 58, 69.

punished Negroes had become extinct with emancipation. Special punishments for freedmen were also recommended. Discriminatory punishments had been used against the free Negro during slavery, and the simple act of emancipation had not caused "any change in the social, legal, or political status" of those already free. Since the emancipated slave occupied no higher position than did the free Negro, it logically followed, said the committee, that the general assembly had authority to discriminate in the case of the freedman. The report recommended that when the law called for fine and imprisonment, there be superadded the alternative of standing in the pillory or thirty-nine lashes or both. The discrimination was based on the difference in the social and political status of the two races. "To *degrade* a white man by punishment," the report stated, would make a bad member of society and a dangerous political agent. To fine and imprison a freedman, on the other hand, would punish the State instead of the individual. The committee also recommended punishment for intermarriage, a vagrancy law, a law to enforce the marriage relation between Negroes, a law regulating labor, and an apprenticeship law.[49]

After ratifying the Thirteenth Amendment, the legislature followed the recommendation of the committee and passed the black codes, some of which were mentioned in a previous chapter. Vagrant freedmen were to be arrested and sentenced to as much as twelve months labor, a provision widely used against the Negroes. All contracts with freedmen had to be in writing and fully explained before two witnesses. If a freedman entered into a contract and was disrespectful or impudent to his employer, or refused to work, he could be arrested and sentenced for vagrancy. If the contract was broken by the white employer, he would be tried by a jury and if found guilty the laborer would be given a first lien on the crops to obtain his legal pay. A tax of three dollars was placed on all males twenty-one to fifty-five. If the tax was not paid, the delinquent could be seized by county officials and hired out to anyone who would pay the tax. This stipulation was to bear directly on the freedmen.[50] Much to the disgust of white citizens, the Freedmen's Bureau prevented the discriminatory laws from being widely enforced. Civil authorities argued that no

---

[49] *Ibid.*, 59-69.
[50] Florida, *Acts and Resolutions*, 1865-66, 28-39; Davis, *op. cit.*, 418.

class legislation had been passed. Florida was a frontier state, they said, the population was restless, there was no penitentiary, and summary punishment was demanded by "the character of the population."[51] Since whites believed the Negro was not equal they probably did not consider the black codes unfair.[52] In their minds, special penalties were necessary to control the "inferior" race.

The freedmen generally accepted the Black Codes with apparent good will. They were well behaved considering the recent date of their emancipation. A few Negroes took advantage of their new status occasionally to elbow a white off the sidewalk, and minor disturbances occurred when they were considered insolent, but generally the whites had few complaints. A New York *Times* reporter wrote in June, 1866, that almost every gentleman with whom he had talked said the late slaves were doing well.[53] A Floridian who had earlier expressed fear of the results of emancipation, claimed in early 1866 that the freedmen had behaved well notwithstanding their disappointment in the belief they would receive the land of their former masters.[54] The Negroes understood the meaning of freedom, and realized they could not break laws without punishment.[55]

Still the former slaves were restive under mistreatment, and were not always in agreement with whites as to what comprised ill treatment. White Floridians had not changed their opinion of the freedmen since emancipation. Colonel Osborn said the whites were opposed to equal or even semi-equal rights for the former bondsmen. The rights of Negroes did "not extend much beyond freedom from the simple condition of absolute bondage," an army officer reported.[56] General Foster asserted that without military rule the position of freedmen would be almost as bad as slavery.[57]

Usually the Negroes were treated correctly if not as equals. Many of the disturbances between whites and freedmen arose be-

---

[51] T. W. Osborn to O. O. Howard, February 4, 1866, in Bureau Records, Florida.

[52] S. A. Swann to D. McRae, June 23, 1865, in Samuel A. Swann Papers; E. Philips to J. J. Philips, August 2, 1865, in James J. Philips Papers.

[53] New York *Times*, June 25, 1866.

[54] E. Philips to J. J. Philips, January 21, 1866, in James J. Philips Papers.

[55] *House Reports*, 39th Cong., 1st Sess., No. 30, pt. 4, 10.

[56] *Ibid.*, 121; T. W. Osborn to O. O. Howard, January 10, 1866, in Bureau Records, Florida.

[57] Davis, *op. cit.*, 431.

cause neither were accustomed to their new position. The whites in some cases expected freedmen to treat them as they did when slaves, while the Negroes believed they were on a level with their masters and frequently demonstrated their belief by words and action.[58] Planters met the changed conditions more adequately than the poor whites. The latter with their "ignorance, prejudice, and pride," of their own whiteness, was the most disturbing element.[59] During the mayoralty of Francis Eppes in Tallahassee a number of "crackers" were enlisted as policemen. These men reportedly used every opportunity to humiliate the freedmen. Negroes were ordered off the streets, beaten and arrested for assembling in small groups. The policemen eventually were discharged at the insistence of whites.[60] The planter class was more generous to freedmen, at least until the Negro became a political force.

White Floridians definitely had not been reconstructed by 1866. Lack of affection for the Union was demonstrated in such ways as refusing to raise the United States flag over the capitol during the legislative session of 1866. Florida was not prepared to accept the Fourteenth Amendment, which was to guarantee the Negroes civil rights and suffrage. The amendment would result, whites believed, either in a race war or the emigration of one or the other race, which would consequently lead to a "total destruction of all interests." No sane man, it was said, would extend suffrage to freedmen without abridgement. A committee appointed to investigate the amendment recommended its rejection, and the legislature unanimously concurred on December 1, 1866.[61]

It is impossible to determine for certain what position the Negro would have held in Florida without federal supervision. Even with supervision freedmen were not treated fairly in the courts. The State appeared to be attempting to give the Negro a position somewhere between slavery and full citizenship. Freedmen were granted the privilege to make labor contracts, to testify in their own defense, to attend school, to assemble, and to sue white men in courts, though these rights were not always scrupulously observed. Moreover, the Negro was excluded as a participant in

---

[58] *House Executive Documents*, 40th Cong., 2nd Sess., No. 57, 82, 90-91.
[59] Abbey, *op. cit.*, 300.
[60] Wallace, *op. cit.*, 38.
[61] Florida, *House Journal*, 1866, 77-80.

politics. By refusing to guarantee equal rights to the freedmen, and by refusing to grant him the right to vote, the seceded states placed ammunition in the hands of the Radical Republicans to be fired back at the South. Florida, like the other Southern states, played directly into the hands of those who advocated a more stringent reconstruction.

CHAPTER XII

MILITARY RECONSTRUCTION AND THE
CONSTITUTIONAL CONVENTION
OF 1868

On March 2, 1867, the first Reconstruction Act was passed over President Johnson's veto. The South was divided into five military areas, with Florida, Alabama, and Georgia composing the Third District. According to the act the states could re-enter the Union after they had formed a constitution framed by a convention of delegates elected by universal manhood suffrage, had guaranteed Negro suffrage, and had accepted the Fourteenth Amendment. Congress reserved the right to examine and approve the proposed constitution after it had been ratified by a majority of voters who were qualified to elect delegates to a convention.[1] General John Pope was commander of the Third District, with Colonel Sprague in command of Florida. General Pope advised civil officials to retain their position until expiration of their terms of office unless otherwise directed. Any vacancies in office would be filled by military appointment.[2] A supplementary act passed March 23, 1867, directed military commanders to register voters including Negroes. Excluded from voting were those persons disfranchised under the proposed Fourteenth Amendment.[3]

Reactions to the Reconstruction Act were mixed. Negroes and Republicans were jubilant. Many Republicans in the State had contended the freedman would not be safe until he was granted the right to vote. Florida Democrats, on the other hand, were generally opposed to the act. One white wrote that "congress intends to grind us as low as possible, and will do it." Whites could do nothing but await the result, he said. "If the Negroes and their devilish white leaders prevail," a resident of Jacksonville asserted, "I think we shall all go to the Devil."[4] A somewhat un-

---

[1] U. S. *Statutes at Large*, XIV, 428-29.
[2] U. S. Congress, *House Executive Documents*, 40th Cong., 2nd Sess., No. 342, 99-100.
[3] U. S. *Statutes at Large*, XV, 2-4.
[4] S. D. McConnell to E. M. L'Engle, March 6, 9, 1867, J. M. Fairbank to J. P. Bouse, November 10, 1867, in Edward M. L'Engle Papers.

informed young lady confided to her diary that the once happy Florida was in a sad state, since "the Negroes are permitted to vote and tha [sic] do not behave as tha [sic] should. . . ." Many Floridians were going to Mexico, she said.[5] The most disturbing factor to whites was Negro enfranchisement, though the editor of the Tallahassee *Floridian* said the whites constituted the class from which Negroes secured their livelihood, so by "acting with promptness and common-sense every freedman" could "be made to vote the Conservative ticket."[6] Some whites still could not accept Negro suffrage. A majority of the old citizens would rather have military rule and no representation in congress than to accept the penalty of freedmen voters, former Provisional Governor Marvin said.[7]

On April 8, 1867, General Pope issued General Order Number Five, which directed commanding officers of the Third District to divide the State into regions for registration. Registrars were to be civilians who would be paid according to the number of registrants. State commanders were authorized to appoint general supervisors of registration and to disseminate information relative to the political rights of citizens.[8] Florida was divided into nineteen electoral districts, which the whites complained were gerrymandered in such a way as to attach counties with white majorities to those predominantly Negro.[9]

On June 18, Colonel Sprague appointed Ossian B. Hart, a native Floridian and office holder in the State since 1849 and later governor of Florida, superintendent of registration.[10] Sprague ordered registration to begin on July 15 and continue through August 20. He recommended that boards of registration be composed of two whites and one Negro. Registrars were civilians, but officers of the army and Freedmen's Bureau were commanded to visit places of enrollment and maintain order. Civil officials were warned against attempting to dissuade anyone from taking an

---

[5] Eliza Horn Diary.

[6] Quoted in Davis, *op. cit.*, 448.

[7] Tallahassee *Semi-Weekly Floridian*, May 28, 1867.

[8] Fleming, *Documentary History of Reconstruction*, I, 430; Bentley, *op. cit.*, 185.

[9] The *American Annual Cyclopedia and Register of Important Events 1867*, VII, 315.

[10] *House Executive Documents*, 40th Cong., 2nd Sess., No. 342, 122; Roster of State and County Officers Commissioned by Governor of Florida 1848-1868, in Florida State Library, Tallahassee; Tallasassee *Sentinel*, August 24, 1872.

active part in Reconstruction.[11] During registration 11,148 white
and 15,434 Negro names were recorded.[12] Bureau agents not only
supervised registration, but urged freedmen to place their names
on the books. The freedmen had a substantial majority, placing
those who could control their vote in a position of power in Florida
politics.

Attempts to organize the Negro politically began soon after the
war—before freedmen were permitted to vote. A New York
Times correspondent found Union Leagues springing up all over
Florida in late 1865.[13] The Union League originated in the North
in 1862, composed of men who declared unconditional loyalty to
the Union. The organization later became a political machine for
Republicans in the South. Making Republicans of the freedmen
was said to have begun in 1865 with the arrival of Osborn in
Florida as assistant commissioner of the Bureau. Osborn had
been a Stephen A. Douglas Democrat before the war, was
sympathetic and helpful to white Southerners, but had believed
from the beginning that universal manhood suffrage was the only
genuine basis for reconstruction.[14] Though he supported Negro
suffrage, Osborn's correspondence revealed little interest in politics
while he was assistant commissioner. He began to demonstrate
more interest after he was succeeded as head of the Bureau by
General Foster on June 11, 1866. The exact date cannot be
pinpointed, but sometime in 1866, Osborn invited a few influential Negroes to a meeting at the home of a freedman in
Tallahassee. An organization, the Lincoln Brotherhood, was formed
with Osborn as president. Meetings at first were held in the Negro
Baptist Church. The Tallahassee society became the parent lodge
for the Lincoln Brotherhood throughout the State.[15]

The Lincoln Brotherhood met in great secrecy, which appealed
to the freedmen. The entrance of the meeting place was guarded
by inner and outer sentinels. At the appearance of a candidate for
admission, the outer guard would determine whether or not he

[11] J. T. Sprague to W. J. Purman, May 3, 1867, in Bureau Records, Florida;
The American Annual Cyclopedia and Register of Important Events 1867, VII,
313.
[12] The Boards of Registration were opened again on October 31 for five
days which brought the number of registered voters up to 28,003. *Ibid.*, 314-15.
[13] New York *Times*, September 5, 1865.
[14] Bentley, *op. cit.*, 61; Cash, *op. cit.*, 51.
[15] Wallace, *op. cit.*, 42.

was a spy. If the visitor passed inspection the guard would so signify by two raps on the door. The inner sentinel then reported the results to the president, who in turn ordered the newcomer conducted in by the "Tylers of the Altar." After an initiation ceremony, the candidates were required to take an oath to protect and defend the Constitution of the United States, and to vote only for members of the league for office.[16] Such an organization appeared harmless, but whites were frightened by any secret Negro organizations. Fear of an armed uprising by Negroes did not end with emancipation.[17]

The mystery of secret organizations impressed the freedmen as it did whites. In the post Civil War period Americans seemed to be inclined toward secret societies and fraternal organizations. Arthur M. Schlesinger wrote that membership in such organizations was greatest in urbanized sections of the country despite "the energy with which the Negroes of the South aped their white brethren. . . ." There were many complaints in Florida about the secrecy of the organizations of freedmen, but whites also had secret societies, some of which perpetrated outrages on former slaves. Experience with their own secret societies might have been one reason why whites were so disturbed by the Lincoln Brotherhood. Some attempts were made to stop secret meetings. In Monticello the mayor permitted private political meetings only if he were given prior notice and the town marshal was in attendance.[18]

In July, 1867, the editor of the *Floridian* charged Osborn with deluding freedmen into the Brotherhood by promising them confiscation of the property of their former owners and social equality.[19] Others accused him of telling the Negroes their former masters desired to return them to some species of slavery. Evidence tends to indicate that Osborn did not promise confiscation. He had not supported confiscation while assistant commissioner, and had been instrumental in returning seized property to whites. Furthermore, freedmen had been provided with their "forty acres"

---

16 *Ibid.*, 43.

17 Tallahassee *Semi-Weekly Floridian*, July 9, 1867; J. A. Remley to A. H. Jackson, May 31, 1867, in Bureau Records, Florida.

18 Arthur M. Schlesinger, *The Rise of the City 1878-1898* (New York, 1933), 288-89; A. B. Grumwell to A. H. Jackson, June 29, 1867, in Bureau Records, Florida.

19 C. E. Dyke to D. L. Yulee, July 22, 1867, in David L. Yulee Papers.

by the Homestead Act of 1866. Osborn was not a demagogue, and probably did not promise social equality, but offices most likely were promised to ex-bondsmen. The allegation that many whites desired some kind of modified slavery was based on sufficient fact to be correctly disturbing to the late slaves.[20]

Floridians who accused Republicans of gaining Negro adherents by purely ulterior means were not realistic. Underhanded methods were not needed. Freedmen considered the Republican Party the source of their emancipation. It was only natural they would turn to the party of Lincoln, and on the basis of experience the Negroes had every reason to believe membership in the Republican Party would be more advantageous to them. This is not to say that Osborn and some other Republicans were not political opportunists like many politicians before and after them. But it is a fact that circumstances threw freedmen into the arms of their emancipators.

Though Osborn generally had the support of officers of the army and Bureau, he had competition in his attempt to organize the freedmen politically. On February 8, 1866, a meeting of freedmen was held in the Baptist Church at Fernandina at which a white Northerner, Liberty Billings, a former Unitarian minister and army chaplain from New Hampshire, told the Negroes that the legislature assembled at Tallahassee was illegal, and that it has recently enacted black codes which, if enforced, would render the condition of freedmen intolerable. A resolution was passed condemning the black codes, and commending Republicans in congress for trying to secure civil rights for all citizens.[21] Billings was later joined by William U. Saunders, Negro, from Maryland, and Daniel Richards, white, from Illinois, who claimed to be representatives of the National Republican Committee.[22] Richards had been in Florida since early 1866, corresponding with Northern Republicans, insisting that Negro suffrage was imperative for the protection of freedmen. A war of races, Richards said, could be avoided only by granting political rights to the ex-slaves.[23] Billings,

---

[20] Davis, *op. cit.*, 376.

[21] J. H. Pratt to T. W. Osborn, February 27, 1866, in Bureau Records, Florida; St. Augustine *Examiner*, January 11, 1868.

[22] Albert Stanley Parks, "The Negro in the Reconstruction of Florida," *Florida Quarterly Journal*, V. (October, 1936), 41.

[23] D. Richards to E. B. Washburne, May 7, 1866, in Elihu B. Washburne Papers.

Richards, and Saunders seemed to more nearly fit the stereotype of a carpetbagger than Osborn and other Republicans. A Republican later charged that Billings was being assisted by Richards in his mad attempt to set up a Negro "empire with himself, Billings, at the *apex*."[24]

In order to compete with the Lincoln Brotherhood, Billings, Richards, and Saunders organized the Loyal League of America in the spring of 1867. Saunders who has been characterized as "one of the shrewdest, most influential, and dangerous negroes in Reconstruction politics," was president of the organization.[25] The League attempted to present a more fascinating program than the Brotherhood. Rituals were elaborate, and it was even more secretive than the Osborn society. Grips, passwords, and secret signs were given to members. Before ex-slaves were recognized as Republicans by leaders of the new organization, they were required to join the League.[26] The property of their former masters would be divided among them, members of the League were reputedly told, and whites had no rights that freedmen were obligated to respect. Saunders and Billings were the primary attractions, Saunders because he was an able, intelligent Negro. Billings made vehement speeches denouncing segregation and black codes, kissed Negro babies, and frequently interrupted his speeches to shout, "Jesus Christ was a Republican."[27]

Democratic charges that Republicans were merely using the freedmen were partially correct. Asked by a white what they did at meetings, an ex-slave replied they had speeches telling them of affairs in Washington, and if freedmen would support the League their future would be secure. They also voted at the meetings, he said. Upon being questioned about how they voted, the freedman gave the following reply:

> Will sar, I'll tell you, you see one man he takes a piece of paper and tars it in little pieces, and gives us all a piece, den

---

24 D. M. Hammond to E. B. Washburne, May 26, 1868, in Elihu B. Washburne Papers.

25 J. Randall Stanley, *History of Gadsden County* (Quincy, Florida, 1948), 113.

26 Caroline M. Brevard, *A History of Florida From 1763 to Our Own Times* (2 Vols., DeLand, Florida, 1925) II, 135; Wallace, *op.cit.*, 45; Parks, *op. cit.*, 41.

27 Davis, *op. cit.*, 471; Wallace, *op. cit.*, 63; Tallahassee *Semi-Weekly Floridian*, October 1, 1867.

another man, he comes round wiff a pencil and writes
somefin on de paper, and gives it to us again den de first
man, he comes round wiff a hat, and we parts em all in;
den he takes em up to de table, and de man up dar counts
em all, and sass carried unanimously.[28]

With allowances for exaggeration on the part of the narrator of
the story, this incident tends to substantiate the claim that some
Republicans were using the freedmen to advance their own
designs.

Tactics of the Loyal League were censured by other Republicans.
Gadsden County had been quiet and orderly, Marcellus L. Stearns,
later governor of Florida, wrote in November, 1867, but was becoming the scene of disorder "under the teachings of certain low
and base men" who fed freedmen with a distrust of whites.
Saunders, Stearns added, "wields the rod of a despot over the
'Loyal League,' and threatens all who oppose his wishes with
immediate excommunication."[29] Another Republican, D. M. Hammond, found a class of men in Fernandina whose "stock in trade of
politics" consisted of inciting gullible Negroes. "It seems to me,"
Hammond added, "that if such apostles of mischief are allowed to
poison the dark superstitious mind of the colored people then are
we about to witness the failure of the Congressional plan of reconstruction." He saw no good coming from the reign of hate,
the object of which, he said, was the elevation of a few men to
places of profit.[30] A majority of the Republicans in Florida did not
sanction the practice of inciting freedmen against their former
masters. Colonel Sprague, who was sympathetic with the Osborn
faction of Republicans, advised the freedmen in May, 1867, not to
permit themselves to be "influenced by designing men' and to
avoid precipitant action.[31]

It was not necessary for freedmen to be in a secret society to
develop an interest in politics. A rash of Negro political meetings
occurred after the announcement of the Reconstruction Act of
March 2. On March 14, a public meeting of Negroes was held in
the Baptist Church in Jacksonville to select candidates for city

---

[28] St. Augustine *Examiner*, November 2, 1867.
[29] M. L. Stearns to A. H. Jackson, November 1, 1867, in Bureau Records,
Florida.
[30] D. M. Hammond to A. H. Jackson, November 14, 1867, in Bureau Records,
Florida.
[31] Tallahassee *Semi-Weekly Floridian*, May 24, 1867.

offices. In a resolution the freedmen declared they were bona fide citizens of Florida and the United States, and they had a right not only to vote, but also to select men to fill political offices. It was the "duty" of Negroes, the resolution stated, to choose men who had been "true to the Union."[32] At a meeting in Capitol Square in Tallahassee in April, a resolution gave thanks to God, the army, congress, and the Republican Party. Participants in the meeting agreed to identify themselves with the Republican Party and to sustain its principles in all their political actions. Southern whites were invited to speak at many Negro meetings.[33] Whites were apprehensive about such mass meetings, fearing they would lead to disorder, but assemblages were held with two to five thousand Negroes in attendance without incident.[34] A visitor from Georgia observed a Negro convention at Gainesville and reported that it was "certainly something rather extraordinary for such a large number of ignorant people, invested so suddenly with such great privilege, to behave so handsomely."[35]

Negroes became so interested in politics that crops were neglected. The cotton crop in the summer of 1867 was discouraging because of worms and too much rain, but corn and potato crops were comparatively good, though they were reported to be suffering from lack of care. Freedmen were advised by the Bureau never to "lose an hour from their labor to attend a political meeting," as they could learn everything they needed to know by talking with others.[36] Moreover, a number of Negro political speakers traveled around the plantations giving advice that Bureau officials believed "considerate, judicious, and temperate." The Bureau attempted to keep freedmen away from the more rabid political meetings.[37]

By mid-1867 there were three factions of the Republican Party in Florida. The most radical clique was the Saunders, Billings, and Richards group, which appealed primarily to the freedmen. Another element, led by Osborn, included the Lincoln Brotherhood

---

32 *Ibid.*, March 26, 1867; Maria Baker Taylor Diary.
33 *Ibid.*, April 23, 30, 1867.
34 J. T. Sprague to O. O. Howard, June 5, 1867, in Bureau Records, Florida.
35 Quoted from the Savannah *News and Herald* by Tallahassee *Semi-Weekly Floridian*, May 14, 1867.
36 A. B. Grumwell to A. H. Jackson, June 29, 1867, in Bureau Records, Florida.
37 J. T. Sprague to O. O. Howard, September 9, 1867, in Bureau Records, Florida.

and a majority of former and active army and Bureau officers. Osborn and friends desired the Negro vote, but refused to engage in violent harangue.[38] The third splinter of the party centered around the Union Republican Club at Jacksonville, organized by Ossian B. Hart in April, 1867. Earlier attempts had been made to organize the Republican or Union Party. Between five and ten per cent of Florida citizens were Union sympathizers during the war, and Union rallies were held in 1863 and 1864 under the protection of federal soldiers. John Hay, President Lincoln's private secretary, went to Florida in 1864, and a small Republican convention was held in May, but divisions among Union men prevented any important success. By June, 1865, Harrison Reed, a newspaper publisher and politician from Wisconsin, who had come to Florida in 1863 as a United States Direct Tax Commissioner, had formed a Union League to make the Union safe "now and forever," but had made little attempt to produce a large political organization.[39] Reed and friends were absorbed by the Jacksonville Republican Club.

On March 27, 1867, a number of Republicans met in Jacksonville in Hart's office to discuss political matters. On April 1, another meeting was held and a committee was appointed to invite those favorable to the organization of a Republican club to attend a meeting for that purpose. A constitution and by-laws were adopted on April 4, which declared that the objective of the association was to aid in establishing and maintaining Republican government in the State. The club also asserted that states were subordinate to the United States; there should be no distinction because of race or color; congress had full jurisdiction over reconstruction; all leaders of the rebellion should be disfranchised forever; and education of the masses was "absolutely necessary to the continued existence of a free government."[40]

Negroes were invited to join the club, and at least two were officers. William Bradwell, a local minister, was one of eight vice presidents, and Jonathan Gibbs was on the executive committee.[41]

---

38 Davis, *op. cit.*, 473.

39 Jacksonville *Florida Union*, July 1, 1865; Tallahassee *Weekly Floridian*, March 10, 1868; Abbey, *op. cit.*, 289-90.

40 Proceedings of the Union Republican Club of Jacksonville, in the Florida Historical Society Collection, University of South Florida, Tampa, Florida.

41 *Ibid.*

By the end of April, Union Leagues had been formed in a dozen counties under Jacksonville leadership, and Negroes had organized clubs in Tallahassee, St. Augustine, Key West, Palatka, and Pensacola.[42] Hart, a native Floridian, was a citizen held in esteem and affection by other whites. "It was with surprise," an acquaintance said, "that his old friends learned that he was affiliating with the aliens. . . ." He had been a Whig before the war, and had opposed secession.[43] Both Southern and Northern men were recruited by the Union Republican Club of Jacksonville.

On July 11, 1867, 125 Republicans representing 30 counties met in Tallahassee at Hart's request in the first state-wide convention of the Republican Party in Florida. About one-half of the delegates were Negroes.[44] Harrison Reed presided temporarily and Osborn was made permanent chairman.[45] A rift had developed in the Republican ranks even before the convention, and was noticeable in Tallahassee. Three divisions already existed, and the Jacksonville Club split when an emmissary of David L. Yulee appeared and presented a resolution to members of the Club asking them to approve a compromise, and suggesting that Yulee was willing to join them if the party designation was dropped. The proposal generated considerable suspicion among the Republicans. Conservative papers charged there were two opinions at the convention, "one appreciative of and admitting the native loyal element to an equality in the works of reconstruction—the other, ignoring that element . . . as unworthy of trust."[46] In reality the "loyal element" was frequently not Republican. Reed had written to Yulee before the convention that Hart, with "mulish tenacity" was determined to organize a Republican party.

Democrats such as Yulee were attempting to infiltrate the party, but could not stomach the title Republican.[47] Influential Democrats, including David S. Walker, Charles E. Dyke, and Yulee, apparently planned to head off the conservative Republican movement and assume leadership of a Union party, thereby dividing the Republicans and lead reconstruction themselves. In

---

[42] Tallahassee *Semi-Weekly Floridian*, April 26, 1867.

[43] Ellen Call Long, History of Florida, 361.

[44] Davis, *op. cit.*, 474-75.

[45] *Ibid.*, 476; Tallahassee *Semi-Weekly Floridian*, July 12, 1867.

[46] St. Augustine *Examiner*, August 17, 1867; H. Reed to D. L. Yulee, May 25, 1867, in David L. Yulee Papers.

[47] H. Reed to D. L. Yulee, May 25, 1867, in David L. Yulee Papers.

April Yulee wrote Reed that they had plans which would benefit
the State and bring prosperity. Yulee claimed to support any
policy which would restore prosperity and peace to the State.
Reed was interested.[48] Governor Walker asked Yulee to determine
the views of Hart on such a plan. But after the Republican convention in Tallahassee, Dyke wrote to Yulee that "all expectations
of a union such as we had hoped might be accomplished is
ended." A majority of the delegates desired the formation of a
Republican party. The only thing the Democrats could do, Dyke
said, was to organize and arouse the State. He suggested putting
forth a platform and asking all citizens of Florida regardless of
color or previous condition to support it.[49]

The Democratic master plan of divide and rule did not work,
partly because it was so obvious, and because some Republicans
simply wanted a Republican party, and were not desirous of
having Florida reconstructed by those who had led the State into
rebellion. This clever plan was probably the brainchild of Dyke,
editor of the *Floridian*, the State's most influential paper. The
editor used the plan with more success later. Yulee received
a sarcastic letter which indicated that at least one Republican
had not been duped by the Democrat's plan. "It appears that
the people of Florida are again to enjoy the benefits of your
statesmanship," the writer said, "and that you supply conven-
tions with ready made platforms and leaders of your choice." The
writer suggested to Yulee that "pabulum should be given in small
and discreet doses, during gestation, otherwise, the fetus may be
smothered." Hart, he charged, had been innocently massacred
under Yulee doctorship; Osborn was "doomed to early strangula-
tion" from his overdoses; and Reed having taken Yulee's "bait,
hook line and pole" would choke. Yulee was reminded that the
precept he followed, Machiavelli's, was applicable to monarchy,
not a Republican form of government. Yulee's false doctrine had
led to secession and war, the writer continued, and would lead to
a war of races. He advised Yulee to comply with the will of congress, and the "mild ultimatum of generous victors." Yulee's
talents, he added, could be used to restore the fortunes of a dis-

---

[48] *Ibid.*, April 18, 22, 1867, D. L. Yulee to P. Frazer, May 17, 1867.
[49] *Ibid.*, D. S. Walker to D. L. Yulee, May 6, 1867, C. E. Dyke to D. L.
Yulee, July 22, 1867, in David L. Yulee Papers.

tracted society, but not unless they were turned to "loyal union."[50] The few men who had ruled Florida for so many years had difficulty in realizing that times had changed.

Democratic leaders were not willing to concede defeat, and despite their denunciations of Republicans for seeking the Negro vote, they also sought the support of their former slaves. With their prejudices, and feelings of superiority, the Southern whites often proved to be ineffective campaigners. They were condescending, and frequently interlarded their pleas to the freedmen with threats. On April 17, a meeting of Negroes and whites was held in Quincy. All of the speakers were ex-slave owners. Governor Walker talked to a mass meeting of freedmen in Tallahassee soon afterwards, and urged whites and Negroes to work together. Democrats advised Negroes to elect Southern whites, rather than "squatters." "You cannot say that the North gave you your freedom." the Negroes were told, "God gave it to you." Freedmen were admonished by Governor Walker to cultivate good relations with whites, as in a few years the Negro would be vastly outnumbered. The statement seemed to contain an implied threat.[51] Sometimes white campaigners were tactless. Freedmen were invited to attend a Democratic political meeting in Tallahassee, one Negro claimed, and then were insulted "some of them saying we stunk."[52] A. J. Peeler, an ex-slave holder and politician participated in a stumping campaign to secure Negro votes, and pointed out to the freedmen they were ignorant and were permitted to cast ballots while intelligent whites were disfranchised.[53] The allegation contained some truth, but was not likely to win many votes.

The Democrats won some Negro adherents. William Martin, Negro, made a speech in Lake City counselling his friends to join the whites. The only way to live happily in the South, he bleakly prophesied, was to avoid a break with Southern whites, for a break would lead to racial strife.[54] Unfortunately he was correct. Freedmen were also threatened with economic retaliation if they did

---

[50] A. Mot to D. L. Yulee, July 24, 1867, in David L. Yulee Papers.
[51] Tallahassee *Semi-Weekly Floridian*, April 23, 30, 1867; St. Augustine *Examiner*, May 4, 1867; Davis, *op. cit.*, 460.
[52] Jacksonville *Florida Union*, September 14, 1867.
[53] Davis, *op. cit.*, 485.
[54] Tallahassee *Semi-Weekly Floridian*, June 25, 1867.

not vote properly.[55] Democratic methods proved unsuccessful in gaining any large number of Negro converts. They could not even arouse white Southerners. Most conservative papers bewailed the apathy regarding the election. The *Floridian* complained that hundreds if not thousands of qualified whites failed to register. Whites were in a majority in a sufficient number of counties to give the conservatives control of a constitutional convention if they would only register and vote, the editor maintained.[56]

With the exception of Democratic leaders, indifference was a characteristic of the whites throughout much of the Reconstruction period. Even so, several Democrats met July 22 to organize, and adopted the name Union Conservative Party.[57] A State-wide convention convened at Tallahassee September 25, and announced for the Union, equal rights, and suffrage for all races. The Democrats were certain, a resolution stated, that since the freedmen's confidence in Southern whites had never been abused, the Negroes would place their confidence in white citizens who had lived among them rather than aliens, who were "seeking a pitiful and ignominious livelihood out of the colored man's honest labor" and who "by their perfidy" would leave the freedman to starve when he became pauperized.[58] Most Negroes seemed to detect a somewhat hollow ring in the Democrats' statement of good intentions. Past actions of the whites spoke more eloquently than campaign promises.

November 14, 15, and 16 were set as days for the election. Qualified citizens were to vote on whether or not to hold a convention, and for delegates in case a convention was held. The Union Conservative Club met in Jacksonville and decided to put forth no candidates for the election because of white apathy. Not only did apathy exist, but "some prominent gentlemen" refused "to cooperate in an active course." Edward M. L'Engle, an influential Floridian, declared the only hope was to defeat the convention since they could not control it. He would not, he said, stoop low enough to try to influence the Negro vote. Other whites including

---

[55] Davis, *op. cit.*, 461; J. E. Quentin to A. H. Jackson, July 12, 1867, in Bureau Records, Florida.

[56] Tallahassee *Semi-Weekly Floridian*, September 17, 1867; Tampa *Florida Peninsular*, August 10, 1867.

[57] *Ibid.*, August 2, 1867.

[58] *The American Annual Cyclopedia and Register of Important Events*, 1867, VII, 314.

Wilkinson Call, urged conservatives to boycott the election.[59] The whites' attitude made it easy for the Republicans. Of the 28,003 registered voters only 14,503 cast ballots, of whom 14,300 favored a convention. Only 1,220 white votes were cast, with 203 of them opposed.[60] Naturally the conservatives charged fraud, but fraud was not necessary. At least 85 per cent, if not more, of the registered whites failed to vote, and many of those qualified had refused to register.[61]

In late December, General Pope announced the results of the election and designated January 20, 1868, as the date for the convention to assemble. Of the forty-six delegates elected, eighteen were Negroes and they demonstrated in the proceedings of the convention a surprising ability.[62] The agriculturist, Solon Robinson, covered the convention for the New York *Tribune* and drew personal sketches of Negro delegates. He was sure, he said, most people would be surprised at the "general appearance" of the freedmen. An observer, Robinson added, would wonder "how it could be possible to select so many men capable of reading, writing, speaking, acting, and thinking, from a race among whom all attempts to learn to read" had been until recently treated as a crime. In Robinson's opinion all of the Negro delegates were literate. All of the freedmen present appeared to be gentlemen, and some of them were "not only well-bred gentlemen . . . but eloquent speakers," he said. Later Robinson claimed to be "sick" of Florida politicians, but added that he was "delighted with the good sense, good conduct, good character, and intelligence" of the Negro portion of the delegates. At the end of the convention Robinson still maintained that fourteen or fifteen of the eighteen freedmen had "behaved discreetly in all things" and had "conducted themselves like gentlemen." He was not a "Negro wor-

---

59 E. M. L'Engle to W. W. Varness, November 5, 1867, W. Call to E. M. L'Engle, November 3, 1867, in Edward M. L'Engle Papers; A. B. Grumwell to A. H. Jackson, October 31, 1867, in Bureau Records, Florida.
60 *The American Annual Cyclopedia and Register of Important Events 1867*, VII, 315; Davis, *op. cit.*, 492.
61 After the voting lists were revised in early November approximately 12,000 whites were eligible to cast ballots.
62 The Negro delegates were Emanuel Fortune, Homer Bryan, William U. Saunders, Frederick Hill, Joseph E. Oats, Charles H. Pearce, John Wyatt, Green Davidson, O. B. Armstrong, Robert Meacham, Anthony Mills, Mayor Johnson, Thomas Urquhart, Josiah T. Walls, Auburn Erwin, Jonathan C. Gibbs, William Bradwell and A. Chandler. Tallahassee *Semi-Weekly Floridian*, December 10, 1867.

shipper," Robinson said, but he was not fearful of having them in government if they were all like the men in the Florida convention. Unhappily, one of the freedmen did not live up to Robinson's expectations, and was arrested and fined for stealing a bottle of whiskey.[63]

Charles H. Pearce and Jonathan C. Gibbs, both Negro ministers, were singled out by Robinson for special praise. Pearce was intelligent and a good speaker. Gibbs was a convincing speaker and the best educated man in the entire convention.[64] Emanuel Fortune, said by some to have a fair education and by others to be barely literate, was a shoemaker and prone to make numerous speeches.[65] Green Davidson was a "violent barber-politician" who was disliked by whites for making speeches on social equality and political rights that were considered inflammatory. Robert Meacham, son of his white master, was an intelligent, able minister and politician, and though the whites considered him troublesome, he was considered an "honest and respected" man.[66] One of the most powerful Negroes in the convention was a former Union soldier, William U. Saunders. He was about thirty-five, and was described as a "bright yellow mulatto, tall and handsome, active and strong," and "charged with eloquence and magnetic influence over a crowd." A New York *Tribune* correspondent said Saunders "would be strong before a great crowd, or in a criminal court, where he could tear the wind, and scatter thunderbolts." He was not the man for a deliberative assembly, for his arguments did not convince, the correspondent added. Gibbs was convincing, which was the difference between the two "colored giants," he continued.[67]

There were able whites at the convention also. The delegates might be inexperienced as legislators, Robinson claimed, but they were not incapable or ignorant of what was needed "for the fundamental rules of government of the State." In point of intelligence the delegates compared favorably with any past legislative body of any Southern state or with any of the new states in the

---

[63] New York *Tribune*, February 5, 8, 31, 1868.
[64] *Ibid.*; Wallace, *op. cit.*, 55; Davis, *op. cit.*, 494-95.
[65] *Ibid.*
[66] Tallahassee *Weekly Floridian*, November 3, 1868.
[67] D. Richards to E. B. Washburne, November 11, 1867, in Elihu B. Washburne Papers; New York *Tribune*, February 5, 1868.

country, Robinson added. Robinson believed the white portion of the convention was a "fair representation" of the people of Florida and was "honestly disposed to act faithfully for the vital interests" of the State.[68] Several white delegates were native Southerners or had lived in the South for many years. J. H. Goss was born in Virginia and was a former slave holder.[69] He was a lawyer and planter, considered to be a capable radical Republican, but not an office seeker. Eldridge L. Ware, was born in New Jersey, but had lived in Florida for many years. He had been a Democrat, but became a strong Republican after the war. He did not appear to be interested in office. C. R. Mobley from Tampa, characterized as a "keen, bold, original Union man," was a native of Kentucky. He had gone to Tampa early in the war for his health. Mobley was a capable man and appealed to the whites.[70] There were about fourteen Southern whites in the convention. Other important whites included former Assistant Commissioner Osborn, William J. Purman, a former officer of the army and Bureau agent, Charles M. Hamilton, ex-Union Army officer, Bureau agent and later United States congressman, Liberty Billings, and Daniel Richards

The convention met January 20, 1868. In the preliminary organization the freedmen seemed to be in control. Pearce was made temporary chairman, and Harry Ford and William Wynn, both Negroes, were selected temporary secretary and doorkeeper respectively. The committee to recommend permanent officers was composed of three freedmen and two whites. Daniel Richards was elected permanent president of the convention, but Negroes held offices of doorkeeper and chaplain.[71] The first business of the convention was to pass ordinances for the relief of Florida citizens. Payment of debts was suspended until after crops were made. It was declared unlawful to sell real or personal property under execution. The ordinance did not prevent collection of debts from wages. Such an act was needed more by native whites than Union men, Robinson averred. If there had not been such a suspension one-half of the people in the State would have been

---

[68] *Ibid.*
[69] Jacksonville *Florida Union*, February 8, 1868.
[70] New York *Tribune*, February 5, 1868.
[71] Tallahassee *Weekly Floridian*, January 21, 1868; *Proceedings of Constitutional Convention*, 1868, 4-5.

ruined, he said.[72] Collection of taxes was also suspended. Such action was not surprising as Florida had a three dollar head tax on males between twenty-one and fifty-five, and an additional tax of one dollar on Negro men. One Negro naively announced that he hoped all taxes would be stopped "for they made the people, both white and colored poor."[73]

A majority of the delegates belonged to the Republican Party, but the rift that had developed before the election was still present. There were two major factions in the convention. The more conservative group, dubbed the "opposition" or "Johnson Party," was composed largely of whites. Osborn and Purman were the leaders of this faction, which consisted of about three Negroes, nine ex-officers of the Union Army and eleven "Southern loyalists." The Radical element led by Saunders, Richards, and Billings was composed of about fifteen Negroes and five whites. At least two of the whites were Southerners.[74] The three most influential Negroes, Pearce, Gibbs, and Saunders, aligned with the Radicals. The division appeared to be between the Loyal League and the Lincoln Brotherhood, with the Reed and Hart followers throwing their support to the latter. Reed was an influential lobbyist for the Osborn faction. Richards, Billings, and company were in complete control from the first day, but the conservative Republicans fought a delaying action.[75] Squabbling and accusations characterized the first few days of the convention with the freedmen appearing to be the moderating influence. Pearce made a speech to the convention which, an observer said, should have convinced any reasonable man of the necessity of ending the angry discussion, and of going to work upon the business for which they were elected. John Wyatt "gave a plain, lucid, manly speech," which would have been a credit to any white man, advising that the quarreling stop and work begin.[76]

The major tactic of the "Johnson Party" was to demand the ouster of Saunders, Billings, Pearce, and Richards on the grounds

---

[72] Jacksonville *Florida Union*, January 25, 1868; New York *Tribune*, February 5, 1868; *Proceedings of the Constitutional Convention*, 1868, 10.

[73] *Ibid*; Jacksonville *Florida Union*, February 1, 1868.

[74] Tallahassee *Weekly Floridian*, February 11, 1868; New York *Tribune*, February 5, 1868.

[75] Jacksonville *Florida Union*, January 25, February 2, 1868; New York *Tribune*, February 5, 1868.

[76] New York *Tribune*, February 8, 1868.

they were ineligible as delegates to the convention, since the Reconstruction law stipulated that delegates must have been a resident in the State one year. Strangers had come into the State, the conservative Republicans complained and had undertaken its reorganization without giving "Southern loyalists" a fair share of the responsibility. Richards, the president, ruled that questions regarding eligibility would not be considered.[77] The 15,000 Negro voters would recognize their friends, Saunders warned the "opposition" party, and if he were forced out of the convention, he would appeal to the freedmen to vindicate his right to be present. Claiming that he was lawfully present and no power in the convention could expel him, Pearce asked for dismissal of the question of eligibility.[78] According to a New York *Tribune* reporter the disgraceful scene at the convention made it "look as though the white race was going backward and the black race advancing in the scale of civilization."[79]

Realizing they could not gain a majority, the Osborn element withdrew on February 4, and went to Monticello, which left the convention without a quorum. Members of the "rump convention" at Tallahassee, maintaining the delegates were absent merely to hold up business, proceeded to draw up a constitution which was accepted; and a copy was forwarded to General George G. Meade, Commander of the Third Military District.[80] Around midnight, on February 10, the "seceders" stole back to Tallahassee and quietly entered the representative hall and proceeded to reorganize the convention. They had left with eighteen members including three freedmen, but had gained enough delegates, two of them Negroes, to raise the number to twenty-four, giving them a majority of one. Richards was deposed as president, and succeeded by Horatio Jenkins, Jr., a white. New committees were formed; and the one on eligibility declared Richards, Saunders, Pearce, and Billings ineligible as delegates to the convention.[81] The Radicals returned and,

[77] Davis, *op. cit.*, 502-503; Wallace, *op. cit.*, 55; Jacksonville *Florida Union*, February 8, 1868; New York *Tribune*, February 8, 1868; *Proceedings of the Constitutional Convention*, 1868, 28.
[78] *Ibid.*
[79] *Ibid.*
[80] *The American Annual Cyclopedia and Register of Important Events, 1868*, VIII, 268; Wallace, *op. cit.*, 57; Tallahassee *Weekly Floridian*, February 11, 1868.
[81] *Ibid.*, Jacksonville *Florida Union*, February 15, 1868.

of course, refused to concur with the declaration on ineligibility. Each group asserted that it was the genuine convention. Again a stalemate was reached. Finally on February 17, General Meade went to Tallahassee and recommended "mutual agreement" on points in dispute and suggested the resignation of both presidents and a reorganization of the convention with Colonel Sprague presiding. The next day, with Sprague in the chair, Jenkins was elected president by a thirty-two to thirteen vote. New committees were formed and after a stormy debate, Billings, Saunders, Richards, and Pearce were ousted.[82] The convention then proceeded to draw up the constitution that served the State until 1885.

The constitution of 1868 was not radical and should have been pleasing to white Southerners. Indeed, native whites played a major mole in making the constitution. Harrison Reed, though not a delegate had been an important influence, and he was working hand in glove with such men as Yulee. On February 16, Reed wrote Yulee that "after the severest and most bitterly contested fight I have ever participated in, I think the destructors [Radical Republicans] have been effectually overthrown. . . ." He promised to confer with Yulee as soon as he could leave Tallahassee, and asked Yulee to send passes to be distributed to members of the convention who had to return over his railroad. "It will be good policy," Reed said.[83] "Mr. Democrat" of Florida, Charles E. Dyke, claimed part credit for the constitution. He had attempted and succeeded in splitting the Republicans, he stated. "We ought to feel grateful to Reed and co. for trying to break the power of such a dangerous faction as was headed by Billings," Dyke continued, and "for framing a constitution so much more liberal than was expected." Billings would have put political power in the hands of the Negroes, and whites could not have lived here, he added, but "we can live under the Reed Constitution" and even control the legislature.[84] Governor Walker said "the constitution I learn is a good one, the chief objection being the Negro suffrage. . . ."[85] Native whites generally agreed the "worst elements" of the

---

[82] *The American Annual Cyclopedia and Register of Important Events, 1868*, VIII, 268- 69; *Proceedings of the Constitutional Convention*, 1868, 34-35, 45-47.

[83] H. Reed to D. L. Yulee, February 16, 1868, in David L. Yulee Papers.

[84] C. E. Dyke to E. M. L'Engle, March 16, 1868, in Edward M. L'Engle Papers.

[85] D. S. Walker to D. L. Yulee, February 24, 1868, in David L. Yulee Papers.

convention had been defeated and the proposed constitution would not "absolutely ruin" them.[86]

Certain features of the constitution were especially pleasing to Florida whites. It offered in effect "universal amnesty" and universal male suffrage. Rebels were not obstructed either in holding office or voting.[87] Moreover, apportionment was arranged in such a way as to assure legislative control to whites. Representation from any one county was limited to a maximum of four. Only eight counties of the thirty-nine had Negro majorities in 1870, and the white dominated counties with small populations were given representation out of all proportion to population figures. Alachua County which had 12,393 Negroes and a total population of over 17,000 in 1870, was given two representatives, while Dade County with a population of 85 was given one. Sixteen predominantly white counties with a population of less than 2,000 each were granted one representative each. While Alachua had two representatives for over 17,300 residents, twelve white controlled counties with a combined population of about 17, 107, had twelve representatives. Furthermore, most of the county offices were appointive which would prevent any large number of freedmen being elected to office. Constable was the only elective county office.[88] There is evidence to indicate the constitution was planned to discriminate against freedmen. In a letter to Yulee, Reed said, "under our Constitution the judiciary and state officers will be appointed and the apportionment will prevent a Negro legislature." I believe, Reed added, "there is a 'God in Israel' and that he will not abandon us to the tender mercies of vagabond adventurers."[89]

Reed, who was usually an astute politician, apparently could not see that the Democrats did not really intend to co-operate with him. He was being used. As Dyke wrote privately, he had labored day and night to intensify the hostility of the "Billings wing

---

[86] E. M. L'Engle to Mrs. Place, March 5, 1868, in Edward M. L'Engle Papers.

[87] Tallahassee *Weekly Floridian*, February 25, 1868; St. Augustine *Examiner*, March 21, 1868.

[88] J. G. Foster reported that only six counties had Negro majorities in 1866. J. G. Foster to O. O. Howard, October 1, 1866, in Bureau Records, Florida; *Ninth Census of the United States*, 1870, I, 19; Florida, *Constitution of 1868*, 12, 15, 30.

[89] H. Reed to D. L. Yulee, February 16, 1868, in David L. Yulee Papers.

against the Reed crowd" and was still trying to widen the breach.[90] By reading Dyke's public declaration it appeared that the Reed group could expect many white converts. There was little possibility of a Negro ever being elected governor of Florida, but such a development was guarded against in the constitution by making nine year citizenship in the United States and three years citizenship in the State a prerequisite for the office.[91] Radical Republicans were incensed and claimed the constitution was formed by "Bogus Republicans" and "Johnson men" who had tried to "swindle the poor Negro. . . ."[92]

Despite Radical criticism the constitution of 1868 was in many respects the most democratic one Florida had ever enjoyed, and unlike the constitution of 1865 it recognized the freedmen as social and political equals. No discriminatory laws could be applied to Negroes; they could testify against whites in courts, and the discriminatory poll tax on freedmen was repealed. No law requiring educational prerequisites for suffrage could be passed before 1880 and then the law would not be applicable to anyone who had registered or voted in a previous election. The constitution provided for insane asylums, a state prison, and public education, important services not provided for in the 1865 constitution. The new charter of government even granted one representative in each house to the Seminole Indians, and the representative had to be an Indian, not a white.[93]

After setting the date for ratification or rejection to be decided by an election held the first Monday, Tuesday and Wednesday, May, 1868, the convention organized itself into a nominating convention and nominated Harrison Reed for governor, William H. Gleason for lieutenant governor, and Charles M. Hamilton for member of congress. The radical Republicans nominated Liberty Billings, Samuel Walker, and Daniel Richards for governor, lieutenant governor, and member of congress respectively, but they opposed the constitution. The Democrats put forward a candi-

---

[90] C. E. Dyke to E. M. L'Engle, March 16, 1868, in Edward M. L'Engle Papers.
[91] Florida, *Constitution of 1868*, 10.
[92] G. N. Atwood to T. Stevens, June 11, 1868, in Thaddeus Stevens Papers, Library of Congress, Washington, D. C.
[93] Florida, *Constitution of 1868*, 17, 19, 22, 26-27.

date of their own, and many of them joined Billings in opposition to the constitution.[94]

The fight for ratification of the constitution was a bitter one. Accusations were thrown back and forth with abandon. Richards wrote Thaddeus Stevens that a deal obviously had been made between Reed and the rebels. Even the Ku Klux Klan favored the constitution, he said. The Democrats, Richards believed, put their own ticket in the field only to frighten the radicals into voting for Reed. They intended to switch to Reed themselves, he said.[95] Many freedmen opposed Reed and the constitution. The African Methodist Episcopal Church of Florida issued a circular calling on Negroes to oppose the constitution, in part because of "its enlargement of the franchise in favor of the disloyal."[96] The resolutions, which backed Billings, accused the Freedmen's Bureau and military personnel of using their influence with the freedmen to secure ratification of the constitution. The Reed ticket won the election and the constitution was ratified by a vote of 14, 520 to 9,491.[97]

The Republicans never recovered from the bitter split which became so obvious during the convention, and the following election. Such a rift made the party vulnerable to Democratic attacks. Conservative Republicans had risked the loss of Negro support to assure loyal Southerners a part in Reconstruction. It was unfortunate that the Democrats would not repay the kindness by performing the role of a loyal opposition, rather than insisting on governing the State at any cost. But, even with bitter opposition and infighting, the Republicans, including many capable Negroes, were able to make important and useful contributions to the State of Florida.

---

[94] Wallace, op. cit., 64.
[95] D. Richards to T. Stevens, May 25, 1868, in Thaddeus Stevens Papers; D. Richards to E. B. Washburne, April 8, 1868, in Elihu B. Washburne Papers.
[96] Tallahassee Sentinel, March 12, 1868; F. A. Dockray to T. Stevens, March 18, 1868, in Thaddeus Stevens Papers.
[97] House Documents, 59th Cong., 2nd Sess., No. 357, pt. 2, 706.

CHAPTER XIII

LAWLESSNESS IN FLORIDA

Florida whites contended that the violence during Reconstruction, which culminated in the Ku Klux Klan movement, was in response to Republican and Negro political domination. This factor undoubtedly aggravated the hostility toward the Negro, but the underlying factors were present before freedmen were permitted to vote. Had outrages never occurred in the South, the ex-slave might not have been granted such sweeping suffrage in the first place. One of the primary arguments in support of granting Negroes the vote was their need for political power to defend themselves. Daniel Richards of Florida wrote to Elihu B. Washburne, Illinois congressman, in May, 1866, that the only thing which would prevent a race war was Negro suffrage. General Foster, when speaking of lawlessness in Florida in October, 1866, said he believed the only remedy was the extention of political privileges. Such arguments were used to convince those to whom freedmen voters did not appeal. Even before the passage of the Reconstruction Act in 1867, when political power was in the hands of Southern whites, a kind of organized warfare was carried out against Negroes and Unionists.[1] Moreover, as Wilbur J. Cash has said, the South became the home of lynching before the Civil War and before hatred of the Negro began to play a part in violence.[2] Florida had bands of regulators before the war, and it was a simple matter to revive such terrorist organizations to deal with emancipated slaves.

Florida was a frontier area and violence seemed to be fairly prevalent against whites as well as Negroes. Among the principle characteristics entitling people to distinction in Marion and Sumter counties, a Bureau agent reported in 1868, were the amount of liquor they could drink and the degree of hostility they held

---

[1] Paul L. Haworth, *The Hayes-Tilden Disputed Presidential Election of 1876* (Cleveland, 1906), 83; Franklin, *op. cit.*, 322; D. Richards to E. B. Washburne, May 7, 1866, in Elihu B. Washburne Papers; J. G. Foster to O. O. Howard, October 8, 1866, in Bureau Records, Florida.

[2] Wilbur J. Cash, *The Mind of the South* (New York, 1941), 43.

toward anyone differing with them on politics. A large majority of the wealthy and influential people in the area were of that class, he said.[3] In 1869, a resident of Gainesville informed a Northern teacher that in his district every man carried a "doubled-gun, a revolver, or a bowie knife. . . ." He carried a gun and had never been without it, he continued.[4]

With the presence of hatred of the Negro and the existence of frontier conditions, it is not surprising that much violence was perpetrated on the former bondsmen. Moreover, many Floridians did not place a high value on the life of a freedman. The attitude of many whites toward the ex-slaves is illustrated by the statement of a Marianna physician who said the thievery and insolence of the Negroes would "make it necessary to kill many." The doctor thought the two races could not live together as free men. The Negro, he added, "must be sent to Africa or be exterminated like the Indian." Other Floridians believed that colonization or extermination were the only alternatives open to the Negro.[5] Such a callous attitude toward killing Negroes was even exhibited by some ministers. When a Methodist clergyman was asked what to do about some freedmen who were foraging the country he suggested they be bushwhacked. The same man threatened to kill two Negro soldiers who made an insolent remark to his wife after she had refused to permit them to draw water from her well.[6]

Violence against the Negro started soon after emancipation and gradually became worse. Many of the early murders and assaults were committed by individuals rather than organized bands. Relations seemed to be especially bad between former slaves and poor whites.[7] Such a development was natural since there had been considerable antagonism between the non-slaveholding white and the Negro while the latter was still a slave. The following

---

[3] J. A. Remley to A. H. Jackson, October 1, 1868, in Bureau Records, Florida.

[4] *The American Missionary*, XII (February, 1869), 32.

[5] E. Philip to J. J. Philips, July 5, August 2, October 27, 1865, in James J. Philips Papers; C. B. Wilder to A. M. A., July 7, 1868, in American Missionary Association Archives.

[6] Simon Peter Richardson, *Lights and Shadows of Itinerant Life* (Nashville, 1901), 181-183.

[7] T. W. Osborn to O. O. Howard, January 10, 1866, in Bureau Records, Florida.

verse known throughout the South, indicated the Negro attitude toward the poor white:

My name's Sam, I don't care a damn;
I'd rather be a nigger than a poor white man.[8]

The poor white hated the Negro when he was a slave. When the Negro became free, the white assaulted him at the slightest provocation.

Many attacks on ex-slaves were made because of supposed impertinence, which was not tolerated by any white class. There were several complaints soon after emancipation that cases of insolence were becoming more and more frequent. There has been "a great change" in the Negroes and "for the worse," a white North Florida resident said in late 1866. An outbreak in Tallahassee was expected at any time. If there should be any disturbance, he added, the freedmen would be killed like sheep.[9] Anytime the Negro attempted to assert himself, trouble could be expected. "There is a terrible state of feeling in this city between the whites and blacks," a New York *Times* correspondent wrote of Fernandina, in June, 1866. He said that in all his travels through the South he had seen no such bitter feeling. The quarrel was between former property owners and Negroes who had acquired their property.[10]

Lawlessness became more widespread after the military was withdrawn and preservation of law and order was entrusted to the civil government. Some of the young white men of the State had threatened to cause trouble with the Negroes as soon as the troops were removed, and they did.[11] Military commanders in the State frequently warned that blood would flow if the army was removed. In October, 1866, General Foster claimed to see each day more necessity for the continued presence of troops.[12] Colonel Sprague reported in December, 1866, that since August

---

[8] Quoted in Vernon L. Wharton, *The Negro in Mississippi, 1865-1890* (Chapel Hill, 1947), 216.
[9] Eppes, *op. cit.*, 344; A. Whitehead to W. H. Branch, August 16, 1866, in Branch Family Papers.
[10] New York *Times*, June 11, 1866.
[11] H. H. Kuhn to J. G. Foster, October 28, 1866, in Bureau Records, Florida; New York *Tribune*, June 7, 1866.
[12] J. G. Foster to O. O. Howard, October 8, 1866, in Bureau Records, Florida.

civil law had been in force without any interference by the military, but the State did not have the power, nor was public sentiment of such character as to bring criminals to justice. Murders were committed, he added, and "the perpetrators well known, but no man has the courage to come forward and expose the parties lest he might share the same fate." The pistol and bowie knife, he thought, were becoming the law of the State.[13] Carrying of pistols and other weapons became so serious by June, 1867, it was made illegal by military order.[14] Bureau and civil officials resigned positions because of fear of retaliation by "prominent parties" who had been arrested for "cruelty to freedmen. . . ."[15] Bureau and army records to 1867 are replete with incidents of murder and assault on Negroes.

Not all the early attacks on freedmen were by individuals. As early as December, 1865, a band of men calling themselves "Regulators" was reported from Fernandina and other areas which discloses that organizations were formed to control the Negro before he ever entered politics. Incidents in which groups of white men took freedmen out and whipped them were reported in early 1866. Negroes were driven from their work, threatened, whipped, and fired upon by so-called regulators.[16] In 1867, an ex-slave was taken to a swamp in Washington County and whipped to death after a white woman reported he had entered her room. Warnings similar to those issued by the Klan were made as early as February, 1867. In that month Robert Meacham of Jefferson County received a letter saying, "Meacham—Sir—Your conduct has become unbearable in this place—and will not be longer tolerated—." He was advised to leave and told that, "one warning is all we give and you have but a few days to leave in beware—you black sun [sic] of a bitch—beware." The note ended with "Death is your doom—beware—." The threat was made because Meacham had written a note asking a white minister not to fill his pulpit in the future, unless invited. The minister had visited Meacham's

---

13 J. T. Sprague to G. L. Hartsuff, December 31, 1866, in U. S. Army Commands, Florida.
14 General Orders No. 4, June 29, 1867, in U. S. Army Commands, Florida.
15 L. M. Shute to O. O. Howard, July 22, 1867, in Bureau Records, Florida.
16 A. E. Kinne to T. W. Osborn, February 13, 1866, F. Thompson to T. W. Osborn, December 17, 1865, T. Leddy to T. W. Osborn, February 24, 1865, in Bureau Records, Florida.

church during his absence and advised his congregation to go elsewhere.[17]

Even though violence, including organized violence, against the freedmen was perpetrated before the advent of Negro suffrage, it did become worse and better organized after the reorganization of the State government under the Military Reconstruction Act. As one Florida historian wrote, by 1868 "the Conservative whites, defeated in the elections, were already beginning to physically assault Republicans, black and white, in desperate efforts to break their grip on the ballot boxes and the government." This meant, the writer added, "violence, often of the worst form. It meant the saddest part of the Reconstruction ordeal—peace sought through means of midnight assassination, riot, and terror."[18] In fact, if the Klan was not already organized in Florida, the Democrats adopted Klan tactics even before the election for state officials in May, 1868.[19] Whether or not it was called the Klan, bands to wreak violence on the freedmen and Republicans appeared to be rather well organized in many localities by 1868.

It is impossible to discern exactly when and by whom the Ku Klux idea was brought to Florida, but there is no doubt the Klan was operative in the State. Sometimes the organizations were called Young Men's Democratic Clubs, rather than Klan, but the ideas were the same. A witness swore before a federal subcommittee in 1871 that he was invited in 1868 to join a "Secret Service" club which he believed was the same organization generally known as the Ku Klux. He had a copy of the constitution of the club which revealed that it was secret, and that members were to learn the name, residence, vocation, appearance, and politics of all voters, Negro or white. If any member of the organization came into conflict with the law, the constitution stated, other members were to aid the fugitive in making his escape.[20] The purpose of the club, the chief of the Leon County organization testified, was to look after "the inciters of riots among the colored voters." If the "inciters" did not heed warnings, they would be asked to leave the county. Anyone ordered to leave would do so,

---

[17] A. B. Grumwell to E. C. Woodruff, February 28, 1867, in Bureau Records, Florida.
[18] Davis, op. cit., 515-16.
[19] Buchholz, op. cit., 143.
[20] House Reports, 42nd Cong., 2nd Sess., No. 22, pt. 13, 156-60.

he maintained, because of fear of violence from the club. The best men of the county, old and young, belonged to the society, he said.[21]

White Conservatives were not completely candid about the Klan in testimny before the sub-committee, but they were in later years. Francis P. Fleming, governor of Florida from 1889 to 1893, later admitted the existence of a Klan which he said "made a bloody chapter" in the history of Florida. The "men who were the actors in them were seldom apprehended or convicted," he added. Fleming freely admitted that the Klan killed and frightened freedmen. "The Negroes, naturally superstitious, were obsessed with dreadful fears," he said, and "their political leaders found it impossible to reassure them"; thus "in ten years the State was restored to Democratic rule. . . ." Fleming gave examples of vicious Klan activity. It apprehended the murderers of a white man of Ocala, he declared, and "took the most summary vengeance upon them." All of those caught were killed, and one, after being shot, was boiled in a sugar boiler, and his skeleton, "articulated" by an ex-Confederate surgeon, "swung for months from a tall pine at a lonely cross-roads near Ocala as a warning of the fate of other evil doers."[22]

Another Floridian, later a professor of law at the University of Texas, W. S. Simkins, also claimed to be a member of the Klan. According to Simkins, most Klan activities were performed at night, and on horseback. Usually men engaging in the lawless acts were from different counties than the one in which the violence occurred so as to avoid detection. The Klan worked "upon the fears and superstitions of the Negroes," Simkins asserted, "performing before their cabin at night apparently supernatural stunts." The Klan was composed of the best young men of the State, Simkins added, and "we could assemble several hundred men at any point of the black belt on short notice and in time to quell any disturbance of a serious nature." If anyone was obnoxious to the community, or was "inflammatory in word or conduct," he was visited at his home at night, a sign was tacked on his door, and "his voice would no longer be heard in the land,"

---

21 *Ibid.*, 228-30.
22 Francis P. Fleming, Reconstruction, typescript in Florida Historical Society Collection.

Simkins claimed. This boastful Klan member illustrated the power of the organization by relating an incident in which he whipped a Negro with a barrel stave, but was not prosecuted, even by the Bureau, because it was known for certain that he was a member or the feared society.[23] Simkins probably exaggerated the close knit organization of the Klan.

Much Klan activity was political. At times it seemed to be an arm of the Democratic Party. To change slightly the cry of the Republicans who waved the "bloody shirt," all Democrats may not have been Klan members, but all members of the Klan were Democrats. The ill opinion held of Negroes and Republicans justified violence in the minds of many Southerners. The Floridian, who wondered how it was "possible that even Yankee villiany [sic] and ingenuity" could make the whites who had "always governed the world subservient to a stinking, deformed race" gave voice to the sentiment of many whites.[24] In August, 1868, an agent from Jefferson County reported the existence of an organization of whites armed and ready for slaughter when the opportunity presented itself. One reason for the organization, white citizens intimated, was to overthrow the State government.[25] "Outlawry and lynch law became part of the political campaign," and even the "aristocracy" did not hesitate to support democratic clubs and the Ku Klux Klan.[26]

The Klan began operating against Republicans of both colors from the time they became involved in politics. Threats of assassination were made to Republican politicians in Madison County in anonymous letters signed K. K. K. in April, 1868. Freedmen who were not active in politics, but had voted Republican were also threatened.[27] Dr. E. G. Johnson, a Republican State Senator from Columbia County, testified that at least seven Republicans had been killed in his county by 1871. In the fall of 1868, Negro Republican Thomas Jacobs was called to the door of his home and killed. L. Johnson, Negro, was taken from his home by disguised men in

---

[23] W. S. Simkins, "Why the Ku Klux," *The Alcalde*, IV. (June 19, 1916), 740-41.

[24] E. Philips to J. J. Philips, December 1, 1867, in James J. Philips Papers; J. C. McLean to Father, February, n. d., 1868, in Burton Papers, P. K. Yonge Library of Florida History, Gainesville, Florida.

[25] J. T. Sprague to O. O. Howard, March 31, 1868, A. B. Grumwell to A. H. Jackson, August 28, 1868, in Bureau Records, Florida

[26] Dovell, *op. cit.*, II, 562; Davis, *op. cit.*, 561.

[27] J. E. Quentin to A. H. Jackson, May 1, June 1, 1868, in Bureau Records, Florida.

the spring of 1869, and was never heard of again, though his clothing was found. Another freedman, Timothy Francis, was threatened by disguised men in the fall of 1869, and was killed two weeks later by a similar group. Ike Ipswick, Negro, was shot and killed in 1869, as was Negro Jones Green, who was taken from his home by disguised men and thrown into a pond. Others were killed, threatened, and whipped, Johnson said.[28] Johnson himself was assassinated in 1875, and it was generally believed throughout the State that it was a political murder. The senate was evenly divided, and his murder gave the Democrats a majority. His successor was expected to be a Democrat.[29] A white Conservative wrote that "if I were on a jury of inquest I would say shot by persons unknown and served him right—who next. . . ." "Death make way for liberty," he added.[30]

Several other leading Republicans were exterminated. An influential radical Negro, Denis Lee, was killed in 1868. James M. Yearty, a Republican of Calhoun County, was murdered in March, 1871, and the Klan claimed responsibility.[31] In the summer of 1870, Robert Jones of Columbia County was killed after being warned to desert the Republican Party. In the same year a Republican member of the legislature, Andrew Mahoney, was assassinated.[32] Others were threatened by the Klan. L. G. Dennis, Republican State Senator from Alachua County, received threats, and attempts were made on his life. A Klan member said Dennis was a man of great courage and resources, but was obnoxious to the whites because he taught social equality. Dennis did not seem to be at all frightened by the threats, and after he retired from politics had many friends among local whites.[33] The so-called carpetbaggers were not nearly so vile when they no longer had political power.

Supposedly responsible newspapers and citizens actually encouraged violence. The Gainesville *New Era* printed such head-

28 *House Reports*, 42nd Cong., 2nd Sess., No. 22, pt. 13, 260-67.
29 Tallahassee *Sentinel*, August 7, 1875; Tallahassee *Floridian*, August 3, 1875.
30 H. A. L'Engle to E. M. L'Engle, July 23, 1875, in Edward M. L'Engle Papers.
31 Fleming, Reconstruction; Proclamation of Governor Harrison Reed, March 7, 1871, in Records of the Department of State, Tallahassee, Florida.
32 *House Reports*, 42nd Cong., 2nd Sess., No. 22, pt. 13, 263.
33 *Ibid.*, 268-69; Fleming, Reconstruction.

lines as "Give Way, Carpetbaggers," and "Death to the Scoundrels." The Monticello *Advertiser* suggested, "Let us remove them now, peacefully if we can, forcibly if we must."[34] By 1870 some of the members of the Klan were active openly. During the election of 1870, a Jefferson countian said, carpetbaggers were warned that in the event of any trouble they would be killed first. The Klan sent to Georgia for "several hundred" men to appear on election day. Whites in Jefferson County said they had little trouble with Negroes afterwards.[35]

Disorder was widespread throughout the State, but was most virulent in Jackson County. A former regulator estimated the number of murders in Jackson County during Reconstruction at 175. Other conservative estimates placed it at about 150.[36] The whites deliberately planned to dispose of the local Republican leaders, and it is estimated they managed to "exterminate" sixty in two years.[37] The whites claimed the war in Jackson County was caused by two Republicans, William J. Purman and Charles M. Hamilton, who were accused of inciting the freedmen. The charges were true if the whites' definition of incitation was encouraging the Negro to assume the rights and obligations of citizens. Full citizenship for the Negro was exactly what white residents of Jackson County did not want. Evidence points to the real motives for violence as political, and the fact the Negroes acted too much like free men. Careful plans were made to assassinate Purman, a political leader, and frighten other Republicans out of the county.[38] An indication that whites were motivated largely by politics and racial hatred is the length to which they went to humiliate Republicans and leaders of freedmen. In 1869 Colonel James Coker, of Marianna, went to the office of John Q. Dickinson, a white Republican and Negro leader, spit in his face, knocked off his hat, and called him a "god damned nigger-loving son of a bitch." Coker was one of the leading figures in the town. Violence did not cease until all leading Republicans had been run out of the county, and the freedmen frightened into political

---

34 Quoted in Tallahassee *Sentinel*, November 26, 1870.
35 Simkins, "Why the Ku Klux," 743-45.
36 Davis, *op. cit.*, 582; *House Reports*, 42nd Cong., 2nd Sess., No. 22, pt. 13, 222.
37 *Ibid.*; New York *Times*, April 13, 1871.
38 Davis, *op. cit.*, 567.

inactivity. It was said, "that an appointment to county office in Jackson was virtually a death warrant."[39]

Many residents of Jackson County were reported to be violently inclined, and several whippings and murders had occurred previously, but opposition to Reconstruction policies "became an actual 'rebellion' against constitutional authority" of the State.[40] The difficulty began in March, 1869, when Dr. John L. Finlayson, Circuit Court Clerk, was murdered and Purman wounded. Purman was the primary objective because he was a leader of the freedmen. Finlayson was a native, but was unpopular because he favored Republican Reconstruction.[41] The political assassination of Finlayson was just a prelude of what was to come, the so-called Jackson County War.

On September 28, 1869, a small group of Negro men and about twenty-three women and children were ambushed on their way to a picnic. A man and a two-year-old boy were killed.[42] On the night of October 1, 1869, some whites sitting on the piazza of James F. McClellan were fired at by what was thought to have been a number of passing freedmen. McClellan was wounded and his daughter killed. There are various suggestions as to why the freedmen fired on McClellan. They may have been seeking revenge for the murders of October 28, and McClellan would have been a natural target because many thought he was one of those responsible. Supposedly the ambush had been made to kill Negro constable Calvin Rogers, who had incurred the enmity of McClellan. A Klan member said the attack was made because McClellan was believed to be the leader of the Ku Klux. It is also possible the Negroes were trying to kill James Coker, who was present, and who was thought to be a ring leader in any political assassination or harassment of the freedmen.[43] Whatever

---

39 *House Reports*, 42nd Cong., 2nd Sess., No. 22, pt. 13, 277; Stanley, *History of Gadsden County*, 111.

40 C. M. Hamilton to A. H. Jackson, December 31, 1867, W. J. Purman to A. H. Jackson, June 30, 1868, in Bureau Records, Florida; J. Randall Stanley, *History of Jackson County* (Marianna, Florida, 1950), 205.

41 *Ibid.*, 206; Fleming, Reconstruction.

42 Stanley, *History of Jackson County*, 209; *House Reports*, 42nd Cong., 2nd Sess., No. 22, pt. 13, 78; Proclamation of Governor Harrison Reed, September 28, 1869, in Records of the Department of State, Tallahassee, Florida.

43 Stanley, *History of Jackson County*, 209; *House Reports*, 42nd Cong., 2nd Sess., No. 22, pt. 13, 78; Fleming, Reconstruction.

the motive of the attack on the McClellan party, the result was an all-out war on freedmen and Republicans. What followed was a nightmare of brutal, cold-blooded murders, and even execution of entire families.

The morning after Miss McClellan was killed, Marianna was filled with armed and mounted men, who offered to "wipe the Negro race out of existence in all West Florida." Residents of Marianna "did not wish the race exterminated," but "there was a carnival of deaths" among the freedmen.[44] Dickinson wrote Secretary of State Jonathan C. Gibbs that human life was counted cheap, but "the frequency and cold blood which have characterized our murders has not been to me so fearful a fact as the carelessness with which the public learn a new outrage."[45] The whites appeared to think the murders were natural or necessary.

Dickinson attempted to keep a record of the outrages and his reports recorded one almost every day. On October 2, Calvin Rogers was chased and wounded, and an attack made on the home of another Negro, wounding one person. The next day was Sunday, and apparently it was decided not to kill anyone on the Sabbath. On October 4, a Negro family was fired upon and escaped, but another Negro was less fortunate. A freedman was wounded October 5. Richard Pooser was forced to leave town and fired at on the sixth. On October 7, William Coker, E. S. Alderman, and Jack Myrick took a Negro, Matt Nickles, his wife and child from their home, killed them and threw the bodies in a lime sink. In a letter of October 11, Dickinson listed the casualties as seven freedmen killed and two wounded, but added a postscript. Another man, Samuel Fleishman, had just been found dead. Fleishman was murdered because he had reputedly sold arms to Negroes and was believed to have favored Reconstruction.[46] By February, 1871, Dickinson knew of about seventy-five people who had been killed in Jackson County. Nine-tenths were Negroes.[47] Several others were driven from the county, and Dickinson himself was later killed.

---

[44] F. B. Chapman, Unpublished Account of Jackson County Affairs, in Call Papers.

[45] *House Reports*, 42nd Cong., 2nd Sess., No. 22, pt. 13, 222.

[46] *Ibid.*, 78-81; Fleming, Reconstruction.

[47] *House Reports*, 42nd Cong., 2nd Sess., No. 22, pt. 13, 221-22.

Some of the freedmen avoided death by giving up their rights. Larry White testified, in 1871, that he was not being harassed because he had promised to quit voting. They seemed to excuse him after his promise and said, "old Larry is a good nigger, they should all do like him," White stated. He had seen so many outrages against freedmen he decided to take the easy way, and stop voting. He had never threatened to kill anyone, he added, and did not want to be killed. "I felt mighty lonesome, mighty dissatisfied when they were doing it," White testified. Emanuel Fortune a Negro politician who left Jackson County after his life had been threatened, believed the main purpose of the Klan was to weed out Republican leaders,[48] but, some of the younger, hot-headed men made war on all Negroes. By 1871, after Republican leaders had been either killed or driven away, and the freedmen were "properly" subservient, violence declined in Jackson County, but not before at least 150 people had been murdered. Since the Jackson County War, a white woman wrote years later, "we have had no serious trouble" with the Negroes. It is not surprising.

The Klan was active in counties other than Jackson. In 1871, Secretary of State Gibbs estimated the murders between 1868 and 1871 by county as: Jackson 153, Madison 20, Columbia 16, Alachua 16, Suwanee 10, Hamilton 9, Taylor 7, and Lafayette 4. Again some of the murders were political. One of the men killed in Lafayette County was John N. Kreminger, a former Republican legislator, and a county judge at the time of his death.[49] Sometimes the freedmen were just frightened and not killed. On election day groups of armed whites would appear to intimidate voters. In Madison County 4 to 5 armed companies of 60 to 100 men each came to town the night before the election of 1870. Some freedmen were, thereby, kept from voting. Similar occurrances took place in other counties. Southern white Republicans were intimidated. Several Southerners said many native whites voted Republican, but would not publicly acknowledge it, or work openly for the ticket.[50]

All violence was not politically inspired. The regulators in Jefferson County, in November, 1868, took a Negro who had been

---

48 *Ibid.*, 94-95, 309-10.
49 *Ibid.*, 177-79, 222-23.
50 *Ibid.*, 70, 103-04, 123, 132-34.

accused of stealing a quarter of beef across the line into Georgia and whipped him. The freedman was ordered to leave the county. Other Negroes were whipped for stealing.[51] About fifteen men went to the home of a freedman in 1868, whipped him, his wife, and four children. The attackers asked the victims if they were unaware that whites did not "allow damned niggers to live on land of their own." The Negro who was living on a homestead was ordered to go to work for a white man the next day. A group of nine men took Samuel and Hanna Tutson of Clay County from their home and whipped them. Four of the men took the woman and five went with her husband. Both were stripped naked and viciously whipped. To add insult to injury, one of the attackers, a deputy sheriff, threatened to kill Mrs. Tutson if she refused to have sexual relations with him. The Tutsons were reputedly whipped because they would not give up their land. When the woman told of the attack, the sheriff of the county put her in jail for a day for falsehood. However, the deputy, George McCrea, was relieved of his duties.[52] Several freedmen were driven off their homesteads.

Regulators acted against whites as well as Negroes. R. W. Cone, a Southerner of Baker County, was whipped by a group of men after being accused of testifying in court against a white for a Negro. When Cone denied testifying saying he was merely on the jury, they replied that it was just as bad because the jury had taken Negro evidence. Another Southern white was stripped and whipped in 1870 in Columbia County apparently because he has associated with freedmen. He had not voted or taken part in politics. In 1871 a Jewish merchant was killed reportedly because he was "in great favor with Negroes." He was not active politically, but had a sizable trade with freedmen.[53] Even the noose was not reserved entirely for former slaves. In May, 1874, a white man living with a Negro woman near Brooksville, was taken out of his cabin at night by a dozen disguised men and hanged to the nearest tree. Two men, a freedman and a white,

---

[51] A. B. Grumwell to A. H. Jackson, November 3, 1868, in Bureau Records, Florida.
[52] *House Reports*, 42nd Cong., 2nd Sess., No. 22, pt. 13, 55-64.
[53] *Ibid.*, 65-73, 197, 307-08.

both accused of rape, were taken from the jail in Milton by local citizens in July, 1875, and hanged in the village.[54]

The question arises, why did not the Republicans who controlled the State government afford protection to freedmen and white Republicans in the lawless counties? The answer is the Republicans simply were not able to protect their party members. Governor Reed requested troops from the federal government in July, 1868, and again in October, 1870, because in several counties law officers were "overawed and set at defiance by organized bands of enemies of the Government. . . ." He requested troops again in 1871, but the federal officials seemed to think any sizable military aid was unwarranted.[55] Reed did not even have an armed state militia. A militia was organized but did not have adequate weapons. Governor Reed ordered arms from New York in 1868, but they never arrived. The weapons reached Jacksonville, were loaded on two railroad cars to be sent to Tallahassee, but disappeared enroute. A former member of the Klan claimed that conductors, engineers, and telegraph operators on the railroads were members and permitted the Klan to board the train. The shipment was thrown off between Lake City and Madison, and destroyed.[56] Reed might not have used the militia if it had been adequately armed. He was fearful the use of Negro troops, and almost half of the militia was Negro, would start a race war.[57]

About the only method the governor had of preserving order was through civil officials, who were unable to carry out their duties because of lack of co-operation and intimidation. William Bryson, Judge of the Third Judicial Circuit, said it was almost impossible to bring criminals to justice because of organizations which intimidated people, and also because many citizens sympathized with the Klan. Bryson himself was once shown a representation of the three K's and told if he held court he would be assassinated.[58] The Klan also threatened anyone who testified

54 Jacksonville *Tri-Weekly Florida Union*, May 16, 1874; Tallahassee *Sentinel*, July 24, 1875.

55 *House Executive Documents*, 44th Cong., 2nd Sess., No. 30, 66-67; *Ibid.*, 41st Cong., 3rd Sess., No. 1, pt. 2, 40; H. Reed to A. Johnson, July 13, 1868, in Andrew Johnson Papers.

56 Simkins, "Why the Ku Klux," 746-47; Stanley F. Horn, *Invisible Empire* (Boston, 1939), 279-80.

57 Otis A. Singletary, *Negro Militia and Reconstruction* (Austin, 1957), 12; Tallahassee *Sentinel*, January 20, 1872.

58 *House Reports*, 42nd Cong., 2nd Sess., No. 22, pt. 13, 258-59.

against them. After Cone had been whipped, he was told that he would be killed if he tried to prosecute his attackers, and he promised he would not.[59] Civil officials received no co-operation, and if they tried too hard to apprehend criminals they were subject to death themselves. Some civil officials, such as the deputy sheriff who helped whip the Tutsons, were actually in sympathy with the Klan. The constable of Marianna, Calvin Rogers, was killed, and his successor was attacked by whites on the street, and was later attacked at his house and wounded. County officials were appointed by the governor, but it was difficult to find enough qualified Republicans, and many Democrats were appointed.

That punishment outside the law was approved by many white citizens is signified by editorials in major newspapers. The *Floridian*, edited by an outstanding Democrat, Charles Dyke, reported an incident in Pensacola in which a group of men took two freedmen from jail and lynched them. Dyke said people did not want to wait for the law, and added it "may or may not be bad for society that such is the case."[60] Governor Reed recognized an existing fact when in a proclamation on August 12, 1870, he said the Klan in its defiance of the law and the overawing of peaceful citizens was the response to "the seditious teachings of an unprincipled press and the treasonable appeals of prominent opponents of the State Government...."[61]

White opposition to enforcement of the law is demonstrated by an incident related by Colonel Robert Bullock, an influential Democratic politician. In January, 1870, he witnessed a fight which was broken up by a Negro marshal. Bullock thought the marshal was to violent in his interference, so he "took him by the throat and hooked him—turned him loose and tried to break his head with a stick. . . ." The marshal "put his hand on me as he said *in* his *official* capacity," Bullock continued, but after "demonstrating to him how nicely my knife would fit his throat he retired." When some freedmen seemed to be considering rendering aid to the marshal, a gun was drawn on them. Earlier

---

[59] *Ibid.*, 65-66.
[60] *Ibid.*, 272-73; Tallahassee *Weekly Floridian*, August 31, 1875.
[61] Proclamation of Governor Harrison Reed, August 12, 1871, in Records of the Department of State, Tallahassee, Florida.

Bullock had written that a Republican in Ocala was "ranting" about an incident in which a Negro had been shot three times by a white. The Republican "ought by all means to be killed," Bullock added.[62] Even the Force Act was unsuccessful in Florida. In 1871 only one person was convicted, and in 1872 there were no convictions, but the threat of federal intervention may have had a sobering influence on the whites.[63]

Violence against Negroes and Republicans did not stop until the Democrats had regained control of the State, though it did decline after 1871. Violence declined in large part because in many counties white Republicans were either killed or driven away, and the Negroes were sufficiently cowed to offer little resistance to the Democrats. The period 1868 to 1871 witnessed a reign of lawlessness which the State government could not put down. All the outrages were not committed by the Klan, but such an extralegal organization, one supported by respectable white people, provided a cover for the brutal, sadistic, and those who murdered and whipped without provocation. The period of lawlessness, night riders, ghostly figures, brutal murders, lynchings, whippings, terrorism, and execution of men, women, and children was the most disgraceful phase of Reconstruction.

---

62 R. Bullock to E. M. L'Engle, September 11, 1869, January 24, 1870, in Edward M. L'Engle Papers.
63 U. S. Congress, *Senate Executive Documents*, 42nd Cong., 3rd Sess., No. 32, 24, 34.

CHAPTER XIV

NEGRO POLITICIANS

Democrats charged that during Republican Reconstruction Florida was controlled by incompetent, illiterate, and venal Negroes. Freedmen were never in a majority in the State legislature, and most of them involved in politics were able and honest men. They did, however, play a significant role in Reconstruction.

Only one Negro from Florida, Congressman Josiah T. Walls, achieved national prominence during this period. Walls was born of free parents in Winchester, Virginia, on December 30, 1842.[1] He learned the trade of a miller at which he was engaged until the outbreak of the Civil War. During the war Walls was pressed into a Confederate artillery battery as a servant. Captured by Union forces at the Battle of Yorktown in May, 1862, Walls went to Harrisburg, Pennsylvania, where he attended school for one year. In July, 1863, he enlisted in the Third Regiment of United States Colored Infantry as a private. He was present at the battle on St. Johns Island, and assisted in taking Fort Wagner. Upon the fall of Fort Wagner, Walls was sent to Jacksonville as a sergeant major and instructor of artillery. He was mustered out in Florida in November, 1865, and settled in Alachua County as a farmer.[2] Walls was a "good farmer," a native white said in later years, and neighboring planters insisted he could get more and better work out of free labor than any man in the vicinity.[3]

Walls first became involved in politics when he was sent as a delegate to the Republican Convention in Tallahassee in 1867.[4] He was then sent as a delegate to the constitutional convention of 1868, where, according to available records, he played a minor role. Elected to the lower house of the State legislature in 1868, he

[1] *Biographical Directory of the American Congress, 1774-1927* (Washington, 1928), 1662; Tallahassee *Sentinel*, August 27, 1870.
[2] William H. Barnes, *The American Government* (3 Vols.; New York, 1874), II, 215-16; Samuel Denny Smith, *The Negro in Congress, 1870-1901* (Chapel Hill, 1940), 75; Tallahassee *Sentinel*, September 10, 1870.
[3] Statement by J. H. Roper in E. C. F. Sanchez Papers, P. K. Yonge Library of Florida History, Gainesville, Florida.
[4] Tallahassee *Sentinel*, September 10, 1870.

remained for two sessions and in 1869 was elected to the senate from the Thirteenth District. While in the lower house he was probably the most active Negro on the floor, and he was one of the two or three most important representatives of his race in the senate. On the basis of the limited reports in the legislative journals, Walls was not only active, but also quite capable of holding his own with the more experienced members.[5] When a convention met in Gainesville in the summer of 1870 to nominate a congressman, Walls was a natural choice for the Negroes who were determined to have a man of their race.[6]

By 1870 Walls was known and respected throughout the State. The Tallahassee *Floridian* said he was a man of "more than average intelligence" though of "limited education." The Conservative Gainesville *New Era* wrote that Walls was "noted for his courtesy, and his efforts to promote peace and harmony" among the races, and predicted he would be successful in his race for congressman. He would, the *New Era* added, "be infinitely more preferable to the people of Florida than the late incumbent," Charles M. Hamilton.[7]

Walls' opponent in the 1870 election was a white Conservative, Silas L. Niblack. After a canvass colored with charges of fraud and intimidation, Walls was declared elected. Democrats used intimidation to keep freedmen from the polls with the result that some precincts were thrown out by the canvassing board. Niblack contested the election, and was eventually declared the victor by 137 votes, but in the meantime Walls had served in congress from March 4, 1871, to January 29, 1873.[8] Renominated and re-elected in 1872 Walls sat in the 43rd congress. He presented credentials to the 44th congress, and served from March 4, 1875 to April 19, 1876, at which time he was succeeded by Jesse T. Finley, who successfully contested his election.[9] Walls had the unhappy distinction of being thrice elected and twice unseated. There were irregularities in the election of 1874, and an accurate count was virtually impossible. By a strict party vote the congressional com-

5 Florida, *House Journal*, 1868, *Senate Journal*, 1869.
6 Wallace, *op. cit.*, 126-27.
7 Tallahassee *Weekly Floridian*, August 23, 1870; Quoted in Tallahassee *Sentinel*, September 10, 1870.
8 U. S. Congress, *House Miscellaneous Documents*, 45th Cong., 2nd Sess., No. 52, 101-107; *Congressional Globe*, 42nd Cong., 3rd Sess., pt. 2, 951-52.
9 *Biographical Directory*, *op. cit.*, 1662.

mittee on disputed elections decided to throw out a primarily Negro precinct in Lake City ousting Republican Walls, and declaring Democrat Finley elected by 234 votes. The precinct not tabulated in the final vote had registered 588 ballots for Walls and 11 for Finley.[10]

When Walls was first elected, he was the State's only member of the House of Representatives. Walls was not educated to deal with many of the important issues on the national scene, but did well under the circumstances.[11] One writer has classified Walls as one of the "twelve most potent colored leaders during the early reconstruction days."[12] An article in the St. Louis *Globe* described him as " 'a good writer but not a good speaker; an effective and tireless worker; tactful, foresighted and practical.' "[13] Others considered Walls an "excellent speaker."[14] "The colored member from Florida," the Washington *Patriot* wrote in 1872, "has been spoken of as one of the brightest of the colored members" of congress.[15] His performance in congress was a credit to his race and his adopted state.

Walls was a "zealous advocate" of the interests of his state, and a Florida "booster." He encouraged settlers to move to Florida, claiming that " 'my own sunny state' " has "a thousand rare and valuable inducements to immigration. . . ." Of all Negro congressmen he was "perhaps the most persistent in the effort to secure improvement for his district and State."[16] He introduced at least fifty-one bills, several of them for internal improvements in Florida.[17] The first bill he introduced called for a land grant to aid in constructing a railroad in Florida, and to secure rail connections with the "nearest available harbor to Cuba" and the West Indian Islands.[18] He introduced several bills to improve harbor and river transportation in the State. Several papers commended

---

[10] *Congressional Record*, 44th Cong., 1st Sess., IV, pt. 3, 2553-2603.

[11] Smith, *op. cit.*, 76.

[12] William H. Ferris, *The African Abroad* (2 Vols., New Haven, 1913), II, 762.

[13] Quoted in Smith, *op. cit.*, 77.

[14] James H. Whyte, *The Uncivil War* (New York, 1958), 240.

[15] Quoted in Tallahassee *Weekly Floridian*, March 5, 1872.

[16] Whyte, *op. cit.*, 240; Alrutheus A. Taylor, "Negro Congressmen a Generation After," *The Journal of Negro History*, VII (April, 1922), 159.

[17] *Congressional Globe*, 42nd Cong., 1st Sess.; 2nd Sess.; 43rd Cong., 1st Sess.; 2nd Sess.; 3rd Sess.; 44th Cong., 1st Sess.; Smith, *op. cit.*, 77.

[18] *Ibid.*, 42nd Cong., 1st Sess., pt. 1, 79.

Walls for his energetic attempts to secure federal funds for internal improvements.[19]

Many other bills were presented by Walls with a view toward aiding the State. He consistently introduced acts for the construction of buildings to be used as custom-houses, post-offices, and other federal offices. The mail system in Florida was greatly improved when he was able to secure the establishment of seven new mail routes.[20] An attempt was made to protect the infant fruit industry in Florida, when he successfully moved to strike from the free list of the tariff of 1872 "fruits, perishable, not dried or preserved, and not otherwise specified."[21]

Education was not neglected by Congressman Walls. On December 16, 1872, he introduced a bill to grant 1,000,000 acres of public lands to the trustees of the Florida Agricultural College. Ninety thousand acres were granted.[22] An attempt was made to secure 1,000,000 acres of public lands for Brown Institute, but the bill was reported adversely from the committee on education. Walls also tried to secure federal buildings not in use in Florida for educational purposes.[23]

On February 3, 1872, he made a lengthy speech in support of a national education fund proposed by the committee on education and labor. He spoke in response to a Georgia representative who invoked state rights in opposition to the bill. Walls pointed out that he too had an interest in his state, but believed the state rights argument was being used not because federal aid to education was unconstitutional or because it would take "reserved rights" from the states. It was, he thought, being used merely as a device to oppose education. This was one of the few times Walls referred to the race question. He gave a brief history of white opposition to Negro education and lack of interest in free schools even for poor whites. He feared that if education was left entirely to the states it would be neglected in the South, especially for Negroes; and education was too important a subject to be disregarded.

---

[19] Jacksonville *Tri-Weekly Florida Union*, February 1, 1874; *The Florida Agriculturist*, I (June 24, 1874), 28.
[20] *Congressional Globe*, 42nd Cong., 2nd Sess., pt. 5, 3939.
[21] *Ibid.*, pt. 4, 3570.
[22] *Ibid.*, 3rd Sess., pt. 1, 220; U. S. *Statutes at Large*, XVII, 397.
[23] *Congressional Globe*, 43rd Cong., 1st Sess., II, pt. 1, 88.

"It has been admitted by every lover of free government," Walls said, "that popular education, or the education of the masses, is necessary to and inseparable from a complete citizenship." Education, he added, made better citizens because it eradicated "prejudices and superstitions so prevalent among an ignorant people." Furthermore, an educated person was generally more industrious and ambitions, Walls continued. It was clear he had his own race in mind when he said,

> . . . education is the panacea for all our social evils, injustices, and oppressions. General diffusion of education among the whole people of the South would render them less submissive to the social and political stigmas under which they are today laboring.[24]

The Negroes were free, Walls said, and it remained for the government "to give them that which will not only enable them to better enjoy their freedom," but also "enable them to maintain, defend, and perpetuate their liberties." In concluding, Walls took to task those who claimed the Negro was uneducable, that he was of an inferior race "with minds unfit for cultivation, with no traits of science, skill, or literature; with no ambition for education and enlightenment; in short, a perfect 'booby brain.'" Such theories, he said, had been "rendered insignificant" by the progress of the freedmen in face of serious obstacles. It was the duty of the national government to provide equal education for all if the state governments were unwilling to do so, and he believed the Southern states would not continue to provide equal facilities.[25]

With the exception of education and civil rights, Walls usually dealt with subjects concerning Florida only, but in December, 1873, he introduced a joint resolution for the recognition of Cuban belligerency. On January 24, 1874, he made a vigorous and somewhat dramatic speech in support of his resolution. He spoke of the "continental patriots of our own land" who "arose in their honesty, their might and majesty, and their devotion to truth and justice to throw off the yoke" of tyranny placed on the colonies by Great Britain. The yoke thrown off by Americans was "less odious than that under which the Cuban patriots" suffered at the moment, he added, and indeed the Cubans had been infested by the "germ

---

24 *Ibid.*, 43rd Cong., 2nd Sess., pt. 1, 809-10.
25 *Ibid.*; Smith, *op. cit.*, 76.

of republicanism" planted by Americans. After discussing the American and French Revolutions, the revolt of Haitian slaves, the Greek revolts against the Turks, the Monroe Doctrine, and slavery in Cuba, he said that Spanish rule in Cuba was "a foul blot at our doors and a disgrace and reproach to the institutions of which we are representative, and a foul stigma upon the civilization of the time." United States recognition of Cuban belligerency "would be fully justified in the eyes of the world and vindicated in history," Walls said, just on the basis of Spanish treatment of the Negro. But in addition, there was the "assassination of the gallant Lopes," the murder of "the brave Crittenden," and "the crowning horror committed upon the *Virginius* prisoners. . . ." The speech should have been sufficient to win votes among the Cubans in Florida. The Cuban question was of considerable interest to Floridians. The State legislature had adopted a resolution requesting congress to render aid to that belabored country.[26]

Walls was vigorous in his attempts to cement relations between white and Negro and North and South. In May, 1874, he made a speech in support of a bill to appropriate $3,000,000 in aid of the centennial celebration and international exhibition of 1876 on the ground it would exhibit to the world "our own satisfaction with the capacities and excellences of our own system of government, thus approved, tested, and favored to be both sufficient and satisfactory. . . ." It would demonstrate the wealth and ability of the United States to the world, and would promote the "general interests of the nation as a whole, as well as the particular interests of each state and section" through the "intimate intermingling of citizens from every section of the country. . . ." He further believed an exhibition of the greatness of the country would "revive" and "invigorate" that "feeling of national patriotism" the late war had weakened.[27]

In addition to his other duties, Walls introduced the usual bills for relief of individuals. He presented a bill for the relief of enlisted men who had fought in the Seminole War. He also attempted to secure the removal of legal and political disabilities of several ex-Confederates in Florida. In December, 1873, Walls introduced a bill to remove "all" disabilities imposed by section

---

[26] *Congressional Globe*, 43rd Cong., 1st Sess., II, pt. 6, 27-29.
[27] *Ibid.*, 250-53 in appendix.

three of the Fourteenth Amendment. He was sometimes criticized by Republicans for his friendliness to Southern whites. He was reproved for his appointment of the son of ex-Governor Walker to West Point.[28] Walker was adamant in opposition to Negro suffrage and participation in government. A letter to the editor of a Jacksonville paper claimed Walls had not supported the Negro enough and he was "fishing for Democratic favor." The attack on the congressman was answered in a later issue by a white who said he had not voted for Walls, but thought he should be sent back to congress, because he had "proved to be a distinguished and active delegate with fine talent. . . ." The Negro should "be proud of such a capable and smart man," he added.[29] Walls was also commended for having voted against "inflation" and opposing the "Salary Grab Act" when a great majority of Southern congressmen had voted for it. He was characterized as honest and independent.[30]

Employment of the race question in politics was opposed by Walls. In a letter published to the citizens of Alachua County in 1874, he said the freedmen had "nothing to gain by an issue" with whites, nor had the "interest of the State anything to gain by an open political issue between its citizens based upon sectional hatred. . . ." He would "in no way . . . be a party to such an issue," he said. "Let us all labor for the financial advancement of our State, and to secure equal civil and political rights to all, irrespective" of race or section.[31] Walls was widely admired by Negroes, but also was respected by whites, who believed him fair and interested in the welfare of all Floridians not just Negroes. Congressman Walls served on the committees of militia, mileage, and expenditures in the navy department.

Though he belonged to a law firm in Gainesville, Walls resumed the occupation of farming after he was unseated by Finley.[32] After he was financially ruined by a frost which killed his orange trees, he took charge of the farm of the State College at Tallahassee, and died there May 5, 1905.[33]

---

[28] *Ibid.*, 42nd Cong., 2nd Sess., pt. 1, 178, 198; Tallahassee *Weekly Floridian*, June 2, 1874.
[29] Jacksonville *Tri-Weekly Florida Union*, June 2, 11, 18, 1874.
[30] Quoted from Gainesville *New Era* in *Ibid.*, September 8, 1874.
[31] *Ibid.*, June 2, 1874.
[32] *Biographical Directory*, *op. cit.*, 1662.
[33] Smith, *op. cit.*, 78.

Walls was the only Florida Negro of national eminence, but there were several able Negro politicians in the State. One of the most capable men in Florida, white or Negro, was Jonathan C. Gibbs. Gibbs was born in Philadelphia of free parents. After his father, a Methodist minister, died, he was apprenticed to learn the carpenter trade, which he followed until he was of age. In the meantime he had joined the Presbyterian Church, and at twenty-one he entered Dartmouth College, with the assistance of the Presbyterian Assembly.[34] Upon graduation from Dartmouth, Gibbs studied for two years at the Princeton Theological Seminary, later becoming pastor of a Philadelphia church.[35] After the War, Gibbs was sent to North Carolina as a missionary to his race. There he opened a private school for freedmen, in addition to ministering to their religious needs.[36] He went to Florida in late 1867. When the freedmen were enfranchised, Gibbs decided there was an "obvious necessity for ability in secular" as well as religious matters.[37]

Gibbs was elected to the constitutional convention of 1868, and aligned with the radical faction of the Republican Party, though his speeches were usually temperate. He was one of the outstanding Negro members of the convention. A New York *Tribune* correspondent wrote that, "I suppose there is no fitter man" in the convention "white or black." He was described as being of medium size with "a good intelligent yellow African face," "active in body and intellect, well educated, and an orator by nature, not a roarer but a convincing, argumentative, pleasant speaker; in this respect the most talented man in the Convention."[38] During the convention, Gibbs preached one Sunday at the Capital. "I have never heard a better address in my life than I did last evening from the Rev. Mr. Gibbs, at the African Church," a Northern correspondent wrote. Another white listener became almost ecstatic saying, "Oh that all the old masters in the South could have heard him this day."[39] A Jacksonville paper stated

---

[34] Gibbs, *op. cit.*, 111.
[35] *House Reports*, 42nd Cong., 2nd Sess., No. 22, pt. 13, 223; New York *Tribune*, February 10, 1868.
[36] *Ibid.*; DuBois, *op. cit.*, 643.
[37] Gibbs, *op. cit.*, 111.
[38] New York *Tribune*, February 5, 10, 1868; Tallahassee *Sentinel*, February 20, 1868.
[39] *Ibid.*

that Gibbs was "a good example of what education will make of his race," adding that he was a man of "pleasing and courteous address."[40] He was probably the best educated and most cultured man in the convention. Despite his adherence to the Billings faction of the convention, he was independent, and even opposed Billings himself on occasion. He labored for a constitution that would protect the rights of Negroes and property in the State.[41]

In 1868 Governor Harrison Reed presented Gibbs' name to the senate for appointment as secretary of state, but the name was incorrectly presented as John. Reed withdrew his name, and for some reason did not resubmit it.[42] Later in the year Gibbs was appointed secretary of state after the first appointee, George J. Alden, a native white Unionist, joined the governor's enemies in an attempt to impeach him. The appointment of Gibbs undoubtedly strengthened Reed's position with the freedmen, who believed the governor had neglected them.[43] As secretary of state, Gibbs was a trusted public servant, and worked closely with Reed. In the governor's absence he served as chairman pro tem of the Board of Commissioners of Public Institutions.[44] He was Reed's right-hand man, and was respected by other cabinet officers.

Even Democrats commended Gibbs for his fairness. In 1873 the Tallahassee *Weekly Floridian* complained of a "legal advertisement law" passed by the legislature which was meant to subsidize Republican newspapers, but under Gibbs, the editor added, "the harsh operations" of the law were "considerably mollified" by the designation of a number of Democratic journals as "official papers."[45] Being fair did not shield Gibbs from the hatred of the Ku Klux Klan. His brother visited him while he was secretary of state, and found him in a "well-appointed residence," but sleeping in the attic where he kept "considerable of an arsenal." Gibbs said he had slept in the attic for several months for better vantage as the Ku Klux had threatened his life.[46]

---

40 Jacksonville *Florida Union*, November 14, 1868.

41 Wallace, *op. cit.*, 55.

42 Florida, *Senate Journal*, 1868, 84.

43 Wallace, *op. cit.*, 90-91; New York *Tribune*, February 8, 1868.

44 Minutes of the Board of Commissioners of Public Institutions, October 26, 1869 to February 13, 1892, February 27, March 2, 23, May 1, 1871.

45 Tallahassee *Weekly Floridian*, March 4, 1873.

46 Gibbs, *op. cit.*, 112.

When Governor Reed was succeeded in January, 1873, by Ossian B. Hart, Gibbs was appointed superintendent of public instruction. According to a Negro contemporary, the freedmen threatened to desert the Republican Party unless a Negro was placed in Hart's cabinet, and as Gibbs was considered the most able Negro in the State, he was invited to join Hart's administration.[47] As superintendent, Gibbs was also president of the board of trustees of a proposed agricultural college. The manuscript records of Superintendent Gibbs demonstrate that he was intelligent and much interested in developing public education. He insisted on full, accurate reports from county superintendents, and supervised them closely. He had some success in securing the adoption of uniform texts in the schools. Previously each student had used any book he could secure.[48] The public school system in Florida experienced rapid growth under the leadership of Gibbs, who was interested in education for all, but the superintendent himself was not satisfied with his progress. A visitor to Florida described Gibbs as "a gentleman of considerable culture, and capacity," but said Gibbs believed he had been able to do little for education. White fear of integrated schools was thought to be the reason for his lack of success.[49] The superintendent was not always so pessimistic. In a speech before the National Education Association in August, 1873, at Elmira, New York, he admitted the shortcomings and problems of public education in Florida, but graphically demonstrated its great improvement and growth since the war.[50] His address received flattering notice from the Elmira newspapers, and "the leading journals of New York seemed to relate with pride" that a Negro from the South "had delivered with the dignity of an educated gentleman," a speech that in "breadth of thought and liberality of sentiment" marked Gibbs as a "worthy son" of Dartmouth College.[51]

Gibbs' sudden death at forty-eight on August 14, 1874, was a loss to the State and his race. His successor as superintendent of public instruction wrote that Gibbs' death "must be regarded as an event of more than ordinary importance, especially when viewed

47 Wallace, op. cit., 268.
48 School Reports.
49 King, op. cit., 420.
50 Copy in School Reports.
51 The Florida Agriculturist, I (January 17, 1874), 20.

in connection with the educational interests of the State." With Gibbs' death, the successor added, the Negroes "have lost one of their noblest representatives, our State one of its most valued citizens, and our public school system one of its most intelligent advocates—one of its best friends."[52] Enjoying apparent good health, Gibbs had delivered a "powerful speech" at a Republican meeting, but died that night. It was whispered and widely believed he had been poisoned. His brother said he died of apoplexy.[53]

The death of one of the State's most illustrious Negroes was regretted by white and Negro Floridians alike. The conservative Tallahassee *Weekly Floridian* wrote, "he was probably the best informed colored man in the State, and would in this respect have stood in the front ranks of his race anywhere."[54] The Jacksonville *Tri-Weekly Florida Union* said it was no injustice to the living to say "that in all the elements that go to make up what is termed a good citizen and a capable and honest public servant, he leaves few superiors."[55] Gibbs was "in many respects a leading representative of his race," the Jacksonville *New South* attested, "and in the State, owing to his education and gentlemenly bearing, he had no superior."[56] The minister-educator-politician was a man of integrity and dedication, and was without question one of the most outstanding men in Florida.

Florida Negroes were also of considerable importance in the State legislature, though they were never in the majority. In the first legislature there were nineteen freedmen present, which was the largest number of Negroes ever sent as representatives to the Florida law making body.[57] The Negroes combined with white Northerners were always outnumbered. In 1868 of 76 legislators 19 were freedmen, 13 were from the North, 23 were white Democrats, and 21 were white Southern loyalists. Southern born whites were always in a majority in the Florida Reconstruction legislatures. In 1868 the composition according to party was 52 Repub-

52 School Reports.
53 DuBois, *op. cit.*, 521; Gibbs, *op. cit.*, 112.
54 Tallahassee *Weekly Floridian*, August 25, 1874.
55 Jacksonville *Tri-Weekly Florida Union*, August 18, 1874.
56 Jacksonville *New South*, August 19, 1874.
57 Tallahassee *Weekly Floridian*, June 9, 1868.

licans to 24 Democrats.[58] Although it has been maintained that Negroes held the balance of power in the State, it would be as logical, and perhaps more so, to say that it was held by the Southern white loyalists, who generally outnumbered Negro legislators.

The Negroes probably exerted more power in the senate than they did in the house. Of the 24 senators freedmen claimed three in 1868, five in 1869-1870, three in 1871-1872, five in 1873-1874, and six in 1875-1876.[59] The number of freedmen in the house ranged from sixteen in 1868 to eight in 1876. There were never more than thirteen in the house after 1868. Only about thirty different freedmen served in the lower house of the legislature during the entire Reconstruction era.[60]

Some of the charges that the freedmen were illiterate and incompetent were true. It has been said that six illiterate delegates were sent to the legislature in Florida during Reconstruction, at least four of them being Negroes and one a white Democrat. Whether the other one was Negro or white is not certain.[61] It is certain that a majority of Negroes in the lower house, and all of the senators were literate. Usually the freedmen appeared to be reasonably intelligent though their lack of experience was occasionally demonstrated. In 1870 Richard Wells of Leon County nominated Fred Douglass for United States Senator from Florida. A white Democrat voted for Jefferson Davis at the same time.[62]

---

[58] *Ibid.*; Dovell, *op. cit.*, II, 557; Jacksonville *Florida Union*, June 18, 1868; Tallahassee *Sentinel*, July 23, 1868.

[59] Negro senators were William Bradwell, Robert Meacham, and Charles H. Pearce, 1868; Bradwell, Meacham, Pearce, Harry Cruse, and Josiah T. Walls, 1869-1870; Meacham, Pearce, and Fred Hill, 1871-1872; Hill, Meacham, Pearce, Thomas W. Long, and Washington Pope, 1873-1874; Samuel Spearing, 1874; Pope, Long, Meacham, Hill, A. B. Osgood, and John Wallace, 1875-1876.

[60] Negroes in the assembly were Josiah H. Armstrong, Columbia; Richard H. Black, Alachua; Oliver J. Coleman, Madison; Singleton Coleman, Marion; Robert Cox, Leon; Harry Cruse, Gadsden; Zebulon Elizah, Escambia; Auburn Erwin, Columbia; Emanuel Fortune, Jackson; Theodore Gass, Alachua; Noah Graham, Leon; Henry S. Harman, Alachua; Fred Hill, Gadsden; Joseph H. Lee, Duval; Robert Livingston, Leon; Ephrain Logan, Jefferson; Daniel McInnis, Duval; J. W. Menard, Duval; Anthony Mills, Jefferson; Alfred B. Osgood, Madison; John Proctor, Leon; Jesse Robinson, Jackson; W. K. Robinson, Jackson; John R. Scott, Duval; Samuel Small, Marion; William G. Stewart, Leon; Benjamin Thompson, Jefferson; Charles Thompson, Columbia; John Wallace, Leon; Josiah T. Walls, Alachua; George Washington, Alachua; Richard Wells, Leon; George W. Witherspoon, Jefferson; John Wyatt, Leon.

[61] DuBois, *op. cit.*, 515; Wallace, *op. cit.*, 323.

[62] Florida, *House Journal*, 1870, 78, 89.

Some of the Negroes were as qualified for voting and holding office as many of the whites. A transplanted Bostonian in Florida claimed the freedmen were not ready for self-government, but thought they were as well qualified as one-half of the white Floridians. He believed Negro suffrage was necessary for their protection and freedmen would "become informed and get qualified faster than the poor whites."[63] Negro legislators served on committees, but usually were not chairman. Lieutenant Governor William H. Gleason said at first he appointed no Negro chairman of committees because they were incapable, but later "many of them fitted themselves to become competent to preside over any committee."[64] Some of the freedmen recognized their incapacity and depended considerably on white Republican leaders, Gleason said. Freedmen served on ten senate committees in 1868.[65] By 1870 Negroes were presiding over some of the committees.[66]

Negro legislators were not always slavishly dependent on white Republicans. They demonstrated independence on several occasions, and frequently co-operated with Democrats in opposition to their own party, especially after 1870. Usually the freedmen were not too active on the house floor, though they were present for voting. A few of them, like Walls, played major roles in legislation and appeared to be at no disadvantage when dealing with their white opponents. Negro senators entered into debates on the floor more frequently than did members of the lower house. Walls, Charles H. Pearce, Robert Meacham, and John Wallace, in particular, refused to take a back seat to their white colleagues.

Education, economic security for the masses, relief and suffrage seemed to be of primary interest to the ex-slave lawmakers. Nearly all of them supported a public education system. Pearce and Henry S. Harman led the fight for a satisfactory school law. Freedmen supported the homestead law and other measures advantageous to the masses, white and Negro. Civil rights were also championed by the ex-slaves.[67] Despite their reputed incapability,

---

[63] *House Reports*, 42nd Cong., 2nd Sess., No. 22, pt. 13, 256-57.
[64] Gleason's memory betrayed him. He appointed Charles H. Pearce chairman of the committee on education in 1868. Edward C. Williamson, "Florida's First Reconstruction Legislature," *Florida Historical Quarterly*, XXXII (July, 1953), 42-43.
[65] Florida, *Senate Journal*, 1868, 32-34.
[66] Florida, *House Journal*, 1870, 32-34.
[67] Franklin, *op. cit.*, 315; Wallace, *op. cit.*, 84.

Negro legislators were a significant factor in Reconstruction politics and legislation. Some Negroes were not qualified just as some whites were not, but several of them were as able as the average white statesman in Florida before, during, and after Reconstruction.

Charges of widespread corruption made against Negro lawgivers are unsubstantiated. In 1870 Governor Reed commended the ex-slaves for their resistance to "extraordinary efforts to mislead, intimidate, or subsidize" them "from the path of duty. . . ." By their resistance, Reed added, they had "preserved the State from the incubus of a corrupt and corrupting power" which had "fastened itself upon so many of the States now struggling to rise from the ruins of war."[68] This is not to say that all freedmen were completely immune to that widespread corrupter of politicians, the bribe. Bribery was extensively employed on the state and national level and Florida was no exception. One Negro legislator, John Wallace, whose statements should be accepted with a good deal of skepticism, maintained that at one time when whites were reportedly receiving bribes a number of Negroes formed a "smelling committee" to search out any scheme which might prove advantageous. Southern whites attempted to bribe Negroes into opposing their white leaders, but with little success.[69] Senator Pearce was expelled from the senate in 1872 after a conviction for bribery. Witnesses against him were two Negro legislators, Fred Hill and Harry Cruse. It is difficult to determine whether Pearce was actually guilty of attempted bribery or was being punished for having supported the wrong side in a Republican squabble.[70] Wallace said at first the freedmen knew nothing about "stealing by legislation" but were taught by whites. Had it not been for whites, he added, Negroes "might have legislated for years before learning to steal by statute."[71] The truth is that "stealing by legislation" was almost non-existent in Florida during Reconstruction. Carpetbag and Negro plundering during Reconstruction has been grossly exaggerated.

Personal information is not available for all Negro legislators in Florida, but brief sketches can be made of a few of the more

---

[68] Florida, *Senate Journal*, 1870, 6.
[69] Wallace, *op. cit.*, 85, 103-04.
[70] Dodd, *op. cit.*, 9.
[71] Wallace, *op. cit.*, 84.

important personalities. One of the most powerful Negro politicians was Elder Charles H. Pearce, commonly known as "Bishop." Pearce arrived in Florida in 1866 as a missionary for the African Methodist Episcopal Church, and became one of the outstanding ministers of the State. He organized churches around the State and made acquaintances which later enhanced his political power. He was a successful pastor and presiding elder. Speaking and debating were among his strong points.[72] In May, 1868, a carpetbagger wrote a Northern friend that Pearce was "a man of great ability, worth, and power," and was doing "a noble Christian work" among the freedmen.[73] Pearce soon became a potent force in the A. M. E. Church in Florida, and that rapidly growing organization became a significant political element, one which Pearce did not hesitate to use. He maintained that one of the duties of a minister was to look out for the interests, including political, of his congregation.[74]

When the new government met in 1868, Pearce was in attendance as senator from the Eighth District. He was quite active in the senate and as a member of the committee on education, held up a bill providing for public schools until one was drawn that did not prohibit integration. Equality for freedmen was always vigorously defended by Pearce in the legislature. When a split occurred between Governor Reed and the more radical Republicans, Pearce was called upon to assure the Negroes that Reed was not selling them out for the favor of Southern whites. He was successful in convincing a large number of freedmen to support Reed, which reputedly earned him the enmity of the Radicals. After a successful campaign for re-election to the senate in 1870 Pearce was indicted for allegedly offering another Negro senator, Fred Hill, $500 to vote against impeaching Governor Reed. The witnesses to the attempted bribery were members of Reed's opposition, and it was widely believed the charge was fabricated to cripple Pearce's political influence. Pearce was convicted, and after the State Supreme Court upheld the conviction, he was expelled from the senate in April, 1872.[75] Expulsion did not destroy

---

[72] Long, *op. cit.*, 195; Arnett, *op. cit.*, 167.
[73] D. Richards to E. B. Washburne, May 7, 1868, in Elihu B. Washburne Papers.
[74] Dodd, *op. cit.*, 6-7; Thrift, *op. cit.*, 109.
[75] Dodd, *op. cit.*, 8-11; Wallace, *op. cit.*, 105; Tallahassee *Weekly Floridian*, December 20, 1870.

Pearce's influence. He remained a political power in the county and was re-elected to the senate in November, 1872. He later went over to the faction that had tried to destroy him. Pearce also served as Leon County superintendent of public instruction in 1869-1870.

Another important minister-politician was Robert Meacham, who served as state senator from the Ninth District throughout Reconstruction. Born in Quincy, Florida, around 1836, Meacham was the son of his master and a slave woman. He learned to read and write though he was withdrawn from a white school to which his father had sent him. The other students objected to his presence. Meacham spent most of his childhood with his physician father, and said he never knew whether he was slave or free. He was left as a servant to his father's sister-in-law upon the former's death.[76] After emancipation Meacham became a minister and formed the first A. M. E. Church congregation in Tallahassee in 1865. In 1867 he entered the political arena when he was made a voter registrar in Jefferson County. He attended the 1868 constitutional convention, and after that time held numerous offices, frequently more than one at a time. He served in the senate throughout Reconstruction, as one of the Republican presidential electors in 1868, clerk of the circuit court of Jefferson County in 1868, and Jefferson County superintendent of schools from 1869 to 1870, and again from 1873 to 1875. He unsuccessfully ran for the United States House of Representatives in 1874.[77] Meacham was an effective legislator, and of sufficient influence to attract the opposition of the Klan. He received warnings from the Klan and at least one attempt was made on his life.[78] He was considered by many of both races as a respected and honest citizen.

Negro politician John Wallace is of interest primarily because in 1888 he wrote a book on Reconstruction in Florida, a book edited for him by an influential Democratic ex-governor, William D. Bloxham. The book contains many inaccuracies and is pro-

---

[76] *House Reports*, 42nd Cong., 2nd Sess., No. 22, pt. 13, 105-07.

[77] Long, *op. cit.*, 57; Davis, *op. cit.*, 541; Tallahassee *Weekly Floridian*, November 3, 1868; School Reports; Smith, *op. cit.*, 135; R. Meacham to G. Alden, August 24, 1868, in Records of the Department of State, Tallahassee, Florida.

[78] A. B. Grumwell to E. C. Woodruff, February 28, 1867, in Bureau Records, Florida; Tallahassee *Sentinel*, August 26, 1876.

Democrat, but is still a useful source. Wallace was born in North Carolina and remained a slave in that state until 1862 when he traveled to Washington with Union forces. In August, 1863, he enlisted in the Second United States Colored troops. He went with the army to Florida in 1864, and was discharged at Key West, January 1, 1866. Lacking formal education, Wallace taught himself to read and write. He later taught school on Bloxham's plantation.[79]

Wallace was elected constable in Leon County in 1868, and was considered by some to be a Radical, and of somewhat violent temperament. As a lieutenant of Pearce, he rallied the freedmen for Reed after Pearce was indicted for bribery. His faithfulness to the Republican Party was rewarded when in 1871 he was elected to the house where he remained through 1874. While in the house Wallace embarrassed his colleagues by being arrested and fined thirty dollars for assaulting a citizen of Tallahassee with a "slung shot." The incident grew out of a collision of vehicles the day before. Soon after he entered the house Wallace began to co-operate with editor Dyke, and the two succeeded in splitting the Republican Party in Leon County. He frequently aligned with the Democrats in the legislature, and campaigned, at times, against the Republican candidate for governor in 1876, though he maintained later he voted Republican. In his own view he was opposing the corrupt faction of his party. To many Republicans it seemed that he had been seduced by "Mr. Democrat" Dyke. Wallace was also a practicing lawyer.[80]

Other Negro politicians were less known and little information is available. Josiah H. Armstrong was born in Lancaster, Pennsylvania, May 30, 1842. He later went to Florida where he became associated with the A. M. E. Church. He was ordained a deacon in 1869, and as elder in 1870. Armstrong served in the house for Columbia County in 1871-1872, and again in 1875-1876. He ap-

---

79 Wallace, *op. cit.*, preface; Tallahassee *Semi-Weekly Floridian*, December 30, 1867.

80 Wallace, *op. cit.*, 182; Tallahassee *Weekly Floridian*, September 15, 1868; Tallahassee *Sentinel*, May 18, 1872; Jacksonville *Daily Florida Union*, February 10, March 29, 1876; R. E. X. to E. M. L'Engle, October 3, 1876, H. Elliott to E. M. L'Engle, February 20, 1875, Memo of H. Reed, October 6, 1876, in Edward M. L'Engle Papers.

parently did not play a major role in the legislature.[81] Armstrong had been "converted" by William S. Bradwell, a minister, who served in the senate from the Eighteenth District in 1868-1870. Bradwell was born a slave in Georgia and preached to other slaves before emancipation. He was a delegate to the constitutional convention where he was not a strong influence. A correspondent wrote that Bradwell was "smart in his way . . . but itching for office, and much more fit for a politician than for a preacher." In the convention he aligned with the moderates. As a minister Bradwell wielded considerable influence over the freedmen.[82]

Emanuel Fortune was sent to the house by Jackson County in 1868-1870. He attended the convention and rendered considerable aid to the Osborn faction. He was literate, a good debater, and was said to be impervious to bribes and promises. Fortune left Jackson County after his life had been threatened by the Klan.[83] Fred Hill of Gadsden County served in the legislature throughout Reconstruction representing his county in the house from 1868, 1870 and was senator from the Sixth District 1871-1876. He was in attendance at the convention and supported the Radicals. A correspondent described him as "an intelligent full blooded African. . . ." Hill was popular with the freedmen.[84] Joseph H. Lee of Duval County was one of the best trained Negro legislators in Florida. Born in Philadelphia in 1848, he attended local public schools and graduated from Howard University Law School in 1872. On the motion of Attorney General William A. Cocke, Lee was admitted to practice before the Florida Supreme Court in April, 1873. He went to the house from Duval County in 1875. Like many Negro politicians, Lee was a minister.[85]

Death cut short the budding political career of Robert Livingston, assemblyman from Leon County. Livingston was born a slave in Leon County, and learned the trade of carpentry. At about twenty he hired his time from his master, and "by industry, econo-

[81] Richard R. Wright, *Encyclopedia of African Methodism* (Philadelphia, 1916), 25.

[82] New York *Tribune*, February 5, 1868; Jacksonville *Florida Union*, July 20, 1867, January 11, 1868.

[83] Wallace, *op. cit.*, 55; *House Reports*, 42nd Cong., 2nd Sess., No. 22, pt. 13, 94.

[84] New York *Tribune*, February 5, 1868.

[85] Tallahassee *Weekly Floridian*, April 15, 1873; *Florida Sentinel*, Tenth Annual Number, 1880.

my, and temperate habits, he accumulated some property, learned
to read, and acquired considerable general information." He served
only one session in the house before his death in 1869.[86] Another
minister-politician was Thomas Warren Long. Long was born near
Jacksonville in 1832. When the war broke out he escaped and
joined the Union troops at Fernandina. He later returned to
Jacksonville and managed to spirit away his wife and two daughters.
As a member of the Twenty-Third United States Volunteer Regiment he was sent to Beaufort, South Carolina. In 1864 Long was
promoted to sergeant for "bravery and strategy in battle" after he
devised a plan and captured a Confederate picket line and led in the
capture of a fort. At the end of the war, he returned to Florida
and joined the A. M. E. Conference. By 1870 Long was Presiding
Elder of the Jacksonville District, and as a power in the A. M. E.
Church he received the political support of the Negroes. He was
senator from the Nineteenth District 1873-1876.[87]

Alfred B. Osgood represented Madison County in the house
during 1868-1874 and was senator of the Tenth District 1875-1876.
Osgood was an able speaker and intelligent. Negro delegates
nominated him for speaker of the assembly in 1874, but white
Republican and Democratic representatives prevented his election.[88]
One Negro legislator, John Proctor, was reputedly born free, but
became a slave. George Proctor, a free Negro, purchased a slave girl
for a wife in 1839 for $1,300 with a down payment of $450. He was
a respectable carpenter, but had difficulty in completing the payments. The mortgage was not paid and his wife and children, including John, were sold in 1854. Proctor served as Leon County
representative in 1873-1876. A contemporary said Proctor considered it ethical to accept a bribe as long as he did not permit
it to influence his decision. Because of his known lack of "honor"
he was apparently "bribed" only once.[89]

One of the leading Negro citizens of Duval County, John R.
Scott, represented his county in the house, 1868-1874. Scott was
more powerful on the county than state level. When the Republican convention met in Jacksonville in 1870, he was elected chair-

---

[86] Florida, *House Journal*, 1869, 138-39.
[87] Long, *op. cit.*, 75-78.
[88] Wallace, *op. cit.*, 228-29.
[89] *Ibid.*, 272, 275; William T. Cash, *The Story of Florida* (4 Vols., New
York, 1938), I, 409-10.

man. He was not active on the floor of the legislature, but was usually present to vote on important issues.[90] Leon sent more Negroes to the legislature than any other county. William G. Stewart, an important member of the A. M. E. Church, represented the county in 1873-1874. Stewart was not a powerful element in Florida Reconstruction politics, but was respected locally for his "modest lamb like nature. . . ."[91] George W. Witherspoon, who in his own words was the "silver-tongued orator of the South" was sent to the house by Jefferson County in 1875. He was described as an "orator-politician" who made up "in a certain eloquent and sonorous cadence of sound what he lacked in knowledge." Witherspoon was unsuccessfully supported for United States Senator in 1875.[92]

There was also a number of Negro officials on the local level though the total has been exaggerated. The only elective local office was constable and Negroes were frequently returned to that position, at least in the early days of Reconstruction. Sprague reported in 1868 that a majority of the constables elected were freedmen. The office became less popular after the Negroes discovered the difficulty of arresting white men. Only four county constables, two magistrates and one unidentified official were listed by the 1870 census as Negroes.[93]

Republican governors in Florida were charged with appointing hoards of incompetent, illiterate Negro officials. Some were appointed, but both Reed and Stearns were hesitant to appoint Negroes. In 1873 Governor Hart admitted this reluctance and added that Negroes could be found who would do well in office if they were accorded "such friendly aid in their new and unaccustomed duties, as was always given before the war to ordinary appointees" by their friends. "We are not apt to trouble ourselves much," Hart said, "to find men who will do for office with some friendly aid, among any but our own color. But we ought to do it. . . ." Hart added that "we ought to act squarely up to our grand political principles, and crush prejudice under our heels."

---

[90] Wallace, *op. cit.*, 128-29.
[91] Long, *op. cit.*, 55.
[92] Davis, *op. cit.*, 644.
[93] *Ibid.*, 536; J. T. Sprague to O. O. Howard, June 30, 1868, in Bureau Records, Florida; Warren Q. Dow Diary; Ninth Census of the United States, 1870, unpublished population schedules for Florida.

In 1876 out of thirty-nine county judges, none were Negro; of thirty-nine sheriffs only two were freedmen; all thirty-nine clerks of the circuit court were white; of thirty-nine tax assessors two were Negro, and all of the thirty-nine tax collectors were white. There were no freedmen in the cabinet.[94]

Some Negroes were represented in city government, and on police forces. In 1870 there were at least five Negro policemen, two of whom were city marshals. At one time Tallahassee was reported to have a Negro chief of police.[95] From 1874 to 1877, Matthew M. Lewey was Mayor of Newnansville, and was commissioned justice of the peace in 1873. Lewey was a school teacher and an able man. Some of the freedmen appointed were incapable and illiterate. Occasionally there was no other choice. In 1867 Hart, who was supervising registration, had difficulty securing men, white or Negro, who could read. In Polk County it was said that "good intelligent" practical men could be found but they had "no education whatever." Another county had only one man who could read and write. Earlier Democratic governors had faced the same problem. An army officer in Lake City wrote in 1866 that many of the white justices of the peace were "entirely illiterate" and incapable of even drawing up contracts. A number of the officers in Volusia County could neither read nor write, and did not understand their duties, a Jacksonville paper reported in September, 1867, and as a result the county was without law. Illiterate county officials were not limited to the Reconstruction period.[96]

Freedmen were permitted to serve on juries in most counties. They were not trained for such duty and there was considerable apprehension on the part of whites, but their forebodings generally proved to be unjustified. A Florida white related an incident in which a Radical in court tried to win a case by securing an all Negro jury. He got a jury composed predominantly of freedmen, but did not win the case. There were few complaints about Negro jurors other than by those who opposed freedmen on the jury,

---

94 O. B. Hart to O. Buddington, March 1, 1873, in Governor's Letter Book, Florida State Library, Tallahassee, Florida; Watchman's Letter No. 11, May 20, 1876.

95 Eppes, op. cit., 351; Bill, op. cit., 84.

96 Jacksonville Florida Union, September 14, 1876; F. E. Grossman to J. H. Lyman, November 1, 1866, in Bureau Records, Florida; R. Comba to O. B. Hart, July 13, 1867, in Records of the Department of State, Tallahassee, Florida.

qualified or not.[97] The number and inability of Negro officeholders in Florida has been magnified.

---

[97] S. D. McConnell to E. M. L'Engle, October 7, 1869, in Edward M. L'Engle Papers; D. M. Hammond to G. W. Gile, December 3, 1868, J. A. Remley to G. W. Gile, November 30, 1868, in Bureau Records, Florida.

CHAPTER XV

AN EVALUATION OF "RADICAL"
RECONSTRUCTION

On June 25, 1868, the United States Congress readmitted Florida to the Union, and so-called carpetbag rule began. In reality, carpetbaggers or even Negroes and carpetbaggers combined, were never in a majority in the Florida legislature. In 1868 Southern whites had a majority of twelve in the assembly, but Republicans were predominant. Twenty-one of the Southern whites claimed Republican sympathies, giving that party a majority of thirty. Only thirteen carpetbaggers and nineteen Negroes were present.[1] No more than twelve carpetbaggers exerted appreciable influence in Florida. Of the twelve, eight were ex-officers of the Union army, five entered the State before 1866, and at least nine were bonafide citizens of Florida before suffrage was granted to the freedmen.[2] There is no indication that all or even most of the Northern Republicans in Florida came to exploit the State. The Democrats steadily gained in power. By 1871 the Republicans enjoyed a majority of only four, though their majority was increased to seven in the election of 1872. In 1875 the Democrats held a majority in the legislature after a murdered Republican senator was replaced by a Democrat. Democrat A. L. McCaskill was made president pro tem of the senate, and Democrat Thomas Hannah was elected speaker of the house. In 1875 Republicans joined to help elect Charles W. Jones, a Democrat, to congress.[3]

The charge that Florida was controlled by outsiders was not true. Northerners were vastly outnumbered in the legislature, and the first native Floridian to become governor of the State was Republican Ossian B. Hart, elected in 1872.[4] Native whites were

---

[1] Tallahassee *Weekly Floridian*, June 9, 1868; Tallahassee *Sentinel*, July 23, 1868; Davis, *op. cit.*, 529.

[2] Davis, *op. cit.*, 477.

[3] Tallahassee *Sentinel*, December 14, 1872, December 19, 1874, March 6, 1875; Tallahassee *Weekly Floridian*, December 17, 1872, December 15, 1874, January 19, February 16, August 3, 1875; Davis *op. cit.*, 641-643; E. W. L'Engle to E. M. L'Engle, November 23, 1876, in Edward M. L'Engle Papers.

[4] Tallahassee *Weekly Floridian*, March 24, 1874; Tallahassee *Sentinel*, January 29, 1870; Jacksonville *Tri-Weekly Florida Union*, March 21, 1874.

also in a majority in local and appointive offices. Governors Reed, Hart, and Stearns all appointed many native whites including Democrats to office. All three of the first supreme court justices were Southern, and two of them, Edwin M. Randall, the Chief Justice, and James D. Wescott, Jr., were Democrats. The third justice was Hart. The important position of comptroller was first filled by a Florida conservative, ex-slaveholder, Robert H. Gamble, and the first attorney general, Westcott, later appointed to the supreme court, was an ex-slaveholder, and had supported the Confederacy. Approximately four-fifths of the other judicial and executive officers were natives of Florida, or at least citizens of the State before the war.[5] Five of the seven appointees to the State Circuit Court were Southern. By August 28, 1868, 198 whites had been appointed to office by Governor Reed; 148 of them were from the South. Southern whites outnumbered Northerners in county offices also. Of 173 white county officials, 134 were Southern.[6]

Governor Reed and the Republicans should be credited with appointing a good supreme court, a better than average cabinet, and county officials about as good as could be secured. Reed sought to establish a strong state government that would earn the respect of citizens.[7] Lieutenant Governor William H. Gleason said that in Democratic counties Reed appointed a Democratic county clerk, a Republican county judge, and a Democratic majority of county commissioners. When Republican legislators were elected from a county, Reed appointed a Republican clerk and democratic judge.[8] Reed's appointments and spirit of conciliation were supposed to be in the interest of building up an impoverished state, but unfortunately the opposition did not co-operate even in legitimate efforts to restore Florida. Democratic leaders, and the press fanned the fires of hate "until a general impression prevailed that Republican government . . . was a hateful tyranny established for their oppression and destruction."[9] Many of the Democrats ap-

---

5 The Republican governors of Florida were Harrison Reed, 1868-1873, Ossian B. Hart, 1873-1874, and Marcellus L. Stearns, 1874-1877. *The Florida Agriculturalist*, I (January 17, 1874), 23; Wallace, *op. cit.*, 81.

6 Davis, *op. cit.*, 534-536.

7 *Ibid.*; Tallahassee *Sentinel*, August 14, 1875.

8 Phillip D. Ackerman, Jr., "Florida Reconstruction from Walker through Reed, 1865 to 1873" (unpublished M.A. thesis, University of Florida, 1948), 249.

9 Tallahassee *Sentinel*, August 14, 1875.

pointed to office, especially Comptroller Gamble, seemed intent on using their position to destroy their benefactors.

A white Democratic officeholder from Taylor County advised Governor Hart in 1873 that Reed had made an error "in his appointments, trying to make Republicans out of Democrats. . . ." If Republicans are in power, he said, appoint Republicans, for we know that if Democrats gain power no Republican will be appointed. He had been appointed by Reed but could not, he said, honestly support the government because of Negro officeholders, and he still voted Democratic.[10] Other Democrats were appointed who were "violently opposed to the Republican party" and worked with the opposition. Some Democrats accepted office with the professed aim of ousting Republicans.[11] Reed appointed at least one justice of the peace who could not take the oath of office under the Fourteenth Amendment. Governors Hart and Stearns also appointed many Democrats. Democratic newspapers sometimes commended Republican governors for their impartial appointments, but the desired co-operation usually was not forthcoming.[12]

Many of the charges against the Republicans during Reconstruction in Florida are either false or exaggerated. The Negroes were not as incompetent as has been said, and though the terms "carpetbagger" and "scalawag" were used with contempt, there is no evidence that these men were less principled or more selfish than other politicians in Florida, or the United States. In 1876 a Democratic politician, Charles Dougherty, defined a carpetbagger as a "man who was reared in the rocks of the North" and who,

> like the black snake, after shedding his skin in the spring of the year, and having become tired of making leather hams, wooden nutmegs, and sharpening shoe pegs, seeks a warmer climate, immigrates to the South to hunt office and live on the labors of others, and without helping themselves, become rich by stealing.

---

[10] S. A. Willcox to O. B. Hart, January 23, 1873, in Records of the Department of State, Tallahassee, Florida.

[11] W. Rogers to H. Reed, July 12, 1870, J. T. Magbee to H. Reed, July 13, 1871, A. C. Lightboan to J. C. Gibbs, October 7, 1872, in Records of the Department of State, Tallahassee, Florida; E. J. Vann to D. H. Hamilton, January 19, 1869, in Ruffin-Roulhac-Hamilton Papers.

[12] Tampa *Florida Peninsular*, January 30, February 6, 1869.

A scalawag Dougherty said was

> one who disregarded his allegiance to his state, and sup-
> ported the general government; he was the meanest creature
> in the world, unfit for society or to associate with decent
> people, [and] ought not to be allowed to live in any com-
> munity.[13]

Of course these definitions were not fair or even rational, but the
words scalawag and carpetbagger were epithets "loaded with op-
probrium and contempt." Such charges were excellent Democratic
propaganda, and many of the misconceptions about Reconstruction
arose because obvious propaganda was believed.

\ A fairer description of the Republicans came from the Jacksonville Tri-Weekly Florida Union in 1871. "The Republican Party
neither North nor South, can be made out to be a congregation of
saints unalloyed of earthly taint," the paper said, "nor are its
leaders everywhere to be regarded with the reverence and homage
which are claimed for the disciples of a higher gospel," but the
party could with justice claim accord with the larger portion of
intelligence, wealth, and moral sentiment of the State. The "itinerant idler and irresponsible adventurer," took a back seat in
Florida, the paper continued, and "if any state in the South has
reason to complain less of either the influence or conduct of a class
of thieving, swindling carpetbaggers, it is Florida."[14] The Tallahassee Sentinel claimed in 1875 it had "never contended that
Republicanism in Florida" had been free from error, or that "all
its individual adherents" had been "models of propriety or para-
gons of honesty," but it had sought to show "that the general results of Republican government" had "been most gratifying" and
the results had been obtained only "through much tribulation" and
opposition.[15]

The scalawags, native whites who reputedly "betrayed" their
state to join the Republicans, were the most heartily hated of the
Republicans. From 1,500 to 2,000 white Floridians fell into that
class, and probably even more would have affiliated with the hated
party had they not feared the resulting intimidation and ostra-

---

13 Jacksonville Daily Florida Union, September 5, 1876.
14 Jacksonville Tri-Weekly Florida Union, June 22, 1871.
15 Tallahassee Sentinel, September 14, 1875.

cism.[16] Undoubtedly some scalawags allied with the Republicans for personal gain, but they actually had good reason to become staunch Union men. Not only were many whites allowed a larger share in government than ever before, but they were also offered services by the Republican party, education, for example, that previous Florida governments had denied them.[17] Furthermore, there had been several Union men in Florida who had opposed secession, and it was natural some of them would become Republicans. A good case can be made that the detested scalawags were more farseeing and statesmanlike than most Democrats. The carpetbaggers brought their progressive ideas ready-made from the North. The scalawags co-operated to put them in operation, and at the same time insured that control of the State would not fall into the hands of outsiders, while many Democrats either sulked and did nothing or determined to destroy the Republican party at any cost. The editor of the conservative Tallahassee *Floridian* wrote in 1868 that "our only hope is in the state's utter financial bankruptcy; and heaven grant that it may speedily come."[18] Many Democrats appeared to be angry not so much at Republican principles and actions, but because Republicans rather than Democrats were in office.

When the Republicans took office in 1868 their position was unenviable. They found "an empty treasury, society in a pathetically impoverished condition and a number of bankrupt railway systems." The public debt was over a half million dollars and the expenditures for the previous year had been $25,000 in excess of receipts. The future of the entire South was uncertain which made the task of financing the government difficult as investors lacked confidence in Florida's ability or willingness to pay its debts.[19] In addition to an acknowledged debt of $600,000 was a much larger sum that had been repudiated, thereby injuring the state's credit. During the war the school fund had been robbed to fight the North, the bankrupted railroads were half completed, revenue laws were inadequate to meet current expenses without paying interest on state debts, there was no school system, no state supported be-

---

[16] Davis, *op. cit.*, 483; *House Reports*, 42nd Cong., 2nd Sess., No. 22, pt. 13, 219-224.
[17] *The Florida Agriculturist*, I (January 17, 1874), 22.
[18] Quoted in Tallahassee *Sentinel*, October 7, 1876.
[19] Davis, *op. cit.*, 652-654.

nevolent institutions or alms houses, no penitentiary, and hardly a jail that deserved the name. The State was desolated by the war, and the Republicans "were savagely opposed by the majority of Southern whites."[20] The Republicans were further handicapped by a party split.

Despite serious obstacles, Republican rule proved beneficial to Florida in many ways. An educational system was devised which by 1872-1873 was reaching 19,196 pupils of all races at a cost of $103,907.06.[21] In 1875 over 32,000 pupils were in school at a cost in excess of $188,000, which was more than the total expenditures of the Florida government in 1867.[22] The "establishment of equal laws and the acknowledgement of equal rights" during Reconstruction was far in advance of anything previously witnessed in Florida.[23] Equality in the courts did not necessarily mean no discrimination against the freedmen, however. They were not always permitted equal privileges in restaurants and on public conveyances. In 1868 Governor Reed vetoed a bill entitled "An Act for the Protection of Citizens of Florida Traveling on Public Conveyances" because, he said, in attempting to secure the rights of one class the proposed law would "afford facilities for infringing the rights of others."[24] Repeated attempts to pass a civil rights bill failed until 1873. The act of 1873 proclaimed that no one should be "excluded from the full and equal enjoyment" of any accommodations "furnished by inn-keepers, by common carriers . . . by licensed owners, managers, or lessees of theatres or other places of public amusement." The law applied to public schools, but specifically exempted private schools and cemeteries.[25] The law was not vigorously enforced.[26] Institutions such as a prison and insane asylum were also created by the Republicans.[27]

One of the most important contributions of Reconstruction was the attempt to educate the State in the workings of democracy.

---

20 Ibid.; Florida, Senate Journal, 1870, 6.
21 Florida, House Journal, 1875, 36-37 in appendix.
22 U. S. Commissioner of Education, Report for the Year 1875, 65; Davis, op. cit., 672.
23 Florida, Senate Journal, 1870, 5.
24 New York Times, August 18, 1868; Florida House Journal 1869, 154.
25 Florida, Acts and Resolutions, 1873, 25.
26 Rerick, op. cit., I, 328.
27 Previously Florida had sent its insane to institutions of other states, and all prisoners were housed in county jails. Florida, Acts and Resolutions, 1874, 88; Florida, House Journal, 1861, 4 in appendix.

The constitution of 1868 disfranchised few whites, and Democrats were given a large number of state and county offices. More noteworthy, "Radical Reconstruction was an assault upon the theory of white supremacy. . . ." Republicans made no persistent attempt to gain social equality for the Negro, but "racial political equality was actually achieved."[28] Republican Reconstruction with all its shortcomings was "preferable to the infamous Black Codes" which in effect virtually nullified the Emancipation Proclamation and the Thirteenth Amendment. Johnsonian Reconstruction seemed to indicate that there was no middle ground. The Southern attitude left a choice between black codes and all they meant or "such free government as could be organized" with the support of Negroes.[29] Unfortunately many of the Democrats did not learn their lesson well. They refused to accept the results of a democratic state government, but the experience in self government was valuable to the Negroes.

In spite of Democratic charges of malfeasance which should have undermined faith in the government, the financial condition of Florida improved during Radical Reconstruction. In 1866 state expenditures were paid in scrip which frequently was not redeemed for as long as ten months, and could be sold at no less a discount than twenty-five cents on the dollar.[30] As late as 1874 it was said that state officials with salaries of $2,500 annually realized no more than $1,500 since they were paid in state scrip which did not sell at face value.[31] Conditions gradually improved. In 1870 the New York *Handels Zeitung*, a German language newspaper, wrote that no state was receiving more attention in the North than Florida. The prosperity of the southernmost state had been steadily advancing since the war, the paper continued, which brought capital from the North to promote railway interests, and to be invested in lands. The state government was "ably and honestly" administered, the *Zeitung* added.[32]

When confidence in the State increased, its financial condition improved. By November, 1875, scrip was selling at ninety cents,

---

[28] Simkins, *A History of the South*, 285.
[29] William A. Sinclair, *The Aftermath of Slavery* (Boston, 1905), 171.
[30] C. E. Dyke to B. F. Allen, January 22, 1866, in Records of the Department of State, Tallahassee, Florida.
[31] Jacksonville *Tri-Weekly Florida Union*, January 10, 1874.
[32] New York *Handels Zeitung*, May 28, 1870.

even in large sums. In April, 1876, it was reported that scrip was selling at ninety-five cents at the lowest, which meant citizens of Florida whether Republican or Democrat assumed the government was reasonably well managed, and had confidence in the present and future of the State. The price of scrip, which demonstrated the trust in the government, was in a sense a strong endorsement of the incumbent administration.[33]

For the first time since 1860 Florida had a balanced budget in 1873. From this time throughout Reconstruction the State enjoyed an excess of receipts over expenditures. By 1876 obligations of the government were being met, the government was being run in a more businesslike manner,[34] the principal of the public debt had been reduced by nearly $500,000, and capital and immigration were flowing into the State.[35] A visitor from New York wrote in 1875 that "few states are officered with more reliable and efficient men than Florida, and the result is peace and prosperity in her borders." Governor Stearns, the writer added, was "wide awake to every interest for the good of the State."[36] Even the Tallahassee *Floridian* admitted in 1874 that "peace, tranquility and a reasonable amount of virtuous industry prevail in this bailiwick at the present time."[37]

The Republicans expended considerable energy in advertising the good qualities of Florida in an attempt to stimulate an inpouring of capital and immigration. The Commissioner of Lands and Immigration published an annual report which was supposed to induce settlers to come to the State. Reconstruction witnessed an influx of Negroes to Florida, but the white population increased even more. The number of white citizens virtually doubled between 1860 and 1880 with growth from 77,746 to 142,605. The Negro population was augmented during the same period by about 64,000. Much of the Negro immigration occurred between 1868

---

[33] E. W. L'Engle to E. M. L'Engle, November 23, 1875, H. S. Elliott to E. M. L'Engle, November 25, 1875, in Edward M. L'Engle Papers; Jacksonville *Daily Florida Union*, April 24, 1876.

[34] In 1861 the comptroller reported that since 1848 there had been no entries made of warrants drawn upon the treasurer, and no accounts had been kept showing expenses for which the State was liable. The treasurer's accounts had never been properly balanced and were not in order. Tax collectors and sheriffs had defaulted to the amount of $107,785.46 without suits being instituted against them to force a settlement. Florida, *House Journal*, 1876, 1-3 in appendix.

[35] Jacksonville *Daily Florida Union*, April 24, 1876.

[36] *The Florida Agriculturist*, II (June 12, 1875), 191.

[37] Quoted in Jacksonville *Tri-Weekly Florida Union*, April 11, 1874.

and 1870. The major portion of white immigrants arrived in the State after 1870, increasing the population by 46,548, within the decade.[38] Many of the newcomers were homesteaders.[39]

Soon after the Republicans took office, Democrats began to charge them with extravagance. It is true that expenditures increased under the Republicans. Annual outlays rose from $187,-667.63 in 1867 to $234,233.80 in 1868 to a high in 1873 of $536,192.55.[40] After 1873 expenditures declined appreciably to $292,037.37 in 1874 and $290,561.43 in 1875.[41] Democratic charges that enlarged expenditures were due to extravagance and incompetence were ill founded. There were many reasons for the increased cost of government. New services offered by the state were expensive. In 1866 the State issued warrants amounting to $3,759.14 for education. In 1874 $139,870.61 was spent. Part of the latter sum came from a county tax and the Peabody fund, but $94,548.28 was spent by the State, which was over twenty-five times the amount spent in 1866.[42] Obviously the cost of public education accounted for a big part of the increased expenditures during Reconstruction. The Republicans also established a state prison, asylums, and built jails. Almost seven times more money was spent in 1874 than in 1866 in care of the insane. In 1866 Florida had no prison system. In 1875 prison expenses added up to $28,296.99.[43]

Cost of government was also increased because there were more officials. The governor's cabinet increased from five to eight, and circuit court judges from five to seven. In addition the legislature was augmented by six members. Not only did the number of officials grow, but salaries were raised. Governor Walker drew an annual salary of $4,000, while Reed received $5,000 in 1868. In 1866, $9,000 was required to pay members of the supreme court, and $21,000 for circuit court judges. In 1869 the supreme court

---

[38] *Tenth Census of the United States*, 1880, I, 378.

[39] J. T. Sprague to O. O. Howard, February 28, 1867, in Bureau Records, Florida; Tallahassee *Semi-Weekly Floridian*, January 11, 29, 1867.

[40] Davis, *op. cit.*, 672; Florida, *House Journal*, 1869, 1, 6 in appendix; 1874, 102 in appendix.

[41] Florida, *House Journal*, 1875, 9 in appendix; 1877, 14 in appendix; 1875, 37-38.

[42] *Ibid.*, 1866, 2-3 in appendix; 1875, 37-88 in appendix.

[43] Jacksonville *Daily Florida Union*, October 3, 1876; Florida, *House Journal*, 1866, 1 in appendix; 1877, 33 in appendix.

drew $12,500 and the circuit court members $24,500.[44] The Republicans themselves took action to decrease expenditures when, in 1869, George E. Wentworth introduced a resolution in the senate to lower the salary of governor to $3,500, chief justice from $4,500 to $3,000, associate justices $4,000 to $2,500, circuit court judges $3,500 to $2,500, cabinet officers $3,000 to $2,000, and lieutenant governor $2,500 to $500. The proposed amendment was accepted unanimously by the senate, and passed 38 to 5 in the house.[45] Even after the amendment decreased salaries, the increased number of officers required more money. Not only did salaries have to be paid to new officers, but operating expenses were necessary for new administrative departments such as the Commission of Lands and Immigration, which published an annual report to be circulated throughout the country.

Greater expenditures were necessary during Reconstruction because of the growth in population. An enlarged population and emancipation increased judicial expenses enormously.[46] Before the war the Negro was punished by his master, and during the Walker administration he was frequently given thirty-nine lashes and dismissed. Furthermore, the Freedmen's Bureau, and the military had borne some of the expenses resulting from Negro crimes. The number of cases before the courts so increased between 1866 and 1872 that the expenses for jurors and witnesses alone multiplied from $780.60 to $68,372.49.[47] The resistance to the courts led by the Ku Klux Klan was responsible for some of the additional expenses of the judicial department.[48] A conservative circuit judge for the Fourth District complained in 1871 that the state government was extravagant. When asked for particulars he answered that it had too many officers and circuit judges. Upon further questioning he admitted there were only seven circuit judges to cover the entire area of 60,000 square miles, and that he himself had not begun to get through his docket for the year.[49]

---

44 Tallahassee *Weekly Floridian*, June 14, 1870.
45 Florida, *Acts and Resolutions*, 1868, 216; 1871, 52; Florida, *Senate Journal*, Extra Session, 1869, 17, 62; Florida, *House Journal*, 1870, 80-81; U. S. Congress, *House Miscellaneous Documents*, 59th Cong., 2nd Sess., No. 357, II, 728.
46 Tallahassee *Sentinel*, September 4, 1875.
47 Florida, *House Journal*, 1866, 2-3 in appendix; 1874, 118 in appendix.
48 Tallahassee *Sentinel*, September 4, 1875.
49 *House Reports*, 42nd Cong., 2nd Sess., No. 22, pt. 13, 217-218.

Ordinary expenses were inflated by the higher prices that accompanied the war and Reconstruction. When, in 1866, the secretary of state told Dyke, Democratic editor of the *Floridian*, that his bid for printing the laws of Florida was *"extravagant"* Dyke replied that "things were not as they used to be." He claimed he paid double for labor and quadruple for paper as compared with 1860.[50] The printing costs of the government more than doubled between 1860 and 1866 before Republicans took office.[51] Printing costs under the Republicans did not rise appreciably. Indeed, the costs of printing in 1868 were considerably less than in 1866.[52] Still, there was generally a slight increase because more printing was done. Some of the appropriations of the Republicans went to pay debts incurred by their predecessors. In 1869 such items as $13,118.72 for interest on the state debt, and $893.53 principal and $355.94 interest on Indian hostilities of 1849 were paid by the State.[53] The necessity of operating on credit magnified the cost of government. The state penitentiary, Comptroller Gamble said in 1871, could have been managed at half the required sum if there had been funds in the treasury to pay necessary expenditures. Instead, the State was forced to sell its own paper at forty cents on the dollar.[54] The financial condition of the State improved by the end of Reconstruction, but in the meantime an empty treasury multiplied costs of government.

Evidence indicates that the Republicans were not extravagant. Increased costs were due to more government and changing times. Even without the services provided by Republicans, expenditures had increased about $50,000 from 1860 to 1867. If the cost of public education is subtracted, expenditures in 1874 were only about $10,000 more than in 1867, a not unwarranted increase with the larger population, more officials, and more services. In some

---

[50] C. E. Dyke to B. F. Allen, January 22, 1866, in Records of the Department of State, Tallahassee, Florida.

[51] Tallahassee *Weekly Floridian*, June 14, 1870.

[52] *Ibid.*; Florida, *House Journal*, 1869, 2 in appendix.

[53] In early 1849, four Seminole Indians murdered a white man on Indian River. There was no hint of concerted action by the Seminoles, but the State was soon in ferment. On January 13, 1849, the legislature requested federal relief. Troops were sent and two companies of the state militia were placed on duty. Before the troops could take action a party of about sixty Seminoles arrived at Tampa Bay with three of the culprits and the hand of the fourth who was killed resisting capture. The state militia saw no action, but had to be paid. *Ibid.*, 1870, 4 in appendix.

[54] *Ibid.*, 1871, 5 in appendix.

ways the earlier conservative Walker administration seemed to be more extravagant than the Republicans. In 1866 the secretary of the senate received $10.00 a day, in 1875 he received $8.00. The enrolling clerk received $9.00 per day in 1866 and $6.00 in 1875. The doorkeeper was paid $8.00 daily in 1866, $4.00 in 1875, while the messenger received $5.00 a day more in 1866 than in 1875.[55] There was a comparable difference in the salary of other legislative officers. Members of the legislature frequently received greater pay under Walker than during the Republican administrations. In 1866 the legislators set their salaries at $8.00 per diem for time in attendance upon the general assembly, including the time taken going to and from the Capital to be estimated by counting every twenty miles of travel as one day.[56] A round trip to Jacksonville, 160 miles from the Capital, could be made in two days. The legislator drew 16 days pay of $128 plus 10 cents per mile travel pay equaling $80 a day for the two day trip. Governor Walker vetoed the bill, but it was passed again despite his objections. Under this law a member from Key West drew $940 in 1866. The largest amount paid to a legislator in 1871 was $666.[57] Under the constitution of 1868, legislators were paid $500 annually and 10 cents per mile for travel.[58]

Increased expenditures during Reconstruction were justifiable, but the Republicans tried with success to lower the cost of government. Annual expenses decreased from $536,192 in 1873 to $290,261.43 in 1875. Two amendments passed in the session of 1874 to save money were accepted in 1875. One provided for biennial sessions of the legislature, and the other abolished county courts. It was estimated that the two amendments would reduce expenditures by $100,000 per year. In 1876 expenses amounted to $188,335.81, less than $1,000 more than spent by the Democrats in 1867.[59]

Another charge against Republicans was that the burden of taxation became intolerable. Increased government necessitated higher taxes. Taxes rose rapidly from 16 2/3 cents per year on

---

55 *Ibid.*, 1875, 9 in appendix; Jacksonville *Daily Florida Union*, October 11, 1876.
56 Florida, *Acts and Resolutions*, 1865, 71.
57 *Ibid.*, 98-99; 1871, 46-52.
58 *Ibid.*, Extra Session, 1869, 49-50.
59 Florida, *House Journal*, 1877, 7 in appendix.

$100 in 1860, to 50 cents in 1867 under the Democrats, and to $1.37 by 1872.[60] All of the tax was not a state levy. In 1869 the state tax was limited to one-half of one per cent on every $100 of property.[61] The tax ceiling was raised in 1872 to permit seven mills for legislative appropriations, one mill for schools, two mills for interest on the state debt and one mill for redemption of state bonds, which permitted a tax of $1,10 on each $100 of property.[62] Combined state and county taxes in 1872 were as high as $2.27 on $100 property in some counties.[63] In 1870 Edward M. L'Engle of Duval County paid $170.55 on $3,045 personal property, 1,038 acres of land and three city lots, which usually would not be considered as unreasonable. Of the total $99.95 was a county tax.[64] The tax was made even less burdensome by paying with state scrip purchased under par. Also, the owner was permitted to set the value of his own property which resulted in drastic underevaluation. In one case an owner who refused to sell a tract of land for $15,000 in 1874, valued it at $1,500 for purposes of taxation.[65] Land that had been sold at 80¢ an acre many years before was still being assessed at 80¢ in 1869 when it was selling for $10 to $20 per acre. Comptroller Gamble pointed out to the Bradford County clerk that in 1869 his county reported 71,237 acres of land valued at $163,296 and in 1870 reported 75,641 acres valued at $125,231, or 4,404 more acres in 1870 with a valuation of $38,068 less. The system of assessing the value of land made it necessary to raise taxes to secure sufficient revenue. Furthermore, the counties frequently failed to levy the full amount of tax directed by the comprtoller. The comproller apportioned the tax, but it was levied and collected by county officials. In 1871 at least fourteen counties levied less than ordered by the State.[66] Making the county responsible for assessments, levies, and collections proved to be one of the most serious weakness of the state financial system.

---

[60] *Ibid.*, 1872, 3 in appendix; Davis, *op. cit.*, 674.

[61] R. H. Gamble to G. P. Canova, August 5, 1870, in Comptrollers Letter Book; Florida, *Acts and Resolutions*, Extra Session, 1869, 13.

[62] *Ibid.*, 1872, 39.

[63] *Ibid.*, 1874, 11, 17; Florida, *House Journal*, 1872, 3 in appendix.

[64] Receipt for 1870, in Edward M. L'Engle Papers.

[65] Tallahassee *Sentinel*, October 10, 1874.

[66] R. H. Gamble to B. E. Tucker, July 23, 1870, in Comptrollers Letter Book; Florida, *House Journal*, 1874, 111 in appendix.

Even if property had been assessed at its full value, and the full amount levied, taxation would not have been excessive in comparison with other states. In 1870 taxes were higher in twelve states than in Florida, and the per capita tax was higher in twenty-nine states.[67] In 1876 the New York *South* reported that there were only four states in the Union with a lighter per capita tax than Florida. In New York each individual paid $11 while in Florida the levy was $2.60 per person.[68] Taxation was actually lighter for some portions of the population during Republican rule than it had been previously. While it increased the tax on the wealthy, the poor, especially the Negroes, paid less. In 1866 a capitation tax of $3 a year had been levied on all males between 21 and 55. Upon refusal to pay, the defaulter could be seized and hired out to anyone who would pay the tax and costs of proceedings. An additional one dollar poll tax was placed on Negroes for support of freedmen's schools. The use of a head tax worked to the advantage of wealthier whites. Besides the capitation tax, a duty of 50 cents on every $100 property was levied.[69] There were complaints about the high rate of taxation before the Republicans took office. In 1866 a man in Jacksonville complained that taxes were not "only onerous, but unequally and unfairly distributed among the inhabitants. . . ." A county judge resigned in 1867 because, he said, his position added to the "already heavy burden of unnecessary taxation placed upon our citizens."[70] If the increased services provided by the Republicans were justifiable so were the higher taxes.

Republicans were accused of running up a phenomenal state debt in Florida during Reconstruction. In reality it was negligible and defensible.[71] The state debt in 1866 was $638,681. In 1875 it was $1,329,690.18, an increase of only $691,009.18.[72] Democrats charged that the debt rose to over $5,000,000, but they were count-

---

67 Tallahassee *Sentinel*, July 3, 1875.
68 Quoted in Jacksonville *Daily Florida Union*, June 24, 1876.
69 Florida, *Acts and Resolutions*, 1865, 65-68.
70 S. R. Bonham to D. S. Walker, August 1, 1867, in Records of the Department of State, Tallahassee, Florida; Jacksonville *Florida Union*, July 21, 1866.
71 Democrats exaggerated the amount and importance of the State debt for political purposes, but many of them were genuinely concerned. They had been disturbed about the high cost of government even before Republicans assumed control.
72 Davis, *op. cit.*, 679; Florida, *House Journal*, 1877, 31 in appendix.

ing the $4,000,000 bonds issued to the Jacksonville, Pensacola, and Mobile Railroad. This sum could not be legitimately added to the debt because the State held a statutory lien on the Road.[73] The bonds were never paid by Florida.[74] The road was sold by the State to pay bondholders.[75] The increased debt does not seem immoderate in view of the increased services of the government, and the added expenses of operating with an empty treasury. Republicans were gradually paying off the debt when they left office. It was decreased by $37,000 in 1876 alone.[76]

Charges of corruption against the Republican regime were sometimes true even if magnified. Plural office holding was permitted. In 1869 C. R. Mobley, senator from the Twenty-Second District, was appointed state attorney for the Sixth Judicial District. A senate committee decided that since Mobley accepted the new appointment he was ineligible to to hold his seat in the senate, but several legislators did hold county offices, including Robert Meacham, Negro, of Jefferson County.[77] Reputedly one of the most widespread abuses was the suborning of legislators. Negro politician John Wallace claimed to know of several cases. In one incident, Wallace said, a Negro, George Witherspoon was given $500 and merchandise to vote for ex-governor Walker for the senate, but voted for Republican Samuel Walker. When Witherspoon was accosted for not voting properly, he claimed to have fulfilled his obligation by voting for "Walker." Carpetbaggers also used bribes, Wallace said.[78] Most of the charges of bribery are impossible to substantiate, but undoubtedly it did occur, though a witness hostile to the incumbent administration testified in 1870 that before the war bribery was common. He concluded, "in this state I am glad to say that we are pretty much free of that kind of thing; there is nobody to bribe or be bribed."[79] Such a device for influencing public officials was peculiar neither to Reconstruction nor the South.

Defaulting tax collectors was another evil existent in Florida. Collectors defaulted to the extent of $48,435.62 in 1866-1867 and

---

73 *Ibid.*, 1874, 100 in appendix.
74 *Florida Reports*, XV, 455-56.
75 Jacksonville *Daily Florida Union*, January 24, 1876.
76 Florida, *House Journal*, 1877, 6 in appendix.
77 Florida, *Senate Journal*, 1869, 40, 43.
78 Wallace, *op. cit.*, 269-70, 273, 276, 300, 317-18.
79 *House Reports*, 42nd Cong., 2nd Sess., No. 22, pt. 13, 252.

there were similar occurences after the Republicans came into office.[80] The revenue law, Comptroller Gamble complained in 1871, was "so incongruous in its provisions and conflicting in its operation" that there could "be no surety that the revenue collected" would find its way to the treasury.[81] In 1873 Gamble said he had reason to believe some of the revenue collected was in the hands of tax officials who were little concerned with making a settlement because of the failure to prosecute them criminally, and the worthlessness of their bonds if a civil suit was initiated.[82] In the same year the legislature enacted a law to tighten the system of collection. Every collector was required to give bond, with at least two sureties, of $2,000 in excess of state and county duties levied the preceeding year. Previously the bonds were approved by the county commissioners, but now they had to be sanctioned by the attorney general and comptroller as well. After the collector received the annual tax list he was required to make a weekly report during November and December and a statement every two months the rest of the year. In the report the collector was required, under oath, to give a return of all money received. Failure to make such a return was deemed a felony and was punishable by imprisonment of not less than six months or more than two years, and a fine equal to the defalcation. A convicted collector was forever disqualified from holding office.[83] The revenue system in Florida was vulnerable to attack before and during Reconstruction.

Another supposed fraud of the period was the disappearance of a sum of state scrip. Responsibility for the loss or theft lay between Comptroller Gamble and Treasurer Simon B. Conover. In 1876 Governor Stearns wrote the attorney general that the comptroller's report for 1875 disclosed a deficiency in the comptroller's office in 1871 and frauds in the treasurer's office. It is of the highest public importance that immediate steps should be taken to investigate these transactions," the Republican governor said, "and the responsible parties held to the strictest accounta-

---

[80] Florida, *House Journal*, Extra Session, 1869, 14; R. H. Gamble to H. Reed, July 15, 1870, in Comptrollers Letter Book.
[81] Florida, *House Journal*, 1871, 8-9 in appendix.
[82] Florida, *Senate Journal*, 1873, 3 in appendix.
[83] Florida, *Acts and Resolutions*, 1873, 9-10.

bility."[84] In January, 1871, Gamble had been ordered by the legislature to turn $37,266 of scrip over to Conover. There was no evidence in the accounts of the comptroller or treasurer to show that the order was obeyed, though Gamble, a Democrat, claimed he had given the scrip to Conover, but had lost his receipt.[85] After suit was brought against Conover, on the evidence of Gamble, the latter decided that Conover was not responsible. Gamble did not know what happened to the scrip. Perhaps, he said, it had never been delivered to Conover, or it had been and was returned, or he had exchanged it for warrants.[86] Gamble later maintained he had exchanged the scrip for warrants, but had neglected to make a record of the exchange, and for some unknown reason "the warrants received as vouchers were lost or destroyed."[87] Probably Gamble did not steal the script, but there is some evidence of incompetence. There were many other errors in his accounts. Conover was also charged with having paid $13,556.01 in 1871-1872 for warrants issued in 1852, which had been previously paid.[88] The Democrats were strangely silent on the issue, preferring that charges of incompetence and fraud be made against Republicans, not Democrats, in office.

The biggest scandal in Florida during Reconstruction involved the attempt to develop a railroad system. Railway schemes in the State before the war and during Reconstruction were accompanied by charges of trickery and inefficiency. A Florida Democrat and ex-Confederate general, Joseph Finegan, wrote in 1868, that before and after the war private agents were used to select the best lands granted the Florida Railroad Company for a favored few. The company had been formed in 1853, and was under the leadership of Senator David L. Yulee. Finegan charged Yulee with swindling the "honest bondholder" of the company in "some of the most gross,

---

84 Conover was born in Middlesex County, New Jersey, September 23, 1840. He studied medicine at the University of Pennsylvania and became an acting assistant surgeon in 1863. In 1866 Conover was assigned to Lake City. He attended the constitutional convention of 1868, became treasurer in 1868, and a United States Senator in 1873. M. L. Stearns to W. A. Cocke, February 17, 1876, in Governor's Letter Book, Florida State Library, Tallahassee, Florida; *Biographical Directory, op. cit.*, 841.
85 Florida, *House Journal*, 1877, 26 in appendix.
86 Jacksonville *Daily Florida Union*, February 25, 1876.
87 Florida, *House Journal*, 1877, 1 in appendix.
88 *Ibid.*, 14 in appendix.

flagrant and unblushing frauds" that had ever been perpetrated. The ex-general, who made the charge directly to Yulee, was not alone in accusing the rebel senator.[89] After the war, Yulee and friends were permitted to bid in lands of the Florida Railroad Company for one cent per acre to be paid for with company bonds. All the lands were ceded to less than "all the bondholders." Some of the railroad builders before the war "had a tendency to make eceedingly liberal use of state financial support."[90] Such practices led Republican Liberty Billings to read a letter exposing some of the "sharp management" of the Florida Railroad Company in the constitutional convention of 1868.[91] A Florida Democrat, Samuel A. Swann, claimed in 1867 that Yulee's railroad was "managed with so little vigor, with such an impolitic penuriousness, that the thing drags along on an old-fogy existence" without life, and with management that "discourages all enterprise among local merchants and capitalists from abroad." Swann added that a proposed railroad from Fernandina to Cedar Keys and from Jacksonville to Lake City, started in 1859-1860, had "proved abortive under the gross mismanagement of incompetent and dishonest men. . . ." By 1868 railroad schemes had cost the State over $3,000,000.[92]

After the Republicans took office in 1868, they were desirous of building a system of railways. In his message to the extra session of the legislature in 1869, Governor Reed maintained that "the railroad system of the state should be prosecuted to completion as early as possible, in order that the business of Florida may not be absorbed by the superior energy and capital" of other states, and so that Florida "may receive her full share of the immigration and capital now flowing southward." The "policy of the legislature," Reed said, "should be to protect the interest of the people" while at the same time fostering the development of internal improvements, which was "the most efficient means of

---

89 J. Finegan and J. C. McGehee to J. McRae, August 22, 1868, J. Finegan to D. L. Yulee, August 5, 1867, E. N. Dickerson to F. Dose, December 19, 1867, in David L. Yulee Papers.

90 J. McRae to J. Soutter, January 18, 1869, in David L. Yulee Papers; Paul E. Fenlon, "The Nortorious Swepson-Littlefield Fraud: Railroad Financing in Florida, 1868-1871," Florida Historical Quarterly, XXXII (April, 1954), 233.

91 New York Tribune, February 8, 1868.

92 S. A. Swann to (?) Boyas, September 12, 1867, S. A. Swann to J. E. Garey, September 25, 1867, in Samuel A. Swann Papers; Florida, House Journal, 1872, 35-36.

strengthening the government and bringing prosperity to the state." Railroads should be given as much aid as could be afforded consistently with the interests of the people and the credit of the State, Reed added. "In all measures the public interests should be first secured," the governor asserted, "and then the widest inducements, within that limit, offered for the profitable investment of capital." Reed suggested the Pensacola and Georgia Railway should be encouraged in order to connect Florida with the Southern Pacific line.[93]

The legislature, Democrats and Republicans, agreed with the governor. On June 24, 1869, an act was approved to incorporate the Jacksonville, Pensacola and Mobile Railroad Company "to secure the speedy completion, equipping, and the maintenance of a connection" by rail between Jacksonville, Pensacola, and Mobile. The major members of the new company were George W. Swepson, a North Carolina railroad financier, Milton S. Littlefield, an agent for Swepson, and J. P. Sanderson, a Florida Democrat and supporter of the defeated Confederacy.[94] Swepson had reputedly already defrauded the State of over $750,000 in the purchase in early 1869 of the defunct Pensacola and Georgia Railroad running from Lake City to Quincy, and the Tallahassee Railroad Company, operating between the Capital and St. Marks.[95] The act incorporating the Jacksonville, Pensacola and Mobile Railroad Company provided for state aid in constructing new track to the amount of $14,000 a mile, state bonds to be issued the company from time to time upon the completion of specified amounts of trackage. To further aid the company its bonds could be exchanged for state bonds which would probably sell for a greater price. As security the State held a statutory lien on all rights, property, and franchises of the company.[96] the act was passed unanimously in the senate and thirty-nine to three in the house.[97]

On the surface there was little to criticize about the incorporation of the J.P. and M. Railroad, but the earlier shady dealings of Swepson should have alerted the legislators. Despite rumors of

---

[93] *Ibid.*, Extra Session, 1869, 9-10.
[94] Florida, *Acts and Resolutions*, Extra Session, 1869, 29.
[95] For an account of the Swepson fraud see Felon, *op. cit.*, 236-242.
[96] Florida, *Acts and Resolutions*, Extra Session, 1869, 31, 32, 36.
[97] Florida, *Senate Journal*, Extra Session, 1869, 70; Florida, *House Journal*, Extra Session, 1869, 78-79.

fraud most citizens seemed ready to accept Swepson's plans for Florida in good faith. The usually critical Tallahassee *Floridian* seemingly expressed the sentiments of most citizens when in September, 1869, it wrote: "Go on Mr. Swepson, in your noble enterprise . . . let us have the happy assurance that the iron horse will carry us all the way to Pensacola."[98] Swepson attempted to gain support in the State by explaining what such a railway could do for Florida, used his influence to make Sanderson vice-president of the J. P. and M. and met for a frank discussion in New York with Sanderson and Edward M. L'Engle, an ex-Confederate officer and lawyer of high repute from Jacksonville. L'Engle and Sanderson both expressed their faith in Swepson's solvency and integrity.[99]

Accusations of fraud against Swepson, and charges that Littlefield had bribed members of the legislature to secure passage of the act, prevented Swepson from exchanging railroad bonds for those of the state. The issuance of state bonds was made possible in 1870 by a law directing Governor Reed to deliver bonds of $16,000 per mile for the entire length of the road owned by the J. P. and M. Railroad. The previous act had provided $14,000 aid. The act of 1870 further ordered the governor to issue bonds for the road already completed to Quincy.[100] Governor Reed was still hesitant to issue bonds to the railroad because Swepson had not yet settled his accounts for the purchase of the two railroads early in 1869. In May, 1870, Reed said he understood that the State had promised no aid before "completion of work on the sections of railroad for which State bonds were to be issued."[101] But, within a few days he issued $4,000,000 of state bonds to Littlefield's agents after Sanderson and M. D. Pappy, a fire-eating Democratic attorney, tendered a written opinion that the issue was legal.

Three million dollars were exchanged for J. P. and M. Railroad bonds and $1,000,000 for those of the Florida Central, which had not been mentioned in the act of 1869.[102] Some of the bonds were never sold. One million dollars of bonds were immediately tied up by Littlefield creditors, but $2,800,000 were sold by S. W. Hopkins and Company of New York to a Dutch syndicate. They sold

---

[98] Fenlon, *op. cit.*, 248-51; Tallahassee *Floridian*, September, 28, 1869.
[99] *Ibid.*, 234-36, 248-51.
[100] Florida, *Acts and Resolutions*, 1870, 10, 13.
[101] Fenlon, *op. cit.*, 253.
[102] *Ibid.*, 254, 255.

for about two-thirds their face value and Littlefield agreed to accept forty-eight per cent, the balance to go to the Hopkins firm for its expenses. From the $1,358,000 supposed to be paid Littlefield, Hopkins and Company deducted $340,000 to pay interest on the bonds and for their commission. Of the $1,018,000 remaining, only about one-third was used to construct or improve the Jacksonville, Pensacola and Mobile Railroad facilities. The rest went to pay Swepson and Littlefield's debts, legal expenses, and for Littlefield's tour of Europe trying to sell the bonds.[103] The State was not liable for the misappropriated money.

In January, 1876, the State Supreme Court declared that the issued bonds were void. Governor Stearns advertised the sale of the railroad to pay the Dutch bondholders, but was ousted from office before the sale could be transacted. Eventually the J. P. and M., and the Florida Central were sold by the State and the proceeds of $355,000 went to the bondholders.[104] An additional $1,000,000 of bonds were issued to the South Florida Railroad on July 1, 1871. The bonds disappeared and malfeasance was charged against the largest stockholder of the road, David L. Yulee, who claimed the bonds were never issued. After an investigation they were located, unnegotiated, $840,000 of them lying in the express office in Jacksonville.[105]

There is no doubt that dishonesty was involved in the transactions concerning the Jacksonville, Pensacola and Mobile Railroad. Littlefield and Swepson, according to the United States Supreme Court, had both "shown themselves capable of the most shameless frauds. . . ."[106] The question is to what extent were officials of the State implicated. It has been charged that Littlefield bribed members of the legislature, and paid Governor Reed $12,500 to support his schemes. Probably there was some bribery, but the money that went to Reed was apparently a loan. In 1871 Littlefield

---

103 *Ibid.*, 255-57; C. K. Brown, "The Florida Investments of George W. Swepson," *The North Carolina Historical Review*, V (July, 1928), 282; Florida, *Senate Journal*, 1873, 198.

104 The issue of the $4,000,000 bonds was declared void because part of the road was to be constructed outside the State. The constitution provided for state aid to internal improvements of an intrastate character. *Ibid.*, 288; Jacksonville *Daily Florida Union*, January 24, 1876; *Florida Reports*, XV, 455-56.

105 L. G. Dennis to D. L. Yulee, February 18, 1873, D. S. Walker to D. L. Yulee, February 18, 1873; H. B. Crosby to E. N. Dickerson, July 22, 1873, C. A. Cowgill to D. L. Yulee, July 23, 1873, in David L. Yulee Papers.

106 U. S. *Supreme Court Reports*, 103, 336.

wrote L'Engle that "at the Freedmen's Bank you will find a mortgage of Governor Reed for $12,500." He asked L'Engle to examine the mortgage and determine if the security was good for an advance.[107] After the New York *World* intimated in 1870 that Reed had been bribed, E. N. Dickerson, President of the Florida Railroad Company, wrote that "there is no truth in the slander upon Governor Reed." He pointed out that Reed had refused to issue the bonds in 1869, and if he had been bribed as charged he would have made the issue then.[108]

That some state officials were involved in the scheme is likely, but cannot be substantiated. "If any mistakes were made," or if there was any "malversation," it cannot be attributed to any one political party or group. If the incorporators had been honorable and had made honest application of the aid rendered, the State lien would have been adequate security. Authorization of the issue of bonds in aid of the J. P. and M. was considered by Republicans and Democrats alike as "a most excellent measure or scheme for . . . developing the western section of the State." The Democrats supported the measure, though Littlefield said one of the Democratic senators "claimed, and was paid, the legislative swag of two members."[109]

Important Democrats in the State worked closely with Littlefield, including Yulee, Sanderson, and L'Engle. They exerted their influence to secure passage of the bill. Samuel A. Swann wrote to a friend concerning railroad lands, while the legislature was in session to pass the bill, that *"everything depends on the action of the Legislature,* and Mr. Yulee's success in manipulating matters in Tallahassee."[110] On June 17, 1869, Littlefield wrote to Yulee that "at the suggestion of several friends of the Railroads I write to ask you to appoint a meeting—private . . . at your earliest convenience."[111] Ex-governor Walker reportedly accepted a $1,000 retainer from Littlefield at the time of the application for state aid

---

[107] M. S. Littlefield to E. M. L'Engle, July 12, 1871, in Edward M. L'Engle Papers.

[108] E. N. Dickerson to Messrs. Drake Brothers, July 15, 1870, in David L. Yulee Papers.

[109] Tallahassee *Sentinel*, September 4, 1875.

[110] S. A. Swann to A. H. Cole, June 11, 1869, in Samuel A. Swann Papers.

[111] M. S. Littlefield to D. L. Yulee, June 17, 1869, in David L. Yulee Papers.

to the Jacksonville, Pensacola, and Mobile Railroad.[112] John A. Henderson, an important Democrat in the senate was an attorney for Littlefield, and as an attorney argued in 1871 that the issue of bonds was constitutional. Henderson was also on the senate committee which unanimously reported in favor of the original bill authorizing the issue of state bonds. In the winter of 1872 Henderson with other Democrats claimed to be horrified at the fraudulent issue of bonds.[113]

So many unfounded charges were made against the Republicans it is difficult to determine which ones are valid. In 1870 Charles E. Dyke wrote an article, "Plundering Rings," in the Tallahassee *Floridian* saying the West Florida Railroad Company was incorporated by Republicans who had divided the capital stock of the company among themselves. Investigation of records show that Charles E. Dyke, Sr., was one of the incorporators.[114]

In January, 1872, the official organ of the administration, the Tallahassee *Sentinel,* accused the J. P. and M. Railroad of fraud. The company had been dealt with generously by the State, the paper said, but the road had not been advanced by as much as twenty miles. "It has proven itself to be a fraudulent, insolent, arrogant, bold, unscrupulous, and remorseless concern," the *Sentinel* added.[115] The *Floridian* had been criticizing the company, but after the *Sentinel* called for an investigation, the Democratic organ maintained that "the character of the trustees, who have the entire disposition of the income, is a sure guarantee of honest and fair dealings."[116]

Republicans, especially Governor Stearns, exerted themselves to protect the interests of the State and the bondholders. The final disposition of the J. P. and M. Railroad by the Democrats was initiated by Stearns. Despite charges which have left a "lasting impression there were few Negroes involved in the Swepson-Littlefield operations." There were venal Negroes, some may have been bribed, but according to Jonathan Daniels, biographer of Little-

---

[112] Tallahassee *Sentinel,* August 12, 1870.
[113] *Ibid.,* September 26, October 3, 1874; Florida, *Senate Journal,* Extra Session, 1869, 68.
[114] Tallahassee *Sentinel,* March 19, 1870; Florida, *Acts and Resolutions,* 1870, 82.
[115] *Ibid.,* January 27, 1872.
[116] Quoted in *Ibid.,* February 3, 1872.

field, "there were plenty of white men, most of them native, insisting as a natural, racial right, upon places first in line." Daniels
said there were no freedmen financiers or politicians involved in
the Swepson plans in Florida in the summer of 1869. At a
strategy meeting in New York in 1869 "Littlefield was the only
stranger" among Southerners.[117] Those most intimately associated
with railroads in Florida, those who were in a position to gain personally were white Florida Democrats. Republican efforts to "restore Florida's transportation and revive her development" were
commendable and "their reports evidenced a genuine perception of
the needs of the state" but unfortunately their ideas were in advance of performance.[118]

Charges of plunder against Republican Reconstruction administrations in Florida have been grossly exaggerated. There was
probably more "pilfering than plunder on a scale to permanently
cripple the State." Most of the testimony concerning corruption
was given "by bitter political opponents who constituted themselves judge, witness and jury. . . ."[119] Democrats who accused the
Republicans of dishonesty apparently forgot that ante-bellum
quarrels "had produced ugly charges of dishonesty, of a deliberate
seeking after monopolistic control of the State resources," and "of
exploitation of the states credit for individual or partisan ends."
Some of the pre-war charges were true.[120]

During Reconstruction native whites were as corrupt as the
Negroes and carpetbaggers. In 1875 a Republican paper admitted its party had some dishonest men, and it had made
some grievous errors, but added, "there is some comfort in knowing
that where the most egregious blunders were made, and where
indications of fraud were most apparent, Democrats were always
as deep in the mud as Republicans were in the mire."[121] Malfeasance was not peculiar to Republicans, the South, or the Reconstruction period.

Republicans were accused of squandering state resources. Before the war the State reportedly sold between 500,000 and 1,000,000
acres of public land, but accounted for only $45,000. In 1881 the

[117] Daniels, op. cit., 212-13.
[118] Abbey, op. cit., 347.
[119] DuBois, op. cit., 615-16.
[120] Davis, op. cit., 664.
[121] Tallahassee Sentinel, September 4, 1875.

state officials sold 4,000,000 acres of land for twenty-five cents an acre to a syndicate headed by Hamilton Disston of Philadelphia. Within the firm was an improvement company which was given an additional 1,000,000 acres of land for draining a 2,000,000 acres area. Disston sold 1,000,000 acres to Sir Edward J. Reed of England "at a price which nearly reimbursed him for his entire expenditure" and sold the rest for $1.25 per acre and above. The Disston land purchase was attended by illegal practices and was responsible for uprooting many squatters. In 1884 a Floridian maintained that the legislature had attempted to grant to proposed railroads 22,360,000 acres out of a public domain which did not exceed 14,831,739.04 acres. Negroes and Carpetbaggers "in all their glory could hardly match such deeds."[122]

In the final analysis "Radical" Reconstruction in Florida was much better than portrayed by most historians. In the first place, it was not very radical. Concessions were made to the Conservatives in the constitutional convention of 1868 and Republicans continued to appoint to office, and attempt to co-operate with their Democratic opponents. No man's rights of person were invaded under the guise of the law, the Democrat's life, property, and business were safe, his path to the ballot box was not obstructed by force, no one attempted to interfere with his freedom of speech, nor was he boycotted because of his political principles. The Negro was more able and less venal than charged. Republicans made significant contributions to the State including public education, a more democratic government, creation of public institutions, rights for Negroes, and an improved financial structure. Taxation was not unreasonable, the state debt was not excessive, and corruption of the period has been exaggerated. The words written in 1870 by a Republican, William B. White, are applicable to the entire Reconstruction era in Florida. He wrote:

> looking back over the history of the State for the last ten years, so full of excitement, and turmoil, we are profoundly impressed with a sense of the value of the results of the reconstruction legislation of the National Government, and

---

[122] C. Vann Woodward, *Origins of the New South 1877-1913* (Baton Rouge, 1951), 117; Francis P. Fleming, Commercial Development, typescript in Fleming Papers, Florida Historical Society Collection, University of South Florida, Tampa, Florida; T. Frederick Davis, "The Disston Land Purchase," *Florida Historical Quarterly*, XVII, (April, 1939), 206.

its subsequent result in the organization of our State government. While we cannot claim that this legislation is
absolutely perfect, or the results to be altogether those that
may have been desired, yet knowing well the thousand
difficulties that, from the peculiar situation and characteristics of the whole South, would necessarily hang around and
embarrass any attempt at adequate legislation at the hand
of merely human law-givers, we believe that as a whole the
legislation of reconstruction originated from patriotic motives, was framed in a friendly spirit . . . and is as well
fitted to promote the ultimate prosperity of the Southern
States, and the well-being of their citizens, as could be hoped
of any legislation that could have been expected under the
circumstances.[123]

As White said Republican legislation was not perfect, and Republican rule was not all that could be desired, but in view of
the many needs of the State, and the unprincipled opposition, they
did as well as could be expected. As far as the future of the Negro
was concerned, and perhaps the State at large, it was unfortunate
that Republicans lost office in 1876.

---

[123] Florida, *House Journal*, 1870, 171.

CHAPTER XVI

THE END OF AN ERA

The election of 1876 and the resulting Democratic victory in Florida marked the end of Republican strength in the State, but the election was merely the climax of a movement that had begun several years earlier. The overthrow of Republican rule did not happen suddenly in 1876. It had been in the making since Republicans took office, and the party itself was partially responsible for its own collapse. The party was divided into three groups as early as 1867. The breach was never fully healed, and it became worse during the constitutional convention of 1868 with the struggle between conservative and radical factions. The radicals lost the battle, and many of them always believed the conservative Republicans had sold out to Democrats. As early as November, 1867, Liberty Billings accused the former Union soldiers in the party of desiring to perpetuate slavery, and claimed the Republican party of Jacksonville was half copperhead (a copperhead being a Northerner with Southern principles). In turn, conservative Republicans maintained that Billings was an ambitious demagogue and a vote for Billings was a vote against the party.[1] Conservative Republicans continued to attack Billings and his cohort Daniel Richards. In January, 1868, Richards was expelled from the Republican State Central Committee, because as a member said, it was believed he was neither a "true radical republican" nor "an honest man" and was "working not for the interest of the people, but for his own personal advancement."[2]

After Reed became governor in 1868 the party rupture was intensified. The governor appointed many Democrats to office much to the disappointment of a few of the carpetbagger type.[3] Even some Republicans who were sincerely interested in the State believed Reed was going too far in his efforts to appease Southern

---

[1] Jacksonville *Florida Union*, November 9, 1867.
[2] *Ibid.*, January 11, 1868.
[3] Cortez A. M. Ewing, "Florida Reconstruction Impeachments," *The Florida Historical Quarterly*, XXXVI (April, 1958), 300.

whites. Especially the freedmen thought the governor was neglecting their best interests. But, the appointment of Gibbs as secretary of state in late 1868 brought the Negroes to Reed's support, and they proved to be a major bulwark between Reed and impeachment.[4]

Some Republicans blamed the party squabble on the "inordinate personal ambition" of a few men, primarily Thomas W. Osborn, who was elected United States Senator in 1868. There was a struggle for power in the State between Osborn and followers and the Reed camp.[5] Throughout Reconstruction there was antagonism between state and federal officeholders.[6] John Wallace in his book *Carpetbag Rule in Florida* claimed the rift was between honest and corrupt Republicans, Reed and followers being honest and Osborn and followers known as the "Ring" being the corrupt element.[7] This explanation is too simple. There were honest men in both factions. Ambition, personal antagonism and a sincere difference of opinion as to how Reconstruction could best be handled, probably played greater roles. Divisions on the local level reputedly developed in some counties between Negroes and carpetbaggers.[8]

The cleavage in Republican ranks was aggravated by the shrewdness of Democrat Charles E. Dyke, Sr. Republican infighting left the party vulnerable and Dyke was able to widen the breach by attacking one group for corruption, while giving qualified praise to the other. He sometimes assailed all Republicans, but usually reserved at least some applause for a few. He was most successful in kindling the flames in Leon County. He convinced John Wallace that he was merely opposing corruption and received considerable support from the Negro legislator. Wallace kept the party divided in Leon County from 1870 throughout Reconstruction. Wallace and cohorts frequently voted with the Democrats in the legislature, and claims in his book to the contrary, Wallace campaigned against the Republican ticket in 1876. Wallace held

---

    [4] *Ibid.*, 303; Wallace, *op. cit.*, 90-91.
    [5] Wallace, *op. cit.*, 271, 295; Tallahassee *Sentinel*, September 5, 1874.
    [6] H. A. L'Engle to E. M. L'Engle, August 1, 1874, in Edward M. L'Engle Papers; Jacksonville *Daily Florida Union*, January 31, 1876; Tallahassee *Sentinel*, May 27, 1876.
    [7] Wallace, *op. cit.*, 295; Tallahassee *Weekly Floridian*, August 4, 1874.
    [8] *Ibid.*, July 22, 1874.

a federal office and was a co-worker with Congressman William J. Purman.[9]

Dyke was aided in his plan by Democrats who were serving under Republicans. Robert H. Gamble for instance was not a loyal subordinate, nor was William A. Cocke, the Democratic attorney general under Hart and Stearns, but they refused to resign.[10] The Democratic editor also formed an alliance with Simon B. Conover, secretary of treasury under Reed. Republicans accused Conover and Dyke of try to bring both parties under their leadership and of seeking spoils of office.[11] Conover was sent to the United States Senate in 1873 with Democratic votes. Even the staunchly Democratic Monticello *Constitution* said there might be some truth in the rumor that Dyke and Conover were trying to assume control of the State, adding, "we must remember that in the memorable Senatorial contest of 1873, certain Democrats proved recreant to their party" and assisted in electing Conover to the senate. Democratic votes were also used to keep Wallace in the legislature as an agitator.[12] Dyke was a shrewd political wire puller and succeeded in virtually destroying the Republican party in Leon County and increasing dissention on the State level. Dyke was probably the most astute politician in the State.[13]

One result of the Republican schism was attempts to impeach Reed. Reed had the unpleasant distinction of being threatened with legislative removal on four different occasions, but served out his term of office. Democrats took advantage of the Republican split to attack the administration for graft. These attacks were not aimed so much at what was thought to be the corrupt element of the party but at Reed. One historian has concluded that to the Democrats "an honest administration was the thing to be most

[9] Wallace, *op. cit.*, 265-67, 293, 295; Tallahassee *Weekly Floridian*, November 1, 1870, July 28, August 4, 1874; Jacksonville *Daily Florida Union*, March 29, 1876; H. Elliott to E. M. L'Engle, February 20, 1875, in Edward M. L'Engle Papers.

[10] Cocke was born in Virginia, practiced law in Richmond, and migrated to Florida in 1863. O. B. Hart to W. A. Cocke, January 2, 1874, in Governor's Letter Book.

[11] Tallahassee *Sentinel*, July 11, 1874; Jacksonville *Daily Florida Union*, April 19, 1876.

[12] Quoted in Jacksonville *Daily Florida Union*, April 22, 1876.

[13] E. W. L'Engle to E. M. L'Engle, November 23, 1874, E. M. L'Engle to E. W. L'Engle, November 28, 1874, in Edward M. L'Engle Papers.

feared and fought."[14] The governor was submitted to repeated attacks and character assassinations.

Democratic attacks gave Reed's Republican enemies an excuse to take action. There had already been "veiled threats that impeachment would be used if the governor did not show more interest in 'Republican welfare.' "[15] The quarrel became worse when the legislature met on November 3, 1868, to choose presidential electors. After the choice was made Reed called a special session at the request of the legislature. It immediately passed an appropriation bill for per diem and mileage, which Reed vetoed on the ground they had already received their salary for the year and were entitled to mileage only.[16] Charges were brought against Reed and with little deliberation a resolution impeaching him was adopted in the house 25 to 6. The governor was accused of falsehood, incompetence, embezzlement, bribery, and of declaring "seats of the legislature vacant before the members duly elected and returned had resigned or legal term of service expired."[17] Reed had tried to prevent plural office holding. Lieutenant Governor Gleason[18] declared himself empowered by the constitution to take over the duties of governor until the outcome of impeachment had been decided. Claiming the senate did not have a quorum when impeachment was reported and received, Reed, on November 9, 1868, appealed to the State Supreme Court for an opinion as to whether he had been impeached lawfully. Secretary of State Alden, a native white, deserted Reed, took the Great Seal of the State and joined Gleason who had established an office in a hotel. Reed cursorily deposed Alden and appointed Gibbs secretary of state. On November 24, the supreme court rendered a de-

14 Ackerman, op. cit., 141.
15 Ewing, op. cit., 300.
16 Ibid.; Wallace, op. cit., 89.
17 Ewing, op. cit., 302; Wallace, op. cit., 89; Florida, Senate Journal, Extra Session, 1868, 24-25; Florida, House Journal, Extra Session, 1868, 41-42.
18 Gleason was born in New York in 1830. In 1848 he emigrated to Wisconsin and became a land surveyor and civil engineer. The Floridian credited him with contributing greatly to the development of Wisconsin. He was a member of the Wisconsin legislature 1853-1855. Gleason amassed a sizable fortune in land and railroad operations, but wartime financial injuries led him to go to Florida at the close of the war. He co-operated with Florida financiers and was reputedly involved in some shady land deals. Tallahassee Weekly Floridian, March 10, 1868; Jacksonville Tri-Weekly Florida Union, January 17, 1874.

cision upholding Reed's contention.[19] In the meantime Reed inaugurated a policy of reprisal. On November 19, through the attorney general, he filed a petition in the State Supreme Court asking for a writ of *quo warranto* against the lieutenant governor, maintaining that Gleason did not qualify for his office as he had not been a citizen of Florida for three years as required by article V section 14 of the constitution.[20] Gleason was disqualified on December 14, by the court.[21]

On January 5, the first day of the 1869 session, Negro Auburn Erwin introduced a resolution to investigate the charges recently presented against Reed. The next day a similar resolution was accepted in the house 30 to 5, all the dissenters being Republicans. On January 26, an investigating committee presided over by a Democrat, George F. Raney, recommended impeachment. A minority report submitted by Erwin and another Republican, announced that papers, documents, and witnesses had produced nothing "upon which the charges of wrongful or illegal conduct of the Governor can be sustained." The majority report was adopted 24 to 19, with 11 Negroes voting nay.[22] On the same day the house voted 43 to 5 to accept a resolution introduced by Negro Emanuel Fortune that the "Assembly finds nothing in said report or testimony justifying an impeachment" of Reed.[23] Daniel Richards claimed credit for saving Reed from Osborn and the Democrats.[24]

A third attempt was made to impeach Reed in January, 1870. The governor sent a message to the legislature saying that in view of the accusations made against him he thought an impartial committee should be appointed to examine all charges himself and other officers.[25] Such a committee was appointed and again the majority report recommended impeachment on the basis of bribery and embezzlement. The minority report written by Republican William B. White said, "while entertaining grave doubts of the propriety of certain acts" of the governor, we find the charges

[19] Ewing, *op. cit.*, 304; Wallace, *op. cit.*, 91; Ackerman, *op. cit.*, 147; New York *Tribune*, February 8, 1868.
[20] Florida, *Acts and Resolutions*, 1868, 200-01.
[21] Ewing, *op. cit.*, 304; *Florida Reports*, XII, 190.
[22] Florida, *House Journal*, 1869, 101-05, 111.
[23] *Ibid.*, 110, 113.
[24] D. Richards to E. B. Washburne, January 7, 1869, in Elihu B. Washburne Papers.
[25] Florida, *House Journal*, 1870, 101.

preferred "in no wise substantiated by the evidence offered" and "there is absolutely no evidence of any criminal intention whatever on the part of Governor Reed." The minority report was adopted 27 to 22.[26] A Democrat wrote that it appeared the "wire-pullers of the Radicals" were willing to leave Reed in office while throwing "the damning blight of the published testimony against him, which must ever stand in the way of his future political fortunes. . . ."[27] Democrats in the legislature generally voted for impeachment, not because they believed the charges against Reed, even though they had made most of them, "but because they knew that every attempt at impeachment would strengthen them and imperil honest Republicanism."[28]

In 1872 the Osborn-Gleason faction and Democrats brought impeachment proceedings against Reed for the fourth time. On February 10, twelve articles were presented charging him with incompetence, malfeasance, and "conduct detrimental to good morals." The articles were adopted 30 to 0.[29] On the same day, Supreme Court Justice James D. Westcott, Jr. administered the oath of office as governor to Lieutenant Governor Samuel T. Day, a Virginian.[30]

Reed's enemies soon encountered disaffection in their ranks. The Democrats who were always eager to bring impeachment charges threatened to support Reed unless two articles concerning the alleged conspiracy of Reed and Yulee, a prominent Democrat, to rob the State of $1,000,000 were withdrawn. The two articles were deleted.[31] On February 14, the senate court, with Chief Justice Edwin M. Randall presiding, was organized to try Reed. The proceedings were political, not judicial. Five of the six prosecuting attorneys, including ex-governor Walker, were Democrats. Reed was wise enough to employ an important Conservative, J. P. C. Emmons, as counsel.[32]

---

[26] *Ibid.*, 173-74, 199.

[27] S. R. Mallory to E. M. L'Engle, February 19, 1870, in Edward M. L'Engle Papers.

[28] Wallace, *op. cit.*, 159.

[29] For the full text of the charges see Florida, *House Journal*, 1872, 257-63.

[30] *Ibid.*, 263.

[31] It was charged that Yulee and Reed had conspired to issue $1,000,000 state bonds to the former's Florida Railroad Company. The bonds were issued under the act to perfect public works of 1869, but were never negotiated. Ewing, *op. cit.*, 308.

[32] Davis, *op. cit.*, 635-36; Tallahassee *Sentinel*, May 11, 1872.

Soon after the court was organized the impeachers began to maneuver for an adjournment of the legislature. Reed requested an immediate trial since an adjournment would postpone the final decision until after his term in office expired, but on February 19, a joint resolution provided for *sine die* adjournment. The senate court was also adjourned.[33] With the governor suspended, and the *sine die* adjournment, Reed, for all practical purposes, was out of office for the remainder of his term. The impeachers were willing to let the issue rest, but on April 8, Reed assisted by Gibbs, took possession of the governor's office thereby forcing the impeachment to an issue.[34] On April 17, Reed submitted the question to the State Supreme Court. By a majority decision the court denied it had jurisdiction, but added that "by all rules of justice, the senate court should decide the impeachment against Reed."[35]

In the meantime Day had called the legislature into special session on April 22. A decision to continue the impeachment trial resulted in reconvening the court on May 2. Emmons requested that Reed "be acquitted and discharged of and from all and singular said impeachment." Democratic Senator John Henderson moved that the request be granted and on May 4 the senate by a vote of 10 to 7 adopted Henderson's resolution.[36] By this time the Democrats were inclined to support Reed. They believed they could win the election of 1872 and thought there was a better chance for a fair canvass under Reed. They had already helped damage Reed's reputation beyond repair, which had been their aim. Actual expulsion was not necessary. The Republicans were no longer eager for impeachment either. The disputed election between Day and William D. Bloxham was being decided by the courts. If the court should decide that Bloxham was the lawful lieutenant governor, and it did, the unseating of Reed would place a Democrat in the executive chair.[37] The disgraceful impeachment attempts opened wounds in the Republican Party that could not be mended. Reed continued to fight his Republican enemies and co-operate with Democrats after he left office.

---

[33] Ewing, *op. cit.*, 309.
[34] *Ibid.*, 310-11; Wallace, *op. cit.*, 183.
[35] Ewing, *op. cit.*, 312; Wallace, *op. cit.*, 203.
[36] Florida, *Senate Journal*, Extra Session, 1872, 37, 68.
[37] G. P. Raney to E. M. L'Engle, February 8, 1872, J. P. C. Emmons to E. M. L'Engle, February 9, 1872, in Edward M. L'Engle Papers; Ackerman, *op. cit.*, 217.

Another reason for the Republicans steady loss of power was the unprincipled Democratic opposition. They used fraud, falsehood, intimidation, and even murder to oust Republicans. "Extravagance, ignorance, and corruption" have been advanced to justify the overthrow of Republican regimes, but malfeasance was not the basic cause. The Conservative or Democratic party in Florida was founded on the principle of white supremacy and Republican Reconstruction was a direct attack on that doctrine.[38] Furthermore, Democrats were angry because they were not in office. A few families had controlled Florida for many years and were unwilling to give up their position of power

There was little difference in the political principles of the two parties. The major sources of disagreement were Negro officeholders, Democrats' desire to be in office, and the extent to which the State should be taxed to support education and other services. Democrats of power were usually of the propertied class and disliked taxation. In 1870 ex-governor Walker announced that there was no diversity between honest Democrats and Republicans.[39] Though Walker's statement was not wholly accurate, the two parties did agree on many issues including the need to improve transportation, encourage immigration and capital to the State, pay off the public debt and make Florida attractive to businessmen. The Democrats frequently joined with Republicans in the legislature especially on bills concerning internal improvements.

Having no really distinctive principles of their own other than white supremacy, the Democrats co-operated at times, but were always on the alert, ready to take advantage of any issue that might divide or destroy their opposition.[40] Since there was no significant policy difference in the two parties, charges of Negro rule, corruption, carpetbaggers, extravagance, and incompetence were necessary to justify the vicious Democratic attacks. Men like Yulee who were more interested in business than in personal political ambition were friendlier to Republican administrations than those seeking political office. The extensive correspondence of Yulee, Swann, and L'Engle seldom mentions the Republican party except at

---

38 Simkins, *A History of the South*, 285; Davis, *op. cit.*, 520.
39 Tallahassee *Sentinel*, August 27, 1870.
40 *Ibid.*, January 8, 1870.

election time and then only rarely. Walker became irritated with Yulee in 1870 because of the latter's inactivity in the campaign.[41]

The Republican rift in 1867 and the concessions made to Democrats in the constitutional convention of 1868 mark the beginning of the Republican decline in Florida, but the election of 1870 was a landmark in their eventual loss of power. By 1870 voting restrictions had been removed from whites and more interest was being demonstrated in politics.[42] The Democrats declared their situation was desperate and as a consequence the most desperate measures were employed. They prepared fraudulent ballots, and "ruthlessly" suppressed freedmen with "halter, shotgun and whip. . . ."[43] The district attorney for the Northern District of the State testified that armed bodies of men appeared at balloting places the day before election and by threats of violence prevented many from voting.[44] The results of the election cut the Republican majority to one in the senate and three in the house.[45]

Similar tactics were used in 1872 though this time Democrats made a more vigorous effort to win Negro votes. William D. Bloxham, Democratic nominee for governor, suggested sending a few Negroes to the Democratic Convention in Jacksonville and was able to secure the appointment of a small number of freedmen delegates.[46] Wallace claimed Bloxham might have won the election if he had been spared by his friends who went about the country denouncing "niggers"[47] The appointment of a few Negro delegates to the convention was not considered sufficient to win the election so the shot-gun and rope were used again. Every

---

[41] D. S. Walker to D. L. Yulee, June 28, 1870, in David L. Yulee Papers.

[42] Margie Trapp Hines, "Negro Suffrage and the Florida Election Laws, 1860-1950," (unpublished M. A. thesis, University of North Carolina, 1953), 22; Davis, *op. cit.*, 629.

[43] Davis, *op. cit.*, 621; Tallahassee *Sentinel*, November 5, 1870.

[44] *Ibid.*, 622; House *Executive Documents*, 44th Cong., 2nd. Sess. No. 30, 67; U. S. *Congressional Globe*, 42nd Cong., 3rd. Sess., pt. 2, 951.

[45] Tallahassee *Sentinel*, December 31, 1870; Davis, *op. cit.*, 629.

[46] Bloxham's running mate was Robert W. Bullock, a native white from Marion County. The Republican candidates were Ossian B. Hart for governor with Marcellus L. Stearns second on the ticket. The congressional candidates were Josiah T. Walls and William J. Purman for the Republicans, Charles W. Jones and Silas L. Niblack for the Democrats. W. D. Bloxham to R. H. M. Davidson, July 30, 1872, in Miscellaneous Letters P. K. Yonge Library of Florida History, Gainesville, Florida; R. Bullock to E. M. L'Engle, July 19, 1872, in Edward M. L'Engle Papers.

[47] Wallace, *op. cit.*, 216.

means, fair or foul, was employed to keep Negroes from the polls.[48] The Democrats sent in false returns and fraudulent counts from four counties, but lost ground in the election, perhaps because the Republicans also used fraud to counter Democratic fraud and violence.[49] The Republican majority was increased to two in the senate and five in the house.[50]

In 1874 the Democrats were able to profit again from Republican division. The Jacksonville *Tri-Weekly Florida Union,* frequently a spokesman for the administration, opposed the election of Congressman Walls, actually announcing for his opponent. A convention held in Tallahassee in August to try to end the party schism proved to be a bitter meeting, with Governor Stearns and Congressman Purman leading opposing factions. Leon County seemed irrevocably split.[51] A cleavage combined with Democratic intimidation resulted in an evenly divided senate and a Democratic majority of three in the house.[52] After winning a majority in the legislature, the Democrats were eager to use their techniques in 1876 to win the executive office.[53] They became expert at intimidating Negroes.

The Republicans were still hopelessly divided in 1876. The split was nominally sealed before the election, but eight years of antagonism could not be easily erased. Stearns, who desired the nomination for governor, was opposed by Conover and Purman. Each side made vicious attacks on the other. Purman maintained Stearns was under the influence of the Democrats and was anti-Negro. "How he does hate, at the bottom of his heart, to see a black man hold office," Purman said. Purman was accused of selling

---

48 Abbey, *op. cit.,* 313.
49 Democrats allegedly sent in false returns from Alachua, Hamilton, Marion, and Hernando Counties. New York *Times,* November 25, 1872; Ackerman, *op. cit.,* 197.
50 Davis, *op. cit.,* 641; Tallahassee *Sentinel,* December 14, 1872; Tallahassee *Weekly Floridian,* December 17, 1872.
51 Jacksonville *Tri-Weekly Florida Union,* August 6, 15, November 3, 1874; Tallahassee *Weekly Floridian,* August 18, 1874; H. A. L'Engle to E. M. L'Engle, August 1, 1874, G. P. Raney to E. M. L'Engle, October 19, 1874, A. Manin to E. M. L'Engle, October 30, 1874, in Edward M. L'Engle Papers.
52 Tallahassee *Weekly Floridian,* December 15, 1874; Florida, *Acts and Resolutions,* 1875, iii–iv; E. W. L'Engle to E. M. L'Engle, November 23, 1874, in Edward M. L'Engle Papers.
53 According to the party listing of the *Floridian,* the Democrats enjoyed a majority in the House; however, the *Sentinel* said December 1, 1874, that three independents held the balance of power.

cadetships to the naval academy and timber agency appointments.[54] Conover was criticized for embezzlement of state funds while treasurer, and for forming an alliance with Dyke to sell out Republicans. Republicans were aware of the damage being done by their internal strife. The Tallahassee *Sentinel* warned that "party unity must and shall be preserved!" but added, "just how we are not prepared to say."[55]

The Republican convention nominated Stearns with David Montgomery as his running mate. The Conover men withdrew and held their own convention.[56] Conover was nominated for governor and a Southern loyalist, Joseph A. Lee, was placed on the slate as lieutenant governor.[57] As late as September 1, Conover continued to campaign, but on September 5 he announced he would withdraw in behalf of Stearns. Wallace maintained that Conover had informed his Democratic friend Dyke he would have to withdraw unless he could get some money for campaigning. Dyke was unsuccessful in securing funds.[58] Conover's retirement enabled the party to present an apparent united front, though Wallace and ex-governor Reed continued to work against the ticket.[59] A few Negroes joined Conservative Clubs and worked openly for the Democrats.[60] Republican nominees for congress were Purman and Horatio Bisbee, Jr., a federal district attorney.[61]

The Democrats met at Quincy and nominated George F. Drew for governor and Noble A. Hull for lieutenant governor. Drew, who was born in New Hampshire, had gone to Georgia before the war. During the war he claimed to be a Unionist, but sold salt and lumber to the Confederacy. In 1876 he was in the lumber business in Ellaville. Some Democrats were less than pleased with Drew, maintaining he was little better than a radical. A Democrat

---

[54] U. S. *Congressional Record*, 44th Cong., 1st Sess., IV, pt. 5, 4940, pt. 2, 1560-61; Tallahassee *Sentinel*, May 27, 1876; Tallahassee *Weekly Floridian*, April 11, 1876; *Watchman's Letter* No. 11, May 20, 1876.

[55] Tallahassee *Sentinel*, May 13, 1876.

[56] *Ibid.*, May 27, June 3, 1876; Tallahassee *Weekly Floridian*, June 6, 1876.

[57] Tallahassee *Weekly Floridian*, June 6, 1876.

[58] Jacksonville *Daily Florida Union*, September 8, 1876; Wallace, *op. cit.*, 333.

[59] Tallahassee *Weekly Floridian*, September 19, 1876; R. E. X. to E. M. L'Engle, October 3, 1876, Memo of H. Reed, October 6, 1876, in Edward M. L'Engle Papers.

[60] Wallace, *op. cit.*, 338; Jacksonville *Daily Florida Union*, June 30, 1876; Tallahassee *Weekly Floridian*, July 4, 1876.

[61] Wallace, *op. cit.*, 332-33.

in Madison County said there had not been a "dirty job" in the county for the last six or seven years in which Drew had not been "conspicuously connected." He was vulnerable to almost every charge made against Republicans. His $10,000 campaign contribution seemed to appease those who were apprehensive.[62] Hull was born in Georgia, had lived in Florida since 1851, and at the time of his nomination was a merchant at Sanford.[63] R. H. M. Davidson and J. J. Finley, both ex-Confederate officers, were nominated for congress.

The 1876 campaign was hard fought with few methods of gaining votes neglected. The "key-note" of the Democratic "campaign method was not persuasion. That had failed." It was "threatened violence and economic coercion" which had already proved successful. The Democrats, according to one writer, "were unscrupulous past-masters in the cunning and demoralizing art of combatting rascality and crushing numbers by counter rascality."[64] The Klan which had been partially repressed since 1873 became active again. Freedmen were taken out and threatened with hanging if they did not vote Democratic. Many testified later they were coerced to swear to vote Democratic and then forced to swear publicly that they had never been coerced. A widespread plan was laid to "starve out" those freedmen who voted Republican.[65] Mounted bands numbering several hundred persons appeared at Republican meetings "in a manner and spirit calculated to create . . . apprehension for the peace of the community and integrity of the ballot-box on election day."[66] Democrats said they intended to carry the State at all hazards. A speaker in Leon County warned Negroes that Democrats had guns and intended to use them at voting time. Wise Negroes "would remain at home and save their lives." he advised.[67] The Monticello *Constitution* boasted that "Democrats are thoroughly prepared for any emergency, and if these Radical hounds want blood, they shall have it

---

[62] *Ibid.*; Tallahassee *Sentinel*, June 24, August 5, 1876; E. W. L'Engle to E. M. L'Engle, May 19, 1876 in Edward M. L'Engle Papers; Jacksonville *Daily Florida Union*, August 29, September 4, 5, 18, 23, 1876.

[63] Tallahassee *Weekly Floridian*, June 13, 1876.

[64] Davis, *op. cit.*, 688, 703.

[65] *Ibid.*, 695-97; Abbey, *op. cit.*, 318; Stanley, *History of Gadsden County*, 121.

[66] Jacksonville *Daily Florida Union*, October 19, 1876.

[67] *Ibid.*; Tallahassee *Sentinel*, October 28, 1876.

to their hearts content." A group of prominent Democrats went to Governor Stearns and personally threatened to kill him if a single white man was killed during the election.[68]

Negro women apparently were more hostile to the Democrats than men. Some women in Jefferson County reportedly threatened to abandon their husbands if they voted Democratic. The Monticello *Constitution* wrote that "a prominent lawyer" directed it to say the legal fraternity would make no charge to secure divorces for men so threatened, and guaranteed that the circuit court clerk appointed by Drew would make no charge for recording the papers. "Thus honest Democratic Negroes," the paper added, "can get rid of their old, ugly, and crazy hags, and be placed in a condition to marry young, sensible, and pretty Mulatto girls."[69] A Democratic railroad official in West Florida sent several groups of Negro workmen into Alabama with the promise they would return before election day, but strangely enough, they spent election day several hundred miles away in Alabama.[70] On election day Democrats destroyed telegraph lines and railroad track to stop communication between state and federal authorities. The Klan and regulators picketed roads with shot-guns to keep Negroes from balloting places.[71] Fraud was also practiced by Democrats. Fraudulent ballots were printed, ballot boxes stuffed and stolen, Republican votes thrown out, and many Democrats voted more than once.[72]

To counter Democratic threats, violence, intimidation, economic coercion, and fraud, Republicans resorted to more fraud. Though Democrats controlled about twenty-nine county canvassing boards, the Republicans by virtue of being in office reputedly had some advantages in the use of fraud. They were accused of manufacturing spurious poll lists, of stuffing ballot boxes, and telling the freedmen to vote as many times as possible for a party loss

---

[68] Quoted in Tallahassee *Sentinel*, July 15, 1876; Albert H. Roberts, "Florida and Leon County in the Election of 1876," *Tallahassee Historical Society Annual*, IV (1939), 90.

[69] Quoted in Jacksonville *Daily Florida Union*, July 1, 1876.

[70] Davis, *op. cit.*, 708.

[71] Marcellus L. Stearns, History of Election in Florida in 1876, microfilm of typescript in P. K. Yonge Library of Florida History; Davis, *op cit.*, 706.

[72] New York *Times*, November 13, 25, 27, 1876; Jacksonville *Daily Florida Union*, November 11, 1876; Davis, *op. cit.*, 703.

would result in the reestablishment of slavery.[73] Wallace, an apologist for the Democrats, maintained that many of the irregularities were in Democratic counties, but were the work of Republican officers.[74] Republican trickery was probably more widespread in the final canvassing after the balloting than on election day. It was reported that Republicans as well as Democrats used intimidation. In Jefferson County, a white Democrat and a group of his Negro followers were pelted with sticks and bricks on their way to cast ballots. Republican intimidation was necessarily rare for the number of Democratic freedmen was small.[75]

Soon after the election both parties began to claim victory though it was widely believed the Republicans had won. Stearns was congratulated by several prominent Democrats upon his triumph.[76] After it became known that the national election might depend on Florida results, both parties began accumulating evidence of fraud. Neither had to look far.[77] One Democrat from Alachua County, however, complained he did not know on what grounds to contest. He had made "diligent inquiry in the county, he added, but could find no more than 50 illegal votes to overcome a 211 majority.[78] After an influx of "visiting statesmen" of both parties, more fraud, deals, and partisan decisions, it was decided that Republicans won Florida's electoral votes, but Democrats won the state slate.[79]

It is difficult to determine who would have won in a fair election. One careful scholar said while a *"fair count"* of ballots "might have resulted in a small majority for Tilden, a *free election* would have with far greater certainty have resulted in a substantial

---

[73] New York *Times*, November 13, 1876; Wallace, *op. cit.*, 338; Davis, *op. cit.*, 703; Abbey, *op. cit.*, 319.

[74] Wallace, *op. cit.*, 341.

[75] Haworth, *op. cit.*, 62.

[76] Stearns, *op. cit.*, 1; E. W. L'Engle to E. M. L'Engle, November 11, 1876, in Edward M. L'Engle Papers.

[77] U. S. Congress, *Senate Executive Documents*, 44th Cong., 2nd Sess., pt. 2, 407; New York *Times*, November 25, 26, 1876; Tallahassee *Weekly Floridian*, November 14, 1876.

[78] T. F. King to E. M. L'Engle, January 1, 1877, in Edward M. L'Engle Papers.

[79] For detailed accounts of the disputed 1876 election in Florida see Haworth, *op. cit.*; C. Vann Woodward, *Reunion and Reaction* (2nd ed. Revised, Garden City, New York, 1956); Jerrell H. Shofner, "The Presidential Election of 1876 in Florida" (unpublished M.S. thesis, The Florida State University, 1961).

majority for Hayes."[80] C. Vann Woodward concluded that "a white majority and a rift in Republican ranks" are "prima facie" evidence that the Democrats had a strong claim to victory.[81] A more recent study supports Woodward's view, while Francis B. Simkins maintained that the Democratic majority was secured by intimidation and lost by the activity of Republican state canvassers.[82] The victor in a fair and free election is not certain, but it is certain that Hayes was inaugurated, the Republicans were ousted in the State, and the Negroes suffered the consequences.[83]

A victory for the Democrats on the State level denoted the end of an era for Negroes. Though the Republicans continued to be active for a few years, the freedmen never again enjoyed the power and rights acquired during Reconstruction. The "saddest picture" in Florida, a New York *Times* reporter wrote in December, 1876, was "the woebegone, appealing face" of the freedman "as he loiters about in the shadows of the trees, in the corridors of the capitol, and at the corners of the street, the mute or weeping embodiment of despair." In his view," the reporter added, "all is lost. . . . His intuitions teach him that darkness is returning, and that he moans in agony."[84]

According to a contemporary the Capital was filled on inaugural day with "large bodies of white men armed to the teeth." As they came into town, she added "a look into their faces . . . was sufficient to tell they were in dead earnest." ". . . The Negroes trembled and began to scatter. Wherever they could find a hiding place they lost no time in occupying it and there was a very noticeable decrease in the black hordes, which had paraded the streets so noisily a short time before."[85] One of the first steps taken by Democrats, Francis P. Fleming, a white Democrat, boasted years later, was to disfranchise freedmen. Soon, he said, the Republicans in Florida were unable to "muster one tenth of the old time party strength."[86] The jubilee for Florida Negroes had ended. The day when they could enjoy political equality, equal

---

80 Haworth, *op. cit.*, 76.
81 Woodward, *Reunion and Reaction*, 19.
82 Shofner, *op. cit.*, 178; Simkins, *A History of the South*, 293.
83 Drew and Hull were sworn in January 2, 1877.
84 New York *Times*, December 29, 1876.
85 Eppes, *op. cit.*, 376.
86 Fleming, *op. cit.*, 18.

educational facilities, and equality before the law was over. An elderly Negro man watching the inauguration of Drew accurately and succinctly indicated the future of Negroes when he remarked "well, we niggers is done."[87]

Despite the regression suffered after 1876, Reconstruction was not a complete loss to Negroes. They had made significant progress in the eleven short years since emancipation. They were no longer slaves, they were recognized by the United States Constitution as citizens, and they had made many adjustments to freedom including a recognition of the importance of law and the family relationship. Negroes had learned to work and care for themselves. Though it would be taken from them they had experienced political equality, being a power in the State, and holding influential positions in government. Negro churches had been founded. Many freedmen owned farms, and were engaged in skilled occupations. They had accumulated considerable personal property and real estate. Great strides had been made in education. There were Negro teachers, ministers, and lawyers. Many of these gains could not have been secured without Reconstruction. Though the Negroes lost many of their rights and privileges after 1876, such things as education, experience, and the knowledge of how it feels to be a free man could not be taken away. The Negro could view Reconstruction as something to strive for in the future, or perhaps to look back on with sadness and longing.

---

[87] Jacksonville *Florida Sun*, January 4, 1877; Shofner, *op. cit.*, 141.

BIBLIOGRAPHY

PRIMARY MATERIALS

MANUSCRIPT

American Missionary Association Archives, Fisk University, Nashville, Tennessee.

James B. Bailey Papers, Southern Historical Collection, University of North Carolina, Chapel Hill, North Carolina.

Eli Whitney Bonney Papers, Duke University, Durham, North Carolina.

Branch Family Papers, Southern Historical Collection, University of North Carolina, Chapel Hill, North Carolina.

Burton Papers, P. K. Yonge Library of Florida History, Gainesville, Florida.

Chapman, F. B. Unpublished Account of Jackson County Affairs, Call Papers, Florida Historical Society Collection, University of South Florida, Tampa, Florida.

Comptroller's Letter Book, April 21, 1870-May 5, 1871, Florida State Library, Tallahassee, Florida.

Court Records, Presentments of Grand Juries and Miscellaneous Papers, Gadsden County Court House, Quincy, Florida.

———————— . Presentments of Grand Juries, Jefferson County Court House, Monticello, Florida.

O. M. Dorman Diary and Notes, Library of Congress, Washington, D. C.

Warren Q. Dow Diary, P. K. Yonge Library of Florida History, Gainesville, Florida.

Fleming, Francis Phillip. Commercial Development, Florida Historical Society Collection, University of South Florida, Tampa, Florida.

————————, Reconstruction, Florida Historical Society Collection, University of South Florida, Tampa, Florida.

Florida. Records of the Department of State, Office of the Secretary of State, Tallahassee, Florida.

Governor's Letter Book, January 11, 1873-February 19, 1875, Florida State Library, Tallahassee, Florida.

Ambrose B. Hart Letters, copy in P. K. Yonge Library of Florida History, Gainesville, Florida.

Edmund H. Hart Letters, P. K. Yonge Library of Florida History, Gainesville, Florida.

———————— . Diary, microfilm, P. K. Yonge Library of Florida History, Gainesville, Florida.

Walter N. Hart Journal, microfilm, P. K. Yonge Library of Florida History, Gainesville, Florida.

Eliza Horn Diary, typescript, P. K. Yonge Library of Florida History, Gainesville, Florida.

Houston Letters, P. K. Yonge Library of Florida History, Gainesville, Florida.

Andrew Johnson Papers, Library of Congress, Washington, D. C.

William J. Keyser Papers, Duke University, Durham, North Carolina.

Long, Ellen Call. History of Florida, Florida Historical Society Collection, University of South Florida, Tampa, Florida.

John Francis Patch LeBaron Diary, Jacksonville Public Library, Jacksonville, Florida.

Edward M. L'Engle Papers, Southern Historical Collection, University of North Carolina, Chapel Hill, North Carolina.

W. J. Lutterloh Papers, Southern Historical Collection, University of North Carolina, Chapel Hill, North Carolina.

Minutes—Board of Commissioners of Public Institutions, October 26, 1869-February 13, 1892, Florida State Library, Tallahassee, Florida.

Ninth Census of the United States, 1870, unpublished population schedules of Florida, microfilm, The Florida State University Library, Tallahassee, Florida.

Ninth Census of the United States, 1870, unpublished social statistics schedules of Florida, The Florida State University Library, Tallahassee, Florida.
John Parkhill Papers, Southern Historical Collection, University of North Carolina, Chapel Hill, North Carolina.
George W. Parsons Diary, P. K. Yonge Library of Florida History, Gainesville, Florida.
James J. Philips Papers, Southern Historical Collection, University of North Carolina, Chapel Hill, North Carolina.
Records of the Bureau of Refugees, Freedmen and Abandoned Lands, National Archives, Washington, D. C.
Records of Deeds, Leon County Court House, Tallahassee, Florida.
A. M. Reed Diary, typescript, P. K. Yonge Library of Florida History, Gainesville, Florida.
Roster of State and County Officers Commissioned by Governors of Florida, 1845-1868, Florida State Library, Tallahassee, Florida.
Ruffin-Roulhac-Hamilton Papers, Southern Historical Collection, University of North Carolina, Chapel Hill, North Carolina.
E. C. F. Sanchez Papers, P. K. Yonge Library of Florida History, Gainesville, Florida.
School Reports of Florida, 1869-1894, Office of State Superintendent of Public Instruction, Tallahassee, Florida.
Stearns, Marcellus L. History of Election in Florida in 1876, P. K. Yonge Library of Florida History, Gainesville. Florida.
Thaddeus Stevens Papers, Library of Congress, Washington, D. C.
Samuel A. Swann Papers, P. K. Yonge Library of Florida History, Florida.
George F. Thompson Journal, P. K. Yonge Library of Florida History, Gainesville, Florida.
U. S. Army Commands, Florida, National Archives, Washington, D. C.
Union Republican Club of Jacksonville.. Constitution and Proceedings, March 27, 1867-July 25, 1867, Florida Historical Society Collection, University of South Florida, Tampa, Florida.
Elihu B. Washburne Papers, Library of Congress, Washington, D. C.
David L. Yulee Papers, P. K. Yonge Library of Florida History, Gainesville, Florida.

GOVERNMENT DOCUMENTS

Bureau of the Census. *Negro Population 1790-1915*. Washington: Government Printing Office, 1918.
Florida. *Acts and Resolutions*. 1865-1877.
Florida, Commissioner of Land and Immigration. *Sixth Annual Report of the Commissioner of Lands and Immigration of the State of Florida for the Year Ending December 31, 1874*. Tallahassee: State of Florida, 1874.
Florida. *Constitution of the State of Florida 1865*.
Florida. *Constitution of the State of Florida 1868*.
Florida, Department of Education. *Bi-ennial Reports of the Superintendent of Public Instruction of the State of Florida for the Two Years Ending June 30, 1894*. Tallahassee, Florida: John G. Collins, 1895.
Florida. *House Journal*. 1865-1877.
Florida. *Journal of the Proceedings of the Constitutional Convention of the State of Florida Begun and Held at the Capital, at Tallahassee, on Monday, January 20th, 1868*. Tallahassee: Edward M. Cheney, Printer, 1868.
Florida. *Senate Journal*. 1865-1877.
Florida, Superintendent of Public Instruction. *Reports 1869-1880*.
Florida. *Supreme Court Reports*. Vol. XIII.
U. S. Bureau of Refugees, Freedmen and Abandoned Lands. *Semi-annual Reports on Schools for Freedmen*. 10 vols. Washington: Government Printing Office, January 1866-July, 1870.

U. S. Bureau of the Census. *Ninth Census of the United States: 1870. Population,* Vol. I.

U. S. Bureau of the Census. *Twelfth Census of the United States: 1900.* Agriculture, Vol. V.

U. S. Commissioner of Education. *Reports for the Years 1870-1876.* Washington: Government Printing Office, 1870-1877.

U. S. Congress. *House Executive Documents.* 38th Cong., 2nd Sess., No. 18.

U. S. Congress. *House Executive Documents.* 39th Cong., 1st Sess., Nos. 11, 19, 30, 47, 66, 70.

U. S. Congress. *House Executive Documents.* 39th Cong., 2nd Sess., Nos. 1, 6.

U. S. Congress. *House Executive Documents.* 40th Cong., 2nd Sess., Nos. 1, 57, 96, 342.

U. S. Congress. *House Executive Documents.* 40th Cong., 3rd Sess., No. 1.

U. S. Congress. *House Executive Documents.* 41st Cong., 2nd Sess., Nos. 1, 142.

U. S. Congress. *House Executive Documents.* 41st Cong., 3rd Sess., No. 1.

U. S. Congress. *House Executive Documents.* 42nd Cong., 2nd Sess., No. 1.

U. S. Congress. *House Executive Documents.* 42nd Cong., 3rd Sess., No. 1.

U. S. Congress. *House Executive Documents.* 44th Cong., 2nd Sess., No. 30.

U. S. Congress. *House Miscellaneous Documents.* 40th Cong., 2nd Sess., Nos. 109, 114.

U. S. Congress. *House Miscellaneous Documents.* 43rd Cong., 1st Sess., No. 15.

U. S. Congress. *House Miscellaneous Documents.* 43rd Cong., 2nd Sess., No. 16.

U. S. Congress. *House Miscellaneous Documents.* 44th Cong., 1st Sess., No. 58.

U. S. Congress. *House Miscellaneous Documents.* 59th Cong., 2nd Sess., No. 357, pt. 2.

U. S. Congress. *House Reports.* 39th Cong., 1st Sess., Nos. 30, 33, 51.

U. S. Congress. *House Reports.* 40th Cong., 2nd Sess., Nos. 10, 30.

U. S. Congress. *House Reports.* 41st Cong., 2nd Sess., No. 121.

U. S. Congress. *House Reports.* 42nd Cong., 2nd Sess., No. 22, pt. 13.

U. S. Congress. *Senate Executive Documents.* 39th Cong., 1st Sess., Nos. 2, 26, 27, 30, 43, 55.

U. S. Congress. *Senate Executive Documents.* 39th Cong., 2nd Sess., No. 6.

U. S. Congress. *Senate Executive Documents.* 40th Cong., 1st Sess., No. 14.

U. S. Congress. *Senate Executive Documents.* 42nd Cong., 3rd Sess., No. 32.

U. S. Congress. *Senate Miscellaneous Documents.* 39th Cong., 1st Sess., Nos. 3, 56.

U. S. *Congressional Globe.* 1865-1874.

U. S. *Congressional Record.* 1875-1876.

U. S. Department of Agriculture. *Reports of the Commissioner of Agriculture for the Years 1865-1876.* Washington: Government Printing Office, 1866-1877.

U. S. Department of War. *The War of Rebellion: a compilation of the official records of the Union and Confederate armies.* 70 vols. Washington: Government Printing Office, 1880-1901.

U. S. *Statutes at Large.* Vols. XIII-XIV.

U. S. *Supreme Court Reports,* 103.

NEWSPAPERS

Fernandina *Observer.* 1876.

Gainesville *New Era.* 1865-1866.

Jacksonville *Florida Union.* 1865-1876. Also published as *Tri-Weekly Florida Union* and *Daily Florida Union.*

Jacksonville *New South.* 1874-1875.

Jacksonville *Weekly Republican.* 1873.

New York *Evening Post.* 1866, 1873.

New York *Hendels Zeitung.* 1870.

New York *Times.* 1865-1876.

New York *Tribune.* 1865-1876.

Ocala *East Florida Banner.* 1876.

Pensacola *Weekly Express.* 1872.
Tallahassee *Semi-Weekly Floridian.* 1865-1876. Also published as *Weekly Floridian.*
Tallahassee *Sentinel.* 1865-1876.
Tampa *Florida Peninsular.* 1866-1871.
St. Augustine *Examiner.* 1866-1874.

BOOKS

Alvord, John W. *Letters from the South Relating to the Freedmen.* Washington: Howard University Press, 1870.
Arnett, Benjamin W. (ed.). *Proceedings of the Quarto-Centenial Conference of the African M. E. Church, of South Carolina, at Charleston, S. C., May 15, 16, and 17, 1889.* Privately Published, 1890.
Bill, Ledyard. *A Winter in Florida.* 5th ed. New York: Wood and Holbrook, 1869.
Brooks, Abbie M. *Petals Plucked from Sunny Climes.* 2nd ed. Nashville: Southern Methodist Printing House, 1885.
Crosby, Oliver Marvin. *Florida Facts Both Bright and Blue.* New York: Privately Published, 1887.
Eppes, Susan Bradford. *Through Some Eventful Years.* Macon, Georgia: J. W. Burke Company, 1926.
Florida, Its Climate, Soil, and Production, With a Sketch of its Natural Features and Social Condition. Jacksonville: L. F. Dewey and Company, 1868.
Gibbs, Mifflin W. *Shadows and Light: An Autobiography with Reminiscences of the Last and Present Century.* Washington: Privately Published, 1902.
Howard, Oliver Otis. *Autobiography.* 2 vols. New York: The Baker and Taylor Company, 1907.
Johnson, James Weldon. *Along This Way.* New York: The Viking Press, 1933.
Jordan, Weymouth T. (ed.). *Herbs, Hoecake and Husbandry The Daybook of a Planter of the Old South.* Tallahassee: The Florida State University, 1960.
King, Edward. *The Southern States of North America.* London: Blackie and Son, 1875.
Lanier, Sidney. *Florida: its Scenery, Climate and History.* Philadelphia: Lippincott, 1876.
Long, Ellen Call. *Florida Breezes.* Jacksonville, Florida: Ashmead Brothers, 1882.
McKinnon, John L. *History of Walton County.* Atlanta, Georgia: The Byrd Printing Company, 1911.
Phillips, Ulrich B. and Glunt, James D. (eds.). *Florida Plantation Records from the papers of George Noble Jones.* St. Louis: Missouri Historical Society, 1927.
Reid, Whitelaw. *After the War: A Southern Tour.* Cincinnati: Moore, 1866.
Rerick, Rowland H. *Memoirs of Florida.* 2 vols. Atlanta: The Southern Historical Association, 1902.
Richardson, Simon Peter. *Lights and Shadows of Itinerant Life.* Nashville, Tennessee: Barbee and Smith, 1901.
Shuften, John T. *A Colored Man's Exposition of the Acts and Doings of the Radical Party South from 1865-1876 and it probable overthrow by President Hayes' Southern Policy.* Jacksonville, Florida: Gibson and Dennis, 1877.
Skinner, Emory Fiske. *Reminiscences.* Chicago: Vestal Printing Company, 1908.
Stowe, Harriet Beecher. *Palmetto-Leaves.* Boston: J. R. Osgood and Company, 1873.
Townshend, Frederick T. *Wild Life in Florida, With a Visit to Cuba.* London: Hurst and Blackett Publishers, 1875.
Wallace, John. *Carpetbag Rule in Florida.* Jacksonville, Florida: Da Costa Printing and Publishing House, 1888.

PERIODICALS

Abbey, Kathryn T. "Documents Relating to El Destino and Chemonie Plantations, Middle Florida, 1828-1874," *Florida Quarterly Journal*, VIII (October, 1929), 79-111.

The American Missionary. 1866-1876.

Andrews, Sidney. "The Negro and His Bureau," *Old and New*, I (February, 1870), 200-207.

Beecher, Charles. "Florida," *Old and New*, I (February, 1870), 178-181.

Bentley, George R. "Colonel Thompsons 'Tour of Tropical Florida,'" *Tequesta*, X (1950), 3-12.

The Florida Agriculturist. 1874-1875.

The Freedmen's Record. 1865-1869.

"Fruit Culture," *The Semi-Tropical*, II (October, 1876), 623-625.

Glicksburg, Charles I. (ed.). "Letters from William Cullen Bryant From Florida," *Florida Historical Society Quarterly*, XIV (April, 1936), 255-274.

"An Itinerary to Miami," *Florida Historical Quarterly*, XVIII (January, 1940), 204-214.

King, Edward. "The Great South," *Scribners Monthly*, IX (November, 1874), 1-31.

The National Freedman. 1865-1866.

Nichols, G. W. "Six Weeks in Florida," *Harpers Magazine*, XLI (October, 1870), 655-667.

"Notes on Reconstruction in Tallahassee and Leon County, 1866-1876," *Florida Historical Society Quarterly*, V (January, 1927), 153-158.

Osborn, George C. (ed.), "Letters of A Carpetbagger in Florida, 1866-69." *Florida Historical Quarterly*, XXXVI (January, 1958), 239-285.

Proctor, Samuel. (ed.). "Yankee 'Schoolmarms' in Post-War Florida," *The Journal of Negro History*, XLIV (July, 1959), 275-277.

"The Problem of the Black Races," *Debows Review*, I (January, 1866), 266-283.

Richardson, Joe M. (ed.). "A Northerner Reports on Florida: 1866," *Florida Historical Quarterly*, XXXX (April, 1962), 381-390.

Rippey, H. C. "Description of Leon County, Florida," *The Semi-Tropical*, II (July, 1876), 396-406.

Simkins, W. S. "Why the Ku Klux," *The Alcalde*, IV (June, 1916), 735-748.

The Spirit of Missions. 1868.

Williamson, Edward C. (ed.). "Florida's First Reconstruction Legislature," *Florida Historical Quarterly*, XXXII (July, 1953), 41-43.

COLLECTIONS, COMPILATIONS AND PAMPHLETS

The American Annual Cyclopedia and Register of Important Events 1861-1874. 14 Vols. New York: D. Appleton and Company, 1862-1875.

Annual Reports of the Freedmen's Aid Society of the Methodist Episcopal Church 1869, 1875, 1876. Cincinnati: Western Methodist Book Concern, 1869, 1875, 1876.

Bethune, Mary McLeod. *An Upward Climb.* Daytona Beach: Bethune-Cookman College, n.d.

Diocese of Florida. *Journal of Proceedings of the Annual Convention of the Protestant Episcopal Church in the State of Florida, 1868-1876.* The printers and places of publication are as follows:
1868, 1870, 1873, C. Drew, Jacksonville.
1869, American Church Press Company, New York.
1871, 1872, Dyke and Son, Tallahassee.
1874, Florida Union Book and Job Printing Rooms, Jacksonville.
1875, 1876, John F. Trow and Son, New York.

Dyke, Charles E. *Republican and Democratic Rule Compared.* Speech to the Hancock and Bloxham Club of Tallahassee, September 6, 1880.

Fleming, Walter Lynwood. *Documentary History of Reconstruction.* 2 vols. Cleveland: The A. H. Clark Company, 1906-1907.
Florida Sentinel. Tenth Annual Number, 1880.
Peabody Education Fund. *Proceedings of the Trustees at their Annual Meeting, 1870-1877.* Cambridge: Press of John Wilson and Son, 1870-1877.
Sixth Annual Report of the Presbyterian Committee of Missions for Freedmen, Presented May, 1871.
Watchman's Letter No. 11, May 20, 1876.

SECONDARY MATERIALS

BOOKS

Abbey, Kathryn T. *Florida, Land of Change.* Chapel Hill: The University of North Carolina Press, 1941.
Barnes, William H. *The American Government.* 3 vols. New York: Nelson and Philips, 1874.
Beale, Howard K. *A History of Freedom of Teaching in American Schools.* New York: Charles Scribner's Sons, 1941.
Bentley, George R. *A History of the Freedmen's Bureau.* Philadelphia: University of Pennsylvania, 1955.
Bethell, John A. *Pinellas: A Brief History of the Lower Point.* St. Petersburg, Florida: Press of the Independent Job Department, 1914.
Biographical Directory of the American Congress, 1774-1927. Washington: Government Printing Office, 1928.
Brevard, Caroline Mays. *A History of Florida From the Treaty of 1763 to Our Own Times.* 2 vols. DeLand, Florida: The Florida State Historical Society, 1925.
Browne, Jefferson B. *Key West The Old and The New.* St. Augustine, Florida: The Record Company Printers and Publishers, 1912.
Buchholz, Fritz W. *History of Alachua County Florida.* St. Augustine, Florida: The Record Company Printers, 1929.
Bush, George Gary. *History of Education in Florida.* Washington: Government Printing Office, 1889.
Carter, Hodding. *The Angry Scar.* Garden City, New York: Doubleday, 1959.
Cash, Wilbur J. *The Mind of the South.* New York: Alfred A. Knopf, 1941.
Cash, William T. *History of the Democratic Party in Florida.* Tallahassee: Florida Democratic Historical Foundation, 1936.
――――――. *The Story of Florida.* 4 vols. New York: The American Historical Society, 1938.
Cochran, Thomas Everett. *History of Public-School Education in Florida.* Tallahassee: State Department of Education, 1921.
Covington, James W. *The Story of Southwestern Florida.* 2 vols. New York: Lewis Historical Publishing Company, Inc., 1957.
Curry, Jabez L. M. *Peabody Education Fund: A Brief Sketch of George Peabody and a History of the Peabody Education Fund through Thirty Years.* Cambridge: University Press, 1898.
Daniels, Jonathan. *Prince of Carpetbaggers.* Philadelphia: Lippincott, 1958.
Davis, Thomas F. *History of Early Jacksonville Florida.* Jacksonville: The H. and W. B. Drew Company, 1911.
Davis, William Watson. *The Civil War and Reconstruction in Florida.* New York: Columbia University, 1913.
Donald, Henderson H. *The Negro Freedman.* New York: H. Schuman, 1952.
Dovell, Junius Elmore. *Florida: Historic, Dramatic, Contemporary.* 4 vols. New York: Lewis Historical Publishing Company, 1952.
DuBois, W. E. B. *Black Reconstruction.* Philadelphia: Saifer, 1935.

Ezell, Boyce F. *Development of Secondary Education in Florida*. DeLand, Florida: privately published, 1932.

Farish, H. D. *The Circuit Rider Dismounts: A Social History of Southern Methodism, 1865-1900*. Richmond: Dietz Press, 1938.

Ferris, William H. *The African Abroad*. 2 vols. New Haven: Tuttle, Morehouse and Taylor Press, 1913.

Franklin, John Hope. *From Slavery to Freedom*. New York: Alfred A. Knopf, 1956.

Gold, Pleasant Daniel. *History of Duval County Including Early History of East Florida*. St. Augustine, Florida: The Record Company, 1929.

——————. *History of Volusia County Florida*. DeLand, Florida: E. O. Painter Printing Company, 1927.

Grismer, Karl H. *The Story of St. Petersburg*. St. Petersburg: P. K. Smith and Company, 1948.

Haworth, Paul L. *Hayes-Tilden Disputed Election*. Cleveland: Burrows Brothers Company, 1906.

Horn, Stanley F. *Invisible Empire*. Boston: Houghton Mifflin Company, 1939.

Jenkins, William S. *Pro-Slavery Thought in the Old South*. Chapel Hill: University of North Carolina, 1935.

Johns, John E. *Florida During the Civil War*. Gainesville: University of Florida Press, 1963.

Johnston, Ruby F. *The Development of Negro Religion*. New York: Philosophical Library, 1954.

Jordan, Weymouth T. *Ante-Bellum Alabama, Town and Country*. Tallahassee: The Florida State University, 1957.

Kennedy, Stetson. *Palmetto Country*. New York: Duel, Sloan and Pearce, 1942.

Lloyd, Arthur Y. *The Slavery Controversy*. Chapel Hill: University of North Carolina, 1939.

Long, Charles Sumner (comp.). *History of the A. M. E. Church in Florida*. Philadelphia: A. M. E. Book Concern, 1939.

Merritt, Webster. *A Century of Medicine in Jacksonville and Duval County*. Gainesville: University of Florida Press, 1949.

Owsley, Frank L. *King Cotton Diplomacy*. Chicago: University of Chicago Press, 1931.

Peirce, Paul Skeels. *The Freedmen's Bureau*. Iowa City: The University of Iowa, 1904.

Pennington, Edgar Legare. *Soldier and Servant: John Freeman Young, Second Bishop of Florida*. Hartford: Church Missions Publishing Company, 1939.

Phillips, Charles Henry. *The History of the Colored Methodist Episcopal Church in America*. Jackson, Tennessee: Publishing House of the C. M. E. Church, 1925.

Pyburn, Nita Katherine. *The History of the Development of a Single System of Education in Florida 1822-1903*. Tallahassee: The Florida State University, 1954.

Randall, James G. *The Civil War and Reconstruction*. Boston: Heath, 1937.

Schlesinger, Arthur M. *The Rise of the City 1878-1898*. New York: The Macmillan Company, 1933.

Simkins, Francis B. *A History of the South*. New York: Alfred A. Knopf, 1959.

Singletary, Otis A. *Negro Militia and Reconstruction*. Austin: University of Texas Press, 1957.

Smith, Samuel Denny. *The Negro in Congress, 1870-1901*. Chapel Hill: The University of North Carolina Press, 1940.

Stanley, J. Randall. *History of Gadsden County*. Quincy, Florida: Gadsden County Historical Commission, 1948.

——————. *History of Jackson County*. Marianna, Florida: Jackson County Historical Society, 1950.

Stowell, Jay Samuel. *Methodist Adventures in Negro Education*. The Methodist Book Concern, 1922.

Swint, Henry Lee. *The Northern Teacher in the South, 1862-1870.* Nashville: Vanderbilt University Press, 1941.
Taylor, Alrutheus Ambush. *The Negro in the Reconstruction of Virginia.* Washington: The Association for the Study of Negro Life and History, 1926.
Thrift, Charles Tinsley, Jr. *The Trail of the Florida Circuit Rider.* Lakeland, Florida: The Florida Southern College Press, 1944.
Wharton, Vernon L. *The Negro in Mississippi, 1865-1890.* Chapel Hill: The University of North Carolina Press, 1947.
Whyte, James Huntington. *The Uncivil War.* New York: Twyane Publishers, 1958.
Wiley, Bell I. *Southern Negroes, 1861-1865.* New York: Rinehart and Company, Inc., 1938.
Woodward, C. Vann. *Origins of the New South.* Baton Rouge: Louisiana State University Press, 1951.
_____. *Reunion and Reaction.* Boston: Little, 1951.
Wright, Richard R. *Encyclopedia of African Methodism.* Philadelphia: Book Concern of A. M. E. Church, 1916.

PERIODICALS

Bentley, George R. "The Political Activity of the Freedmen's Bureau in Florida," *Florida Historical Quarterly,* XXVIII (July, 1949), 28-37.
Brown, C. K. "The Florida Investment of George W. Swepson," *The North Carolina Historical Review,* V (July, 1928), 275-288.
Cox, John and La Wanda. "General O. O. Howard and the "Misrepresented Bureau,'" *The Journal of Southern History,* XIX (November, 1953), 41-56.
Davis, T. Frederick. "The Disston Land Purchase," *Florida Historical Quarterly,* XVIII (April, 1939), 200-210.
Dodd, Dorothy. " 'Bishop' Pearce and the Reconstruction of Leon County," *Apalachee,* (1946), 5-12.
Ewing, Cortez A. M. "Florida Reconstruction Impeachments," *Florida Historical Quarterly,* XXXVI (April, 1958), 299-318.
Fenlon, Paul E. "The Notorious Swepson-Littlefield Fraud," *Florida Historical Quarterly,* XXXII (April, 1954), 231-261.
McKelvey, Blake. "Penal Slavery and Southern Reconstruction," *The Journal of Negro History,* XX (April, 1935), 153-179.
Palmer, Henry E. "The Proctors—A true Story of Ante-Bellum Days and Since," *Tallahassee Historical Society Annual,* I (February, 1934), 14-16.
Parks, Albert Stanley. "The Negro in the Reconstruction of Florida," *Florida Quarterly Journal,* V. (October, 1936), 35-61.
Pennington, Edgar Legare. "Some Experiences of Bishop Young," *Florida Historical Society Quarterly,* XV (July, 1936), 35-50.
Richardson, Joe M. "An Evaluation of the Freedmen's Bureau in Florida," *Florida Historical Quarterly,* XLI (January, 1963), 223-238.
_____. "The Freedmen's Bureau and Negro Education in Florida," *The Journal of Negro Education,* XXXI (Fall, 1962), 460-467.
_____. "The Freedmen's Bureau and Negro Labor in Florida," *Florida Historical Quarterly,* XXXIX (October, 1960), 167-174.
Roberts, Albert H. "Florida and Leon County in the Election of 1876," *Tallahassee Historical Society Annual,* IV (1939), 88-96.
Scroggs, Jack B. "Carpetbagger Constitutional Reform in the South Atlantic States, 1867-1868," *The Journal of Southern History,* XXVII (November, 1961), 472-493.
Smith, George Winston. "Carpetbag Imperialism in Florida 1862-1868," *Florida Historical Quarterly,* XXVII (January, 1949), 260-299.
Taylor, Alrutheus Ambush. "Negro Congressmen A Generation After," *The Journal of Negro History,* VII (April, 1922), 127-171.
Tebeau, C. W. "Some Aspects of Planter-Freedman Relations, 1865-1880," *The Journal of Negro History,* XX (April, 1936), 130-150.

UNPUBLISHED MATERIALS

Ackerman, Philip D., Jr. "Florida Reconstruction from Walker through Reed, 1865-1873." Unpublished M.A. thesis, University of Florida, 1948.

Cushman, Joseph D. "The Episcopal Church in Florida: 1821-1892." Unpublished Ph.D. dissertation, The Florida State University, 1962.

Hines, Margie Trapp. "Negro Suffrage and the Florida Election Laws, 1860-1950." Unpublished M.A. thesis, University of North Carolina, 1953.

Shofner, Jerrell H. "The Presidential Election of 1876 in Florida." Unpublished M.S. thesis, The Florida State University, 1961.

Federal Writers Program. Florida Slave Interviews. Typescript in P. K. Yonge Library of Florida History, Gainesville, Florida.

INDEX TO

THE NEGRO IN THE RECONSTRUCTION
OF FLORIDA, 1865-1877